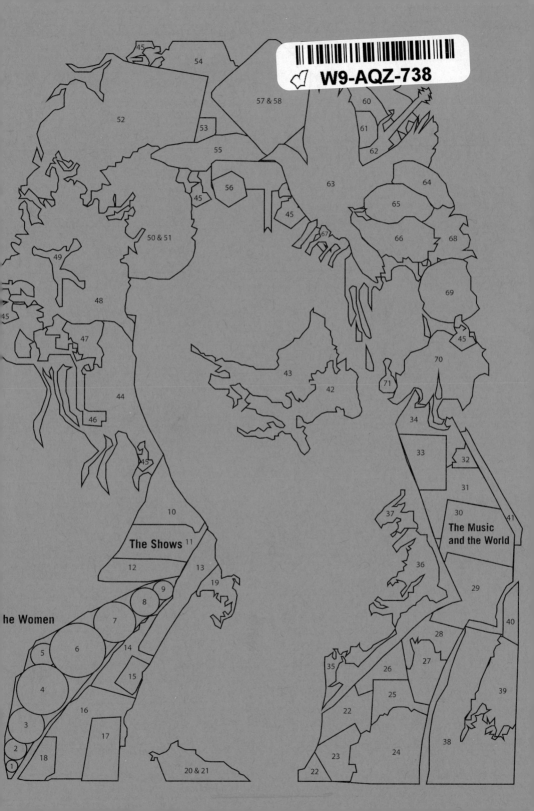

W9-AQZ-738

The Women

The Shows

The Music
and the World

Also by Ben Greenman

DIG IF YOU WILL THE PICTURE

Funk,

Sex,

God,

and

Genius

in the

Music of Prince

DIG IF YOU WILL THE PICTURE

Ben Greenman

Henry Holt and Company
New York

Henry Holt and Company
Publishers since 1866
175 Fifth Avenue
New York, New York 10010
www.henryholt.com

Henry Holt ® and ® are registered trademarks of Macmillan Publishing Group, LLC.

Foreword by Questlove originally published in *Rolling Stone*, 2016, reprinted by permission

Library of Congress Cataloging-in-Publication Data

Names: Greenman, Ben.
Title: Dig if you will the picture : funk, sex, god, and genius in the music of
    Prince / Ben Greenman.
Description: First edition. | New York : Henry Holt and Company, 2017. |
    Includes bibliographical references.
Identifiers: LCCN 2016054759| ISBN 9781250128379 (hardcover) |
    ISBN 9781250128362 (electronic book)
Subjects: LCSH: Prince. | Rock musicians—United States—Biography.
Classification: LCC ML420.P974 G74 2017 | DDC 781.66092 [B]—dc23
LC record available at https://lccn.loc.gov/2016054759

Our books may be purchased in bulk for promotional, educational, or business use. Please contact your local bookseller or the Macmillan Corporate and Premium Sales Department at (800) 221-7945, extension 5442, or by e-mail at MacmillanSpecialMarkets@macmillan.com.

First Edition 2017

Designed by Meryl Sussman Levavi

Printed in the United States of America

10 9 8 7 6 5 4 3 2 1

To Gail, Daniel, and Jake—
Forgive me if this goes astray.

CONTENTS

FOREWORD

By Questlove

When I first got *1999*, it was 1982, and I was eleven, newly in charge of my own record-buying habits. I couldn't resist the cover, with Prince's name floating on a purple field of stars. Plus, there were so many hidden meanings in the illustration: Was that a football or a smile? And how phallic was that "1," anyway? My parents were born-again Christians at that point, and Prince was a bridge too far. For starters, when you turned the album cover upside down, the "999" became "666," the mark of the beast. They didn't need more than starters.

I bought the record and hid it, but my mom found the record and threw it away. When winter came, I shoveled snow until I had enough money to buy it a second time. That one went into the garbage, too. There was a third record that just vanished without a trace and a fourth that got broken over my father's knee. I got smarter, meaning sneakier: I found a friend to make me cassettes of Prince's albums. At home, I loosened the heads of my drums and hid the contraband in them. I listened to the tapes when I was practicing, playing something totally different on the drums so that my parents wouldn't know what I was actually hearing.

Prince was in my ears and he was in my head. Starting then, I patterned everything in my life after him. I studied his fashion; I studied his affect. I studied his taste in women. He began to mentor me in musical matters, too: when Prince mentioned someone in an interview, I became voracious in my pursuit of their music. I wouldn't have started listening to Joni Mitchell without him. She led me to Jaco Pastorius, who led me to Wayne Shorter, who led me to Miles Davis. I had a simple rule: if Prince listened to it, I listened to it.

Before *Purple Rain*, I kept my Prince obsession close to the vest. But the day after the video for "When Doves Cry" premiered, I was shocked to see that my secret was out. Everyone suddenly knew what I knew, which was that Prince was everything.

✦ ✦ ✦

Prince was singular in his music. He was his own genre. That same singularity extended to everything: he went the other way in life, too. As he got older, the way he managed his career showed off that contrary streak. It came to the forefront in the way he mastered his records, in the way he handled reissues, in the way he used (or didn't use) the Internet and online streaming services. Control was job one to him, which allowed for amazing things in the studio and onstage, unprecedented leaps of inspiration and synthesis and an energy so prolific it seemed like it would never be shut off. But it also created mistrust when it came to letting the outside world in.

I don't know. There's so much we all don't know about Prince's life, and how he lived it, and why it ended, and what that will end up meaning for us all. This book will help, not to solve the mysteries necessarily, but to frame them, to give them life beyond Prince's life. This book will help to show us how much we need to know, and how much we can never know. This is what I do know: much of my motivation for waking up at 5:00 a.m. to work—and sometimes going to bed at 5:00 a.m. after work—came from him. Whenever it seemed like too steep a climb, I reminded myself that Prince did it, so I had to also. It was the only way to achieve that level of greatness (which was, of course, impossible, but that's aspirational thinking for ya). For the last twenty years, whenever I was up at five in the morning, I knew that Prince was up, too, somewhere. When Prince went away, 5:00 a.m. felt different. It wasn't a shared experience anymore. It was just a lonely hour, a cold time before the sun came up.

DIG IF YOU WILL THE PICTURE

INTRODUCTION

The End

THE PHRASE IS STUCK IN MY HEAD. IT'S THE GREAT GREG TATE WEIGH-ing in on Miles Davis's passing. Talking about it, Tate wrote, "seems more sillyass than sad." I think that's what Tate wrote. I went looking for my copy of *Flyboy in the Buttermilk*, Tate's 1992 essay collection, and I can't find it. I've looked everywhere. Still, I have the sentence in my mind, and it's not coming out. It's a good way of explaining how the departures of some people from the world make it seem like the world is disappearing rather than those people. It throws the whole question of existence into flux: If they're not here, how can we be sure that we are?

On the morning of April 21, 2016, I was at a sandwich shop, unwrapping lunch. First, I got an e-mail from my brother. Subject: "Prince." Body of message: "Noooo!" The next message was a link from my mother, who was passing along news from KTLA in Los Angeles that authorities had been dispatched to Paisley

Park to remove the body of an unidentified decedent. The dots connected themselves.

I was stunned into something more than silence: I was stunned into clamor. All at once, I heard Prince's music, not snatches of a few songs in medley but all of them, brutally overlaid. I heard the volcanic guitar from "When Doves Cry." I heard the scraping percussion from "Kiss." I heard the keening synthesizers of songs like "Automatic" and the rubbed-raw passion of "The Beautiful Ones." It was impossible to endure the music in that form, everything coming in at one time. It was a violence being done to some of the things that I loved the most.

✦ ✦ ✦

The first Prince album I bought was *1999*, which I picked up on cassette in a Peaches Records store in Miami. This was back in November of 1982, when it was new and I was new to Prince. I bought it for the cover art—his name and the record's title sinuously lettered on a field of purple stars, the dozens of hidden icons and messages—and listened to the music obsessively for weeks. After that, I was hooked. I went back and bought all the earlier albums, and from then on I never missed a release. In high school, I went directly from school to the store. In college, I showed up before the store opened. I remember getting *Around the World in a Day* in April of 1985, in the rain in Miami, and *Sign O' the Times* in March of 1987, in the midst of a surprise New Haven warm spell. I bought singles, too: the "Glam Slam" seven-inch, with "Escape" on the B side, came out in 1988, when I was back in Miami for the summer. The presidential election season was in full swing; the clerk at Peaches was a Gephardt guy and was saying so to the girl ahead of me in line. When I got to the cash register, I braced myself for more political talk. Instead, the clerk tapped the single, which was packaged in a transparent sleeve. "Wouldn't have been my choice," he said. "I would have picked 'Dance On.'"

I agreed. "Glam Slam" was a little airy for my tastes. "Dance On" was tougher funk. "He'll probably release that as the next single," I said.

"You're probably right," the clerk said.

I wasn't. He released the even airier "I Wish U Heaven." I bought that one, too.

A great deal of my (my parents') money went into Prince's (his record label's) pocket over the years. He released more than forty albums and almost a hundred singles and charted on the *Billboard* Hot 100 every year between 1978 and 1993. Nineteen of his songs made the top ten. Five went to number one: "When Doves Cry," "Let's Go Crazy," "Kiss," "Batdance," and "Cream." His signature song, "Purple Rain," peaked at number two, kept from the top spot by Wham!'s "Wake Me Up Before You Go-Go."

Those are just statistics, though—and sales statistics at that, the worst kind. They set the lower bound for his significance. Prince was, as Eddie Murphy said of Stevie Wonder, a musical genius. He was also, as he said of himself, a star. But he was several other things as well: lickerish pup, doe-eyed Jeremiah, peace cowboy, jazz-age sweetie, sylvan sprite, slam-bang funk bricoleur, spiritual pilgrim, sexual puppeteer, husband (twice), father (once, too briefly), man. For me, for most of my youth, he was something to defend fiercely. Adults—and plenty of other kids, for that matter—didn't seem to understand him. They didn't like the way he dressed, or underdressed. They made fun of his creepy little mustache (the dad of a kid I knew said that it looked like "someone's horribly wrong guess at something that someone else might find attractive"). They dismissed his music as pornographic, or hubristic, or melodramatic. They acted in error.

+ + +

In the summer of 1989, I rented a small bungalow in Key Largo for a month. It was just after my junior year of college, and I was trying to write a novel. I wanted to be alone. That was how art got made, right? My girlfriend drove me down and dropped me off. About two days later, I called her: I had made a terrible mistake with this "alone" stuff. Could she visit me? And, oh, by the way, before she drove down to see me, could she pick up Prince's new album, the soundtrack to that summer's blockbuster, *Batman*? We could listen to it together. My motives were impure, in that they were oddly pure. I wasn't motivated by sex or even really by loneliness. I wanted the record.

Batman started with "The Future," a slice of simmering dystopian funk that sampled the movie's dialogue, and then it was on to "Electric Chair," an aggressive rock song noteworthy less for its sound (thudding bass, screeching guitar, verse-chorus-verse structure) than for its psychology. "If a man is considered guilty / for what goes on in his mind," Prince sang, "then give me the electric chair / for all my future crimes."

"That's quite an idea," my girlfriend said. And it was. Prince didn't explicitly mention Matthew 5:28 ("everyone who looks at a woman with lustful intent has already committed adultery with her in his heart") or Orwell's notion of crimethink, but he was wrestling with the same ideas, wondering about the relationship between personal transgression and social control. That night, I turned on the TV for the first time that summer and we watched the video for "Batdance," the lead single from the album. It was directed by Albert Magnoli, who had directed *Purple Rain* and who was, by the late eighties, also Prince's manager. The "Batdance" video was staged like a Broadway musical—and not a good one, either—with a glut of colored lights and floor fog. Prince appeared as a character named Gemini. It was his actual astrological sign, but also an ontological model: half purple and half green, half hero and half villain, Gemini was the literal embodiment of something that had been in Prince's work from the start, a deep and abiding commitment to exposing internal contradictions in the human experience. The "Batdance" video wasn't good, but it was great.

It all was, for a while. When I started off with Prince—when anyone my age did—he was operating at a level that few other pop artists could even see, let alone reach. From *Dirty Mind*, in 1980, through to *Batman*, he rarely if ever put a foot wrong, and in the glorious middle of that period (from *1999*, in 1982, to *Sign O' the Times*, in 1987), he was perfect, the equivalent of Bob Dylan from 1965 to 1969, the Rolling Stones from 1968 to 1972, Talking Heads from 1980 to 1985, or Public Enemy from 1988 to 1991. At some point, the seams began to show. He made wobbly records, like *Graffiti Bridge*, and wearying ones, like *Diamonds and Pearls*. The awe we all felt at his talent turned to something else—to estimation, to the realization that he could be dropsical at times, fussy at times, incoherent at times. Rather than see him as a factory of genius that never faltered, I came to understand that even Prince sometimes had to get up on the step stool and, sighing, reset the "Days Since Last Accident" sign. As it turns out, that intensified my interest in him rather than erasing it. Perfection in artwork turns the contents cold. Flaws are what make for beauty, the way a stray strand tumbling out of an impeccable hairstyle ignites the heart.

So what is this book? It's an attempt to suture the laceration left by his death, to repair the rip in the world. It's an investigation. It's a celebration. In some ways, it's a frustration as well.

I wish I could transfuse the joy of hearing all Prince's albums over all the years—the great ones, the mixed bags, the duds—onto the page. But that experience can't be fully recaptured. It happened and then passed into the has-happened. So, this is not the gold itself, pulled up from the ocean floor as the treasure hunters wait breathlessly on the ship. Nor is it a detailed technical account of how the gold was located, extracted, and lifted. It's the footage of that moment. It's a visit to the museum where that gold is on display, a full-faith-and-credit description of the glow.

✦ ✦ ✦

I met Prince once. It was 1999. I was an editor at *Yahoo! Internet Life,* and we had started an awards show for musicians who were taking advantage of the then-nascent digital medium. Prince was nominated for an extended funk jam called "The War" that he had released on his website. We invited him to the ceremony at Studio 54, and he shocked us all by accepting the invitation, and then shocked us again by agreeing to do an online chat with fans on the afternoon of the show. He came in wearing a light suit, with a cane and, I think, a stickpin in his collar. He sat and talked while a young female assistant typed his answers. He was curious, pleasant, and funny, but he was not there very long.

That night, Spike Lee presented the award for the Best Internet-Only Single category. He read some introductory remarks I had written, in which he gave an overview of the format wars at the time, and then he introduced a video montage of the nominees. "I've been very fortunate to work with two of the nominees," he said, "Public Enemy on *Do the Right Thing* and The Artist on *Girl 6.*" The video montage ended. "The winner is," he said, opening the envelope, "from Minnesota." The crowd cheered. "The Artist, for 'The War.' And here to accept, The Artist." The crowd cheered louder.

Prince strode to the stage, dressed in black now, wearing sunglasses, sporting at least one large earring. He hugged Spike Lee. He briefly cradled his award, a round Lucite disc engraved with a speaker icon, after which he set it on the podium next to him. Then he spoke, using his natural tone, which was soft, precise, and unexpectedly deep.

> Thank you. Let me first say that I don't believe in the word "best." I appreciate it. I appreciate appreciation. Art's perception. One person's peanut butter is your jelly. This award should read "the NPG"; New Power Generation helped me make this record. What was cool about the song is that they didn't know what I was going to do. We started jamming, I had some lyrics, and the song just organically turned into what it turned into, tonight's so-called winner. The one thing I want to say is, don't be fooled by the Internet. It's cool to get on the computer, but don't let the computer get on you. It's cool to use the computer, but don't let the computer use you. You've all seen *The Matrix*. There's a war going on. The battlefield's in the mind. The prize is the soul. Thank you.

His speech—not quite an acceptance speech, more a defiance speech—touched on so many things, one after the other: the folly of judging art, the importance of collaboration, the value of spontaneity, the false lure of technology, the reality of soul and also of *the* soul.

The next year, he won another *Yahoo! Internet Life* award for an Internet-only single called "One Song." He didn't attend that ceremony, but he sent a speech in the form of a new song, joking that he didn't know why he won awards because he "only [knew] two chords," but adding, "thank U just the same." Then he sang Yahoo's name, a little dipsy doodle at the end. Later that year he released another online single called "My Medallion" that used the same instrumental backing. The original leaked soon enough—he was right about the Internet—under the title "Thank U Just the Same."

You're welcome. And thank you.

Section One

MAN, MUSIC

LIFE CAN BE
SO NICE

His Life and Its Beginnings

Beginnings consume us. Or rather, we consume them. We gobble them up hungrily, certain that they will explain all that follows. We break time into segments so that it can be apprehended and, if not overtaken, at least undertaken.

And, so, we start with the start of one particular segment: Prince was born on June 7, 1958. *Prince* was *born*. That's important to remember. In a life filled with so many achievements—lyrics written, songs sung, instruments played, concerts performed— that they seem to require an army, or a mystical being, we should begin with a reminder that they belong to exactly one person, who arrived on the earth via normal channels rather than descending into our realm from the empyrean plane.

Prince lived in music from the first. His mother, Mattie Della Shaw, was a singer. His father, John Nelson, was a piano player and composer. The two of them, African-Americans in mostly white Minneapolis, floated around the city's jazz scene in the fifties, and for a time Mattie sang with John's band, the Prince Rogers Trio. It's unclear how or why John thought of his stage name, though royalty was a common theme in jazz nicknames. Buddy Bolden was known as "King Bolden," and there were others: King Oliver, King Watzke, King Kolax. Princes were rarer.

When he met Mattie, John Nelson had a long-term girlfriend named Vivian. Though he and Vivian never married, he had five children with her, beginning in the late forties and continuing through the late fifties. Somewhere in there, John's relationship with Vivian wilted, and his relationship with Mattie bloomed. Mattie got pregnant. Their baby entered the world, and John transferred the name of his act to that baby: Prince Rogers Nelson.*

The world that Prince entered was a fragile one, at least as far as American identity was concerned. Sputnik had launched the previous October, kicking off the space race with the Soviets. The United States was just emerging from the Eisenhower recession, the first major economic downturn since the Great Depression—unemployment had soared; steel and auto production had dropped. Minneapolis was at the tail end of a decade of transformation. In 1950, the city reached the half-million mark in population—still an all-time peak—but legislation like the Housing Act of 1949 and the Federal-Aid Highway Act of 1956 were pushing population toward the near-ring suburbs and beyond. General Mills, one of the city's industrial anchors, moved out to Golden Valley.

---

* Prince's birthday was also the launch day of another homegrown Minnesota luminary that would make a mark in North American popular music—the lake freighter *SS Edmund Fitzgerald*, which spent seventeen years hauling taconite iron ore from mines near Duluth before it wrecked and sank on Lake Superior, inspiring Gordon Lightfoot's ballad.

Faced with a new family to feed, John took work as a plastic molder at Honeywell, the industrial conglomerate that was the city's largest employer. A daughter, Tyka, was born in 1960. Though the life of a plastic molder was more stable than that of a jazz musician, the marriage was not a happy one. John and Mattie fought frequently, separated more than once, and eventually split; over that period, Prince moved several times, always adjusting to new neighborhoods and new schools, making new friends while trying to keep in contact with the old ones.

Prince was smart and sensitive and a good athlete, but he was also shy and small. Early on, he took solace in music; it had been a source of joy for both his parents and it was a source of joy for him as well. When his mother brought him along to Dayton's, a local department store, in the early sixties, he would sneak away to the musical instruments section. His mother would find him there, a four-year-old, plinking out melodies. In the early sixties, he saw his father perform. "It was great," he said. "I couldn't believe it. People were screaming. From then on, I think, I wanted to be a musician." But if his father was inspiring onstage, at home he could be demanding and discouraging. "He was so hard on me," Prince told Tavis Smiley in 2009. "I was never good enough. It was almost like the army when it came to music . . . I wasn't allowed to play the piano when he was there because I wasn't as good as him. So when he left, I was determined to get as good as him, and I taught myself how to play music. And I just stuck with it, and I did it all the time. And sooner or later, people in the neighborhood heard about me and they started to talk."

Success has many fathers. In April of 1968, a few months before his tenth birthday, Prince went with his stepfather, Hayward Baker—his mother had remarried quickly, to stabilize a shaky situation—to see James Brown at the Minneapolis

Auditorium. "Yeah," James told the crowd, "I was just a shoe-shine boy and I'm still one of you; I haven't changed. Can you feel it?" Prince could.

✦ ✦ ✦

There are conflicting stories about what caused Prince to leave home. Some cite general instability, the wear and tear of too many moves. Others suggest that he was driven away by his mother's sternness, which kept him from hanging out with his friends and bandmates. The most salacious rumor holds that Prince's step-father, a devout Christian, found him in bed with a girl and promptly kicked him out of the house. What is certain is that Prince left his parents' home in his early teens and went to live with the family of his best friend, André Anderson, in the 1200 block of Russell Avenue. At first, he and André shared a room, but André was far messier, to the point where Prince had to move to the basement.

In that north-side neighborhood, kids streamed from their houses on Saturday morning to play football in the street. Walter Banks, who lived nearby and later became a local radio personality, remembered those games. "Prince was that athletic guy. He was unbelievable," Banks said. "He had an afro so big, it was more like his afro wore the uniform because his body was so small. He was a little giant within his own right." Prince also played basketball, and played well, a fact that would gain wide currency later on through the release of junior-high-school team photos and (more importantly, and more hilariously) a *Chappelle's Show* sketch. He was quick and funny, though he tended to work out his jokes in advance, in notebooks. He was highly produced even then.

At the end of junior high, Prince and André—who was now calling himself André Cymone—formed a band, Grand Central, with Chazz Smith (Prince's second cousin) on drums and André's sister Linda on keyboards. Within a year, Chazz Smith was out and a new drummer, Morris Day, was in. Grand Central practiced in André's basement, which was still Prince's bedroom. Morris Day's mother started managing the band, securing them gigs in local high school gyms, community centers, and hotels. Some were even paying gigs, after a fashion. In a late-nineties interview with Mel B. of the Spice Girls, Prince said that the band was compensated with Snickers bars: "That's how we exchanged money back then. It was currency." Grand Central's main competition was Flyte Tyme, another group made up of Minneapolis teens. Flyte Tyme's repertoire leaned toward soul artists like Al Green and James Brown; Grand Central also incorporated the work of rock and funk acts like Mandrill, Jimi Hendrix, and Santana, and even the songs of pop singers like Carole King. The two bands were on each other's radar, and then some; Flyte Tyme would later take on Morris Day as a front man and morph into The Time, Prince's greatest side project and one of his worthiest competitors. Jimmy Jam, who was then in a band called Cohesion but would later serve as Flyte Tyme's keyboardist, remembered playing in a small combo that backed the junior-high choir. Prince showed up, too, casually wandering over to a guitar and magically reproducing the fuzzed-out solo from Chicago's 1970 hit "Make Me Smile." The guitar stunt was impressive, but it was only the start. Jimmy was sitting at the drums, and when he stood up, Prince took his spot. "He sat there," Jimmy said, "and he killed 'em."

✦ ✦ ✦

Prince must have seemed like a perfect subject for a profile in the high school newspaper, and that's exactly what he became, on February 16, 1976. His high school, Central High, was the oldest in Minneapolis, founded in 1860; since 1913, it had occupied a four-story Collegiate Gothic building at Fourth Avenue South and East Thirty-Fourth Street. The school colors were red and blue, which Prince would later combine to great effect. (The lyrics of the school song, not written by Prince, began, "Oh, red and blue, dear red and blue, our hearts are true to you.")

In the school paper, Prince—identified as "Prince Nelson, senior at Central"—was pictured in the music room, his wide collar flared beneath his even wider afro. The piece didn't explore his personality, which was shy but playful (André Cymone would later say that "everybody who really knew him [knew] that he was a funny dude"). It didn't mention his participation in a student film, in which he played a shy but playful musician competing with a muscle-bound jock for the affections of a pretty cheerleader—the musician failed repeatedly until he learned a secret kung fu move and got the girl. Rather, the piece focused mainly on Prince's accomplishments as a musician: he had started playing piano at age seven, guitar "when he got out of eighth grade"; at the time of the article, he was also proficient on bass and drums, and he regretted having given up the saxophone, which he had played in seventh grade. He played by ear, though most budding musicians, he advised, should invest in lessons. "One should learn all their scales too," he said. "That is very important." He did not, the article noted, play in the school band. "I really don't have time to make the concerts," he said. After a brief mention of Prince's "more enthusiastically athletic" brother Duane, a member of both the football and basketball teams, the article returned to musical matters. Prince liked the school's music teachers—Mrs. Doepke and Mr. Bickham were especially supportive—but he felt stranded in Minneapolis. "I was born here, unfortunately," he says. "I think it is very hard for a band to make it in this state, even if they're good. Mainly because there aren't any big record companies or studios in this state. I really feel that if we would have lived in Los Angeles or New York or some other big city, we would have gotten over by now." Still, he was determined not to be marooned. Grand Central, the article concluded, was "in the process of recording an album containing songs they have composed. It should be released during the early part of the summer."

It wasn't, though there is evidence that Prince, André, and Morris visited ASI Studios on West Broadway in early 1976 to cut a set of tracks that included "39th St. Party," "Lady Pleasure," "You're Such a Fox," "Machine," "Whenever," and "Grand Central." Tom Waits, touring behind *Nighthawks at the Diner*, his first live album, played a show at ASI for FM broadcast about a month before Grand Central's session. There's no evidence he knew anything about Prince at the time, but a decade later, he would name him as one of the few popular artists who consistently impressed him: "Prince is rare, a rare exotic bird . . . To be that popular and that uncompromising, it's like Superman walking through a wall." Waits also said, "Writing songs is like capturing birds without killing them." Triangulate accordingly.

✦ ✦ ✦

In early 1976, a studio owner named Chris Moon hired Prince and André to record background music for an educational slide presentation. Bespectacled and bearded, Moon was also an aspiring songwriter—or rather, a poet in search of songs. He had notebooks filled with lyrics, and he noticed that Prince had a head filled with melodies. He gave Prince a key to his Moonsound studio, and Prince started to record there at night.

At around the same time, Prince struck up a relationship with a veteran R&B musician named Pepé Willie. Pepé Willie came from Brooklyn, but he had spent time in Minneapolis since the early seventies as a result of his on-again, off-again relationship with Prince's cousin, Shauntel Manderville. He had first met Prince in 1970 and over the years served as a kind of informal mentor to him. In 1974, back in Minneapolis and now married to Shauntel, he attended a ski party for which Grand Central had been hired as entertainment. He was impressed with Prince's progress:

> He would take off his guitar and go over to Linda and play the chords on the keyboard he wanted her to play. And I'm like, "Wait a minute, this guy plays keyboards too?" Then he would take André's bass and play like he had been doing it for twenty years, playing the funkiest lines.

By the end of Prince's time in high school, Grand Central was at a crossroads. For starters, their name had become a liability—they were too often confused with Graham Central Station, the popular Bay Area funk band led by Larry Graham, the former bassist with Sly and the Family Stone (and a distant-future collaborator of Prince's). When the band rebranded itself as Champagne, Prince began to distance himself from the group, first to work with a local musician named Sonny Thompson and then, with André, to support Pepé Willie and his group 94 East. Some of Prince's earliest recordings date from this period, songs like "Lovin' Cup," "Dance to the Music of the World," and "One Man Jam." Prince didn't sing on the tracks and cowrote only one of them, "Just Another Sucker." Still, he was instrumental in the sessions, contributing on guitar, bass, keyboards, and drums.

In the meantime, his partnership with Chris Moon had started to bear fruit. One of their songs, "Soft and Wet," became a new favorite in Prince's set. It wasn't the crowning jewel of his early catalog, though. That honor was reserved for "Just as Long as We're

Together," a sparkling demonstration of his singing, playing, and songwriting. Prince put together a demo and briefly went to New York to shop it, without much luck. At the same time, Moon sent the songs to a local music impresario named Owen Husney. Husney had been the lead guitarist of the mid-sixties Minneapolis garage-blues band the High Spirits—a forerunner to Twin Cities groups like Hüsker Dü and the Replacements—and he had gone on to work in various aspects of the music business, everything from catering to advertising. Husney liked what he heard of Prince's music, though he thought the songs were too long; most were extended soul-funk workouts designed to showcase all of Prince's instrumental skills. Husney felt that they weren't going to attract veteran A&R men, and he called Prince with a pitch: he would help shepherd Prince through the process if Prince would come back to Minneapolis and work on the songs. Prince agreed. Husney was instantly impressed by Prince's intensity and intelligence, as he told Kim Taylor Bennett of Noisey:

> I've seen pictures of Little Richard when he was in a band before he was Little Richard. They're all sitting around, one of them is looking off right, one's looking off left, one's looking down, and then there's a very young Little Richard, and his eyes are laser focused on that camera. You can see the burning; you can see there's something else. That was the feeling I had about Prince. There was a focus, there was a brilliance of intelligence.

Husney also took note of Prince's massive afro, which he dubbed a J7, because it dwarfed the afros of the Jackson 5, which were themselves significant. Husney wanted to get Prince his own apartment and some recording equipment, so he sought out local professionals whom he knew—a doctor, a lawyer—and signed them up as investors. While Prince set about shortening and sharpening his songs, Husney started to package him for major labels. He created press kits in which he lowered Prince's age by a year: whatever he was worth as an eighteen-year-old wunderkind, Husney figured, he was worth that much more as a seventeen-year-old. He outfitted Prince in a three-piece suit to distinguish him against the prevailing fashions, which tended toward casual dress, jeans and open shirts. He sent out demos not on cassettes but on reel-to-reel tapes, coloring them silver for maximum impact. Finally, he played labels off each other: He called Warner Bros., where he knew people through his advertising work, and told them that he had already secured a meeting with Columbia, which was flying him to California, and would be interested in stopping by Warner's offices while he was out west. He then did the same thing in reverse, calling Columbia and telling them that Warner was flying him out but that he'd love to stop by and give Columbia a look at his client as well. He ran the game a third time, on A&M Records, and called two other labels for good measure, RSO and ABC/Dunhill.

Husney's plan all along was to place Prince at Warner Bros., the most artist-friendly of the labels, and Warner was receptive, though the label wanted to assign him a producer. They suggested Maurice White of Earth, Wind & Fire, and there were some backup ideas as well: Norman Whitfield, Nick Ashford and Valerie Simpson. Prince put his foot down. It wasn't that he didn't respect their suggestions, but he wanted to make a record that sounded only like himself. Husney understood Prince's perspective, but he thought it would be a tough sell. "I had the great job of going to the chairman of Warner Bros. and saying that an eighteen-year-old artist, who has never made an album before, is going to be producing his own album and having complete creative control," Husney later told NPR. "I didn't relish that meeting." Warner agreed to a kind of test. Bring the kid in, they told Husney. Let's see what he's got.

On a summer morning in 1977, Prince was ushered into a Warner studio. He sat down immediately at the drums and created a rhythm track, after which he started in on the bass. As Husney stood in the hall watching, Lenny Waronker came around the corner. Waronker, the head of A&R for Warner, was an industry vet who had produced hits like the Mojo Men's "Sit Down, I Think I Love You" and signed artists such as Randy Newman and Ry Cooder. Waronker stopped to watch Prince, who had by now moved on to guitar. Husney couldn't read Waronker's expression. Was Warner going to scotch the deal?

They weren't. "By the time the drum part was recorded, it was clear," Waronker told the Minneapolis *Star Tribune* in 2004, as part of a tribute to Prince for his induction into the Rock and Roll Hall of Fame. "We didn't want to insult him by making him go through the whole process, but he wanted to finish. As I was walking through the studio, he was on the floor. He looked up and said, 'Don't make me black.' I thought, 'Whoa!' He said, 'My idols are all over the place.' He named an array that was so deep in terms of scope of music that for an eighteen-year-old kid to say what he said was amazing. That, as much as anything, made me feel that we shouldn't mess around with this guy."

Warner extended the gangway, and Prince came aboard. In the September 1 issue of the *St. Paul Dispatch*, the signing was the subject of a short news story. It began with the facts, such as they were (Husney's age deception was not exposed): "A just-turned-eighteen-year-old Minneapolis youth has signed a six-figure recording contract with Warner Bros. and is scheduled to begin recording his first album today in Sound 80 studios, Minneapolis." The article reviewed Prince's bona fides (he played "drums, bass, lead and rhythm guitar, piano, synthesizers, and percussions," and sang "lead as well as all the backups"), engaged in some myth-making regarding his career to date (Prince and Husney pretended that he had not performed yet in the Twin Cities because his "ambition was to be a national recording star and he did not want to wear out his talent in local clubs"), and remarked upon the unusual terms of the contract (the grant of full creative control, plus the fact that three albums were guaranteed rather than the customary one or two). The piece ended with an assessment of his prospects:

> Do you think Prince will become a star? "I know he will," shot back Husney. But after a pause, he said, "Maybe I shouldn't use the word star, but I know Prince is a legitimate talent and he'll do well."

He was a legitimate talent. He did well. There would be false starts, but they would pass quickly, and once his star began to rise, it went so quickly that it was as if everyone else was falling away. Life unfolded in a series of rapidly accelerating moments, a flip-book under time's thumb.

Moment: It's 1985, the night that the American Music Awards are broadcast on ABC. The ceremony takes up most of the evening, running an interminable three hours. Lionel Richie hosts. The producers entrust the job of presenting Favorite Black Single to the whitest performers imaginable—the country singer Janie Fricke, then at the height of her popularity, and the Beach Boys. There are only three nominees per category, because that's how business is done at the American Music Awards: there's Billy Ocean, for "Caribbean Queen"; Tina Turner, for "What's Love Got to Do with It"; and Prince, for "When Doves Cry." Al Jardine announces the winner; it's Prince. "Big Chick" Huntsberry, Prince's blond, Hulk Hogan–like bodyguard, clears the way for the band. Prince—hair curly, one eye covered, decked out in an Edwardian blouse and purple jacket—accepts the award. "Outrageous," says Lionel Richie, happily. Later, Huey Lewis and Madonna present Favorite Black Album; the nominees are Lionel Richie's *Can't Slow Down*, Michael Jackson's *Thriller*, and *Purple Rain*. Huey Lewis pretends that he can't remember Prince's name and snaps his fingers for recall. "Well, what is it?" Madonna says. "This is going to come as a surprise," Huey Lewis says, "but it's *Purple Rain*, by Prince and the Revolution." The whole band returns to the stage for the second award, Prince bringing up the rear, walking like George Jefferson, trailed by Big Chick. Wendy Melvoin, Prince's guitarist in the Revolution, takes the second award and says some nice things about vinyl. Lionel Richie says "Outrageous," again. The word has lost much of its meaning by now. The third time, it's Favorite Pop/Rock Album, presented by Vanity and two members of Night Ranger, one of them chattering ceaselessly just off-mic. Vanity reads Prince's nomination and then announces him as the winner. "I Would Die 4 U" plays on the PA system as Prince comes to the stage again. This time, he finally speaks; it's as if he knew he'd have a third shot at the mic. "For all of us," he says, "life is death without adventure, and adventure only comes to those who are willing to be daring and take chances."

Moment: 1991, the MTV Video Music Awards. Arsenio Hall is hosting at the Universal Amphitheatre in Los Angeles. Much of the night is spent handing trophy after trophy to R.E.M. for their "Losing My Religion" video, which firmly establishes the ascendancy of so-called alternative rock. There are a dozen performances, and many of them are sexual in nature, including Van Halen's "Poundcake" and Poison's "Talk Dirty to Me." But only one is sexy. "This is the one," says Hall, wearing a sweatshirt with way too many colors. "This is the reason I took the gig again."

The opening scream of "Gett Off" sounds in the hall. Dancers appear. There's (safe) fire on the stage. Then Prince strides out: swoop of hair, ventilated yellow suit, Yellow Cloud guitar. He lip-syncs the scream a second time, falls to the ground, magically rises to his feet via a reverse split, approaches the mic, and snags his sleeve on the stand, botching a word or two in the process. (I contend this was at least partly on purpose, to remind the audience that he's singing live.) Midway through the song, he spins around to reveal that his outfit is entirely assless. The song proceeds, with plenty of full-bacchanal dancing, a lead vocal that finds a lovelier melody than the one on the album, guitar played while spinning, and a closing chant of "peace and love," but all anyone will ever to be able to remember is the assless pants. "What'd I tell you?" Arsenio says afterwards. "I told y'all it was funky like doo-doo." The next year, Howard Stern appears as Fartman (Wikipedia offers a helpful taxonomy: "Species: Human") and displays the second most famous ass in MTV Video Music Awards history.

Moment: 1999, *Larry King Live* on CNN. Larry King's is the first voice we hear. "Tonight: he's rocked, he's shocked, and he's been telling us to party like it's 1999 for seventeen years . . . a music world original, The Artist Formerly Known as Prince." It's hard to tell who dressed more flamboyantly for this interview: Larry is sporting a wide white collar, purple-and-green suspenders, and a green tie. Prince wears a black jacket with a gold decorative edge. On the chyron, he's identified by his now famous glyph. Larry opens by discussing the relative scarcity of Prince releases in the late nineties, and Prince explains that he has been discouraging bootleggers by releasing his own versions of leaked songs. Larry calls him "unusual." Prince begins to protest. Larry calls him "different." Prince protests again. "Well," Larry says, "most people don't get famous with one name and

then change it. What's the story about that?" Prince speaks softly
and quietly, like he's thinking as he goes: "Well, I had to search
deep within my heart and spirit, and I wanted to make a change
and move to a new plateau in my life. One of the ways I did that
was to change my name. It sort of divorced me from the past and
all the hang-ups that go along with it." He mentions the fact that
he is in a "deep dispute" with his record label, and Larry inter-
rupts. "That's Warner Brothers, right? Which owns this network,
I might add." Prince recoils a bit. Larry presses the name issue.
Larry says that the only other person who changed names after
achieving fame was Muhammad Ali—he doesn't remember
Kareem Abdul-Jabbar, and Ron Artest hasn't yet become Metta
World Peace. Finally, Larry endorses the symbol. "It's pretty
cool," Prince says, pretty cool himself. "It makes for great jew-
elry, too." The name issue seems settled, though a little later
on Prince confuses matters again: "I'm still Prince. I just use a
different sound for my name, which is none." Larry asks about
Spain, where Prince is living at the time. Prince likes the Iberian
pace, the fact that everything shuts down in the afternoon. Larry
says, hilariously, "Siesta—fiesta—siesta." When Prince says he
doesn't like to live in the past, Larry says, "You're not a reminis-
cer." Prince leans in. "Is that a word, Larry?" But Prince is a rem-
iniscer for a little while, recapping his Minneapolis origins,
throwing shade at Owen Husney in the process ("I was taken
out to Los Angeles by my first manager, whose name escapes
me"). Finally, Larry King asks a predictable but good question:
How would Prince describe his own music? "The only thing
I could think of, because I really don't like categories, is 'inspira-
tional.'" Then Prince talks about the origins of "1999" (including
the claim that he will retire the song on New Year's Eve, which
turns out to be as ridiculous as Larry King's suspenders), takes
a backseat during a secondary interview with Larry Graham,

who has just been signed to Prince's label NPG Records, and fields questions from callers. A woman on the phone asks Prince what different people in his life—his wife, his bandmates—call him. He answers, still speaking softly and quietly: "Larry [Graham] calls me 'baby brother,' Mayte calls me 'honey.' Let's see, my enemies call me 'squiggle,' and, you know, all kinds of crazy."

2

BABY I'M A STAR

His Music and Its Beginnings

ON AUGUST 10, 1979, MICHAEL JACKSON RELEASED *OFF THE WALL*. Jackson, who had shot to fame a decade earlier as the eleven-year-old lead singer of the Jackson 5, was now a few weeks shy of his twenty-first birthday, and he was ready for his close-up. The lead single and first track, "Don't Stop 'Til You Get Enough," opened with a pulsing synth bass that started the album on its relentless march toward the top of the charts. No one could get enough, and it didn't stop.

Two weeks later, Prince released "I Wanna Be Your Lover." The single was the first song from his eponymous second album, which was a reintroduction of sorts. Prince's debut, *For You*, had been released the previous April—*Dallas* had just debuted on CBS; Cher was on the cover of *People* magazine. While it had showcased a virtuosic musician and singer, especially in the falsetto mode, the lasting impression was of an artist still finding his footing. The album had no big hits. "Soft and Wet," a naughty little burble released as a single on Prince's twentieth birthday (nineteenth, by Husney's false count), got to number ninety-two on the *Billboard* Hot 100. For an immensely talented, immensely determined young artist like Prince—not to mention for Warner Bros., the label that had invested heavily in him—it wasn't enough. Prince had retrenched, holing up in Alpha Studios in Burbank, California, in late spring 1979 and cutting nine tracks in quick succession. A few years later, Prince would plan and then abandon a semi-fictionalized tour documentary called *The Second Coming*, but Prince's second album was his first second coming.

Prince, the album, was released in October of 1979. *Dallas* had just started its third season, which would conclude with the "Who shot J.R.?" cliffhanger, and once again, Cher was on the cover of *People* magazine, this time dressed in a Bob Mackie show girl–style outfit. Prince was on the cover of *Prince*, dressed in nothing at all (at least down to the nipples) and showing mostly hair—head, chest, and a stippling of mustache.

The album was alive on arrival. "I Wanna Be Your Lover" burst from the gate with a taut, danceable guitar line and a confident falsetto. The lyrics addressed a woman, but they also seemed to be Prince's appeal to his not-yet-seduced audience—though he didn't have much money, not like "those other guys you hang around," he was promising unconditional devotion. The real revelation was the song's second half, which sped away on twin outboards of keyboard and guitar. "I Wanna Be Your Lover" entered the charts at number eighty-five, higher than "Soft and Wet" ever got, and kept going for sixteen weeks. In mid-December, 1979, Prince taped an episode of *American Bandstand*; by the time it aired, in January 1980, the song had climbed all the way to number eleven.

American Bandstand certified Prince as a star on the rise, but he wasn't on his own. He had, the previous summer, rented space in Del's Tire Mart, a warehouse near the University of Minnesota, to audition a backing band. He brought aboard the drummer Bobby Rivkin (who went by "Bobby Z," maybe to conflate himself favorably with fellow Minnesotan Robert Zimmerman), the guitarist Dez Dickerson, and two keyboardists, Matt "Dr." Fink and Gayle Chapman. André Cymone played bass. They hadn't been taking the record out live for very long: the group had showcased it for Warner in August, at a rehearsal space on Hollywood Boulevard, and debuted it onstage at the Roxy Theatre, on Sunset Boulevard.* On *Bandstand*, Prince wore pants that were gold and tight and a shirt that was pink and open. He danced and spun and played guitar; when he strutted and high-stepped, he looked like Mick Jagger's long-lost cousin. Directly after tearing through "I Wanna Be Your Lover," Prince was interviewed by *Bandstand*'s longtime host, Dick Clark. Clark would later insist that Prince was the "single most difficult interview" he had ever done. On the strength of available video, that seems like an exaggeration. Prince admitted that his music wasn't what people expected to hear from a Minneapolis-based artist, identified his band (Dick Clark, repeating names chummily, called Gayle Chapman "Dale"), lied about his age ("Nineteen," he said, shaving off two years now), held up fingers to indicate how long ago he had

---

* The opening act at the Roxy was the magician turned stand-up comic Judy Carter. Before the show, Carter staged a guerrilla performance outside the theater, pretending to be a blind accordionist and playing "Lady of Spain" over and over again. When she took the stage, still holding her accordion, the audience groaned, but the set went well. Years later, she would recall that Prince stopped by her dressing room to tell her how much he liked her act and to pose for a photo. "I was struck by how tiny he was," she wrote in *Psychology Today*. "Onstage he'd had such a huge presence. It was obvious that he was painfully shy as he said, 'Thank you for opening for me. You were really terrific.'"

shopped his demos (four years), and clouded the question of how many instruments he played ("Thousands," he said, before humblebragging that it was far fewer, maybe only a half dozen or so). All along the way, he was a small weather event of insouciance, all hair flips and doe eyes. It seemed calculated to increase his mystique, and it achieved that effect perfectly. Then the band got back to playing. "Why You Wanna Treat Me So Bad?" opened with a shot of the show set's disco ball, rotating overhead. The guitar slid from Prince's shoulders into his hands, where it ignited. A microphone stand was knocked to the floor in the fervor.

✦ ✦ ✦

After "I Wanna Be Your Lover" scraped the top ten, Prince didn't get back there for four years. He wasn't happy about it. His third and fourth albums—*Dirty Mind*, in 1980, and *Controversy*, in 1981—generated tremendous critical goodwill, but the closest they came to a hit was the latter record's title song, which reached number seventy in 1980. Along the way, he parted company with Husney. He made another record that year, too—an arrest record. In Jackson, Mississippi, on tour, Dr. Fink decided that the band needed a bullhorn for an onstage prop, and Prince borrowed one from an overhead compartment of their airplane. A stewardess saw him putting it into his bag and called the police.

Then *1999*, released in 1982, began to move the needle. The title song, helped along by a sexy video (Prince playing live, surrounded by ladies in lingerie), hit the top twenty. "Little Red Corvette" went top ten, as did "Delirious," the album's third single—partly because it drafted behind "Little Red Corvette" and partly because DJs, desirous of a little time to themselves, often cued up the first three songs of the record and let them play as one fifteen-minute sequence. The album sold surprisingly well for a double album: more than four million copies in the United States and almost another two million internationally.

There was no Prince album in 1983, a year dominated by Michael Jackson's *Thriller* and the Police's *Synchronicity*. *Thriller* maintained its stranglehold on the top of the charts for the first four months of 1984, eventually giving way to the *Footloose* soundtrack and Bruce Springsteen's *Born in the U.S.A.* Then, in August, Prince returned to the top of the charts with his fifth album, *Purple Rain*. For many people, that's where Prince began, or where they began with him. And for many of those people, *Purple Rain* began with the release of "When Doves Cry."

✦ ✦ ✦

He bathed, purple flowers strewn around the tub, a mushroom cloud of steam hanging over him. He crawled across the floor. He stood at the mirror looking pensive. He stood at the mirror looking petulant. He disappeared and was replaced by an illustration of a face: two eyes, two nostrils, one red lip, eventually one purple tear streaking downward across that face. He dreamed a courtyard and asked everyone else to do the same.

The first time I saw "When Doves Cry," I didn't hear it. I was at a friend's house doing homework and MTV was on in the background, the sound turned all the way down. That night, the radio corrected the error. The song opened with a squall of guitar and a precarious beat. The rhythm was the musical equivalent of a Dutch angle: the horizon line of the song wasn't straight, and psychological tension was everywhere. There was a kind of astringency in the vocals, a choked-up or choked-off quality; it was a song that said plenty but was still mostly filled with what could not be said. Like *Dirty Mind*, like "1999," the song straddled reality and fantasy: the "Dig if you will the picture" verse was framed as an act of imagination, as was the "Dream if you can a courtyard" verse. In those fantasies, Prince—Prince, the narrator of the song, who was significantly similar to but not identical to Prince, the man—asked his lover (and, by extension, the rest of us listening to the song) to join him in a vision of romance. He had pulled off great lines before, sometimes for an entire song ("Little Red Corvette"), but here his lyrical abilities intensified. "An ocean of violets in bloom" was as powerful an image, as succinct and mysterious, as anything Prince (or anyone else) wrote in an eighties pop song, and the way he characterizes his romantic anxiety as "butterflies all tied up" lagged only slightly behind. Then there were the animals, striking curious poses, feeling the heat between Prince and his lover (or was it his audience?). But the request to join him in these images wasn't casual. He employed the imperative mode ("dig this," "dream this"), and what initially sounded like confident instruction was quickly revealed as desperation: "Can you, my darling, can you picture this?" The chorus shifted to a tone of actual betrayal ("How can you just leave me standing / alone in a world that's so cold?"): Prince (again, as Prince, the narrator) took responsibility for the romantic breakdown for only a moment before laying blame at the feet of his parents—his too-bold father and his never-satisfied mother. Self-absorption couldn't be held off for long. While *Purple Rain*, the film, lingered on the violence between the parents, "When Doves Cry" shifted quickly back to the narrator: the chorus wondered not "why do *they* scream at each other," but "why do *we* scream at each other." Just past the four-minute mark, after singing the title phrase, Prince unleashed a series of unearthly shrieks. There were six short ones—a hex of them—and then a four-second showstopper. The show didn't stop, of course; Prince vocalized along with the stuttering rhythm and then closed up shop with a dazzling keyboard solo. When you heard the song on the radio, it eclipsed the first few seconds of the song that followed. That's how powerful it was.

✦ ✦ ✦

"When Doves Cry" was not only an aesthetic triumph but a commercial one as well, a song that spent more than a month atop the charts and was the last single by a solo artist to be certified platinum when platinum still meant two million in sales. The song's size and scope was no accident: Dr. Fink, the same keyboard player who had goaded Prince into stealing an airplane bullhorn, encouraged him toward more overt pop music during the *1999* tour. "We kept running into Bob Seger and the Silver Bullet Band," Fink later told *Spin*. "After one of the shows, Prince asked me what made Seger so popular. I said, 'Well, he's playing mainstream pop-rock.' Michael Jackson and Prince were breaking ground, but there was still a lot of segregation on mainstream radio. I said, 'Prince, if you were to write something along these lines, it would cross things over for you even further.' I'm not trying to take credit for anything here, but possibly that influenced him."

"When Doves Cry" was followed, just two months later, by its fraternal twin, "Let's Go Crazy." It opened with a churchy organ surging beneath a spiritual monologue ("Dearly beloved, we are gathered here today to get through this thing called 'life' "), after which it erupted into a welter of calliopelike synthesizers and full-throated rock-and-roll singing—and guitar. Prince had stepped back from the guitar slightly on *1999* in favor of more outré keyboard and drum programming. For "Let's Go Crazy," he stepped forward again, wearing seven-league boots. Suddenly, the eighties got their own Jimi Hendrix, and black rock got its own Eddie Van Halen. Melodically similar to another hit of the time, the J. Geils Band's "Freeze-Frame," the song was bracingly buoyant, less an axe for the frozen sea within us than a raft for the roiling one. Lyrically, the balance of the song made good on the sermon of the opening moments. The theme of pursuing adventure despite the inevitability of death—"look[ing] for the purple banana until they put us in the truck"—recalled the dance-in-the-face-of-the-apocalypse message of "1999" and would be echoed again a few years later in its tie-dyed cousin, "Play in the Sunshine," in which Prince insisted that he would love all his enemies "till the gorilla falls off the wall." (It was a Donkey Kong version of the end, but still—game over.)

"Let's Go Crazy" entered the charts with "When Doves Cry" still perched at number one. It arrived at number two in late September, spent a week eyeing John Waite's "Missing You," and then swept past it, remaining at number one for two weeks before giving way to Stevie Wonder's "I Just Called to Say I Love You" (see also: "when you call up that shrink in Beverly Hills"). It also topped the dance chart, where it was replaced by Stephanie Mills's "The Medicine Song" (see also: "thrills and pills and daffodils"). Neither of those songs was a highlight for the charting artists; nor were some of the other songs "Let's Go Crazy" bumped up against in the top five: Laura Branigan's "Self Control," Dan Hartman's "I Can Dream About You." It was a lightship among the flotsam of the radio mainstream.

The rest of the record was electric as well. "Computer Blue" was a sizzling techno-rocker whose guitar solo grew out of an untitled piano piece written by Prince's father. "Darling Nikki" channeled pain and loss through a character study of a licentious woman (or was it a character study of a disappointed man?). The last stretch of the album documented a live performance from an August Wednesday at the Minneapolis nightclub First Avenue. The show opened with "Let's Go Crazy" (though that version was not used for the album), included a cover of Joni Mitchell's

"A Case of You," and debuted the mysterious "Electric Inter-
course," which was bumped from *Purple Rain*, both the film and
the album, in favor of "The Beautiful Ones." But everything else
made the cut. Prince and his band tore through "I Would Die 4
U" and "Baby I'm a Star." Both were up-tempo. Both were messianic. Both were Rorschachs, of a sort. If you were the kind of
listener who preferred the former, you liked your Prince pinned
down by his own erotic and spiritual suffering, reveling in the
idea of being rooted to the spot. If you were the kind of listener
who preferred the latter, you liked your Prince up off the mat and
triumphant. My own preference has changed over the years.
At first, I skipped "I Would Die 4 U" because the melody had a
narrow range; I went straight to "Baby I'm a Star," which seemed
like a superior funk composition. Later, when Prince was locked
in battle with Warner Bros., I listened more to "I Would Die 4 U."
Over the last year, for obvious reasons, I've been back to "Baby
I'm a Star."

The concert at First Avenue ended the way the album would
end, the way the movie would end, with the title song of *Purple
Rain*, as grand and lovely a ballad as Prince ever wrote. He poured
it all out. He never meant to cause us any sorrow, he never meant
to cause us any pain. He would take it all on himself. Those were
the terms of his martyrdom, of his stardom, of his kingdom.

+ + +

Before there was an end of the movie, there was a beginning of it,
in the form of a screenplay. It wasn't the *Purple Rain* screenplay
but an earlier version called *Dreams*, created at the behest of the
Prince camp by a screenwriter named William Blinn. Blinn had
worked mostly in television—he had written the TV movie *Brian's
Song* and been heavily involved with shows like *Starsky and Hutch*
and *Eight Is Enough*. In the early eighties, Blinn was writing for

Fame, the television series adapted from the film about students at the New York High School for the Performing Arts. Robert Cavallo, Prince's manager at the time, approached him with the idea of writing a movie loosely based on Prince's own life; in May of 1983, Blinn went to Minneapolis to watch Prince and his band and collect material for the project. The script came together quickly. It was about the Kid, an up-and-coming musician who was struggling with the recent death of his parents by murder-suicide. There was also a battle for local supremacy between the Kid's band and a competing outfit, an idea that occurred to Blinn after he observed the fierce fraternal rivalry between the Revolution and the Time.*

Many directors passed on *Dreams;* they dismissed it as over-wrought and excessively dark, a dreary melodrama without enough pop appeal to make it commercially viable. One of them, James Foley—who would later helm such tense dramas as *At Close Range* and *After Dark, My Sweet*—mentioned the project to a friend at USC's film school, another aspiring director named Albert Magnoli. Magnoli read *Dreams* and came to the same conclusion as the others. While certain elements of the script excited him, he thought that he could find another way into the story. For starters, he wanted to eliminate the murder-suicide subplot, or at

---

* In a later interview with *Spin,* the Time's stalwart drummer, Jellybean Johnson, remembered a typical early-eighties night: "We're onstage, and all of a sudden, Morris Day's big bodyguard grabs Jesse Johnson and snatches him offstage. And Prince takes his place playing guitar. They take Jesse backstage, chain him to a coatrack or whatever, and proceed to pour syrup, or whatever food was in their dressing room, all over him. Now the band is wondering what the hell's goin' on: Prince is still playing guitar, and Jesse's gone, and then they got Jerome [Benton] too. So when we got done with the last song, we decided, 'We're gonna kick their ass[es].' We took all our suits off and got into some dirty clothes, and we got eggs and everything, and we made them quite uncomfortable. We wouldn't do it while the show was going on, 'cause we figured we would've got fired, but the minute the show was over, it was on. We got all of them. We didn't discriminate."

least back it up in time: he thought the Kid's parents should be alive and in the midst of their tumultuous relationship. That way, he could develop the Kid's character by contrasting his confidence onstage with a more fragile and fearful home life. He also felt that Minneapolis club culture should be more central to the story. He contacted Cavallo and sketched out his plan for retooling the script. By that point, Blinn had gone back to Los Angeles to resume work on *Fame*. Cavallo, impressed with Magnoli's ideas, agreed to send him to Minneapolis to explore the new direction.

When Magnoli arrived in Minneapolis, he was met by another of Prince's managers, Steve Fargnoli, who informed him that he was probably wasting his time. They had scraped together a million dollars in financing, half of which was coming from Prince himself, who was determined to put *Dreams* on film. Fargnoli was cordial, almost apologetic. He didn't send Magnoli home. They drove to a hotel, where Magnoli waited in a suite with Big Chick Huntsberry. Finally, a door opened, and Prince emerged. The group went to a restaurant, where Prince ordered spaghetti and orange juice, one of his favorite meals at the time. Prince asked Magnoli what he thought of *Dreams*. Magnoli tried to read the room. Prince's manner was quiet and thoughtful. He seemed as though he really wanted Magnoli's opinion. Magnoli inhaled deeply and then took a chance, pitching Prince on the idea he had mentioned to Cavallo on the phone, adding in details and texture as he went: Much of the film would focus on the young musician's problematic relationship with his father, who had himself been a talented pianist but hadn't gotten the necessary breaks to make it in the music world. The father would be domineering and abusive. Maybe the young man would discover a secret stash of songs the father had written. Prince got up from the table. "Let's go," he said. He sent Fargnoli and Huntsberry in one car and took Magnoli in his blue BMW.

On that ride, Prince veered off the highway onto a street that was pitch black on both sides. Magnoli later surmised that it ran through a cornfield. Prince asked if Magnoli knew his music, and Magnoli said not really, except for the few big singles from *1999*. Prince blinked and asked how, if Magnoli wasn't familiar with his work, he could pitch a script that was so close to Prince's essence. Prince was especially interested in the violence of the story; he asked if it was important that the Kid be hit by his father. "Yes," Magnoli said. Prince nodded. They then spoke briefly about the music; Prince said that he had almost a hundred songs finished and told Magnoli to drop by the next day to hear them. He did, and even received a care package from Prince in the form of a box of cassettes.

The next hurdle was finding a studio. Warner Bros. was interested, but executives wanted to cast someone else to play the Kid, possibly John Travolta. They also wanted to soften the script so that it wouldn't earn an R rating from the Motion Picture Association of America.* Prince and Magnoli dug in their heels. They had their star; that was nonnegotiable. And they didn't want to sacrifice the story's darkness or sexuality: *Flashdance*, the previous year's most popular movie musical, had been rated R. Eventually, Warner conceded on both points, and Magnoli embedded himself in the Minneapolis scene the same way that Blinn had, observing and interviewing Prince and his band to build the story. Filming began on Halloween. The budget was seven million dollars; the shoot was scheduled for forty-two days. Winter intervened, making second takes impossible and sending the

---

* The PG-13 rating was new at the time. In the early eighties, films designed for young audiences were starting to incorporate more profanity and violence, drawing criticism from parents. On the heels of especially intense PG releases like *Gremlins* and *Indiana Jones and the Temple of Doom*, Steven Spielberg proposed a new intermediate rating, PG-13, that would further warn parents about content.

production to Los Angeles to pick up most of the interior shots. Still, as long as *Purple Rain* stayed in Minneapolis, Minneapolis stayed with *Purple Rain*. "We had over nine hundred extras who came to the set every day excited," Magnoli said. "They gave the whole scene a tremendous amount of realism."

Prince saw the rough cut at a private showing in Los Angeles, on Santa Monica Boulevard. He didn't attend any test screenings, though he heard from executives that enthusiasm was through the roof with crowds from Culver City, in California, to rural Texas. *Purple Rain* was released in July of 1984. Reviews were mixed on the merits of the film. Vincent Canby, in the *New York Times*, wrote, "The offstage stuff is utter nonsense"—but it was nonsense America wanted. It made back its entire budget in its first weekend, after which Warner expanded the release to a thousand theaters. Over the course of the year, it grossed more than seventy million dollars.*

+ + +

Purple Rain wasn't where purple first appeared in Prince's work; it was all over *1999*, from the star-filled sky on the album cover to the first verse of the title song. But *Purple Rain* was where it became inseparable from Prince's image. On the album cover and throughout much of the film, Prince wore what would come to be his trademark look: a neo-Edwardian purple suit with a chain-mail patch on the right shoulder, a ruffled white shirt, and black pants with an asymmetrical fly. The outfit

---

* James Foley ended up directing his own pop-star movie. Unfortunately, it was *Who's That Girl*, starring Madonna, a project that he joined as a result of his friendship with Madonna's then husband, Sean Penn. (Foley had directed Penn in *At Close Range*, served as best man at the pair's wedding, and been responsible for two Madonna videos, "Papa Don't Preach" and "Live to Tell.") *Who's That Girl* earned seven million dollars, a tenth of *Purple Rain*'s gross.

was created by Louis Well and Terry Vaughn, who had also designed costumes for Earth, Wind & Fire. (Prince hadn't wanted Maurice White to produce his music, but clothes were a different matter.)

The color was a good match. Purple was, after all, the royal color, fit for a Prince. It was the color of the Minnesota Vikings, Prince's hometown football team. And while it was the color with the shortest wavelength, it had a long tradition in rock and soul music: not just Jimi Hendrix's "Purple Haze" but also Stevie Wonder's "Purple Rain Drops" and Marvin Gaye's "Purple Snowflakes." Outside of music, purple's history went back even further. The Phoenicians were the first culture to isolate purple, producing it by extracting pigment from a gland in certain mollusks. Roman emperors began to dye their cloaks in the hue. When the Roman Empire fell, the color was lost, and it remained scarce through the Middle Ages. Imperial France tried to restore it to its high standing; Napoleon was preoccupied with the aristocratic implications of the color, and the nineteenth-century French biologist Henri de Lacaze-Duthiers located mollusks in the Balearic Islands, including *Murex trunculus*, which yielded purple pigment when milked. Then, in London, in 1856, a young chemist named William Henry Perkin rediscovered the color via a different route. He was trying to synthesize quinine for the treatment of malaria when he accidentally discovered that it produced, when combined with alcohol, a vivid purple substance he called "mauveine." The color caught on widely in France: It was used in fashion. It was used in painting. Claude Monet was an enthusiastic proponent.

Mauveine ran its course; by the late nineteenth century, the ease with which it could be produced made it less rare and consequently less valuable. The Dutch scholar Herman Pleij, in his book *Colors Demonic and Divine*, traces its rise and fall:

Another sign of the times is the regimentation in sports-
wear, as evidenced by the sight of whole families stroll-
ing around holiday resorts and shopping malls in jogging
suits of glowing purple.

Pleij's book makes no mention of Prince, unless you count the
phrase "sign of the times." But Prince also had to contend with
the overpurpling of his world. When *Purple Rain* blew up, the
color went everywhere. Headline writers used it whenever
possible in reference to the artist—"Purple Reign" was a particular favorite that quickly became cliché. Nicknames incorporated
it—the best one, popularized years later by the Minneapolis
Star Tribune and incorporating a reference to the suburb where
Prince's Paisley Park complex was located, was "the Purple
Assassin of Chanhassen." Prince tried to broaden the palette:
Around the World in a Day introduced a rainbow color scheme and
a raspberry single; *Parade* was black and white, and under a
cherry moon. On *Sign O' the Times*, he made an explicit appeal
on behalf of peach and black ("Color you peach and black / Color
me taken aback"). He dressed to avoid typecasting as well. In
normal life, there was no such thing as a normal outfit: he went
for velour jackets and platform shoes and lavender perfume even
to head out to the store. And onstage he was always on display.
One of the online message boards devoted to Prince collected fan
reports of aftershow outfits: "Coral/red suit with musketeer style
hat same color" . . . "Lemon-colored attire, the top had a hood,
big gold necklace on and sunglasses at the beg" . . . "Red suit,
black shirt, shades." None of the alternatives took, and by degrees
he made peace with his purple past. In 2007, he released *Indigo
Nights*, a live album cobbled together from aftershow performances.
Indigo, of course, is a vegetarian version of purple, derived not
from mollusks but from flowers.

+ + +

Buoyed by the movie's July 1984 release, *Purple Rain*, the album, was a massive success. In August, it took over the number-one spot on the *Billboard* chart and didn't relinquish it until the following year. Over the years, it has sold more than twenty-five million copies worldwide, and after Prince's death, the first official release from his catalog announced was a long-rumored expanded reissue of the record.

There were five albums before *Purple Rain*, and more than thirty after. The first one that followed, *Around the World in a Day*, did impressive if inconsistent things with psychedelic rock and pop, spawning a number-two hit with the lilting "Raspberry Beret." The second one, *Parade*—the soundtrack to Prince's second film, *Under the Cherry Moon*—included "Kiss," which stayed on the charts for four months and hit number one the week that "Manic Monday," which Prince had written for the Bangles, hit number two. In a creative sense, though, all of that was just the run-up to the watershed. Prince had been planning a massive new album that he originally titled *Dream Factory*. Begun before *Parade* even hit stores, it ballooned quickly, and more than eleven songs were in place at the end of April. By June, there were nineteen. By July, Prince had removed four from the running order and added in three new ones. He kept working, and the album kept evolving: come November, it was called *Crystal Ball* and it incorporated not only a number of tracks salvaged from *Dream Factory* but a handful picked up from the likewise unreleased *Camille*, in which Prince's vocals were manipulated into a higher pitch. The album, when it emerged, was called *Sign O' the Times* (written that way, with the "of" as a contraction of peace sign and apostrophe, the title was an anagram, probably accidentally, for "Mightiest Ones"). It was a classic double album, like *London Calling* or *Exile on Main Street*—or *1999*, for that matter. It yielded four hit singles, including two that went top five. But those songs only hint at its achievement. *Sign O' the Times* is not the equal of *1999*, or even *Purple Rain*, but it is unsurpassed as a demonstration of acrobatic versatility. The album's musical style ranges across spooky political R&B, full-throated psychedelic pop, bone-rattling skeletal funk, and pocket soul so gentle and nuanced you could almost call it folk—and that's just in the first four songs. Moreover, *Sign O' the Times* ushered in a glorious, if brief, period in which Prince's creative floodgates were thrown fully open: there were B sides to spare, remixes, extended versions, concert films. To be a Prince fan at that time was to be in a state of constant elevation, with no fear of ever coming down. We could hardly believe what we were hearing, and we were hearing it all the time.

3

BRAND NEW GROOVE

His Music and Its Properties

BEFORE *PURPLE RAIN*, THERE WAS "PURPLE MUSIC." RECORDED IN 1982, never released, performed only once, the song, built around an insistent electronic beat and monotonous vocals, was a ten-minute-long manifesto in which Prince compared the intoxicating effect of his music to that of drugs and judged his music to be superior ("Don't need no reefer, don't need cocaine / Purple music does the same to my brain"). But what was Purple Music, exactly? It started as a bundle of borrowings: From James Brown, Prince took a taskmaster's precision. From George Clinton, he took an interest in empire building. From Duke Ellington, he took a mix of closely guarded personal privacy and musical expansiveness. From the Beatles, he took a visionary bravery regarding the possibilities of arrangement. From Joni Mitchell, he took a flinty intelligence and a delicacy that he could deploy when it was least expected. From Todd Rundgren, he took an understanding of the adrenaline rush that came from working as a one-man-band. From Little Richard, he took falsetto shrieks and flamboyant androgyny. From Sly Stone, he took pop smarts and the benefits of an integrated band. From Jimi Hendrix, he took guitar pyrotechnics. From Carlos Santana, he took more guitar pyrotechnics. From Stevie Wonder, he took mastery. From David Bowie, he took mystery. All of these influences were ingested and digested until Prince, nourished, went about making something new. Prince used many instruments, many production techniques, many vocal and lyrical strategies. It's important to examine the ingredients, at least briefly. But it's also important to remember that these are just ingredients, and Prince *cooked*.

✦ ✦ ✦

Where should a consideration of Prince's music start? What lies at the foundation of his foundation? During his studio tryout with Warner Bros. in 1977, Prince made a beeline for the drums. Rhythm was at the heart of what he did, but it was rarely just a heartbeat. Much Western music uses 4/4 time, four quarter notes per measure, which is also called "common time" because it's so, well, common. Classical music tends to stress the first beat of the bar, the downbeat, and then the third. Most African-American-derived music, whether it's blues, jazz, or rock and roll, uses syncopation, or a shift in emphasis, to stress the second and fourth beats of the bar. This is called the "backbeat." Chuck Berry celebrated it in "Rock and Roll Music," released the year before Prince was born ("It's got a back beat, you can't lose it"), and Prince agreed more than thirty years later on "Escape," a *Lovesexy* B side ("Snare drum pounds on the two and four / All the party people get on the floor").*

---

* Backbeat is a culturally specific rhythm. There's a joke that it's impossible to teach Germans to clap along with rock and roll. And there's a recording that proves that

Over his first few albums, Prince used relatively conventional rock and disco beats. Starting with *1999*, that changed. Prince had a new collaborator for much of the record: the Linn LM-1 drum machine (1980 retail price: $4995), which let him program rhythms, shift their pitches, and so on. The more experimental second side of the album illustrated how kaleidoscopically electronics were expanding his sense of possibility. "All the Critics Love U in New York" clattered along, "Lady Cab Driver" added handclaps over its drum program, and the skittering "Something in the Water (Does Not Compute)" was especially visionary—electroclash twenty years before the fact.

Purple Rain, engineered for arena dominance, returned in large part to traditional rock rhythms; "Let's Go Crazy," for instance, was a master class in the two-four. The conspicuous exception was "When Doves Cry," on which Prince syncopated further and more drastically: the first measure stressed the first beat, the second beat, the midway point between the second and third beats, and then the third beat; the second measure arrived at its second stress a tiny bit earlier. When listening to it, it's impossible to settle into an easy pocket; the rhythm advances unsteadily, tripping a bit as it goes, and its refusal to achieve a pleasing symmetry mirrors the song's theme of romantic mismatch.

Though *Around the World in a Day* emphasized melody, the side one closer, the almost avant-garde "Tamborine," was mostly just drums and bass. Rhythm came roaring back on *Parade*, which opened on the staggered beats of "Christopher Tracy's Parade." The second track, "New Position," added in crisp stick-tick and

---

it's not a joke: In 1993, the blues guitarist Taj Mahal played a concert in Bremen that was later released as *An Evening of Acoustic Music*. As he starts to play "Blues with a Feeling," the majority of the crowd claps on the one and the three. He stops playing and explains the concept of the backbeat, telling the crowd that it's *schwarze*, or black, music. A few understand and switch to the two and four. Most do not.

steel-pan percussion and slowed its pace at the end so it could pick up the beat of the next song, "I Wonder U." Prince was also broadening the sonic palette of his rhythm tracks, with cowbell in "Life Can Be So Nice" and an echoing clap that elevated "Mountains." And the album after that, *Sign O' the Times*, introduced the "Housequake" beat, a specific and indelible tattoo that came to serve as Prince's equivalent of the Bo Diddley hambone.

Prince's willingness to take risks with rhythms worked hand in hand with the second major ingredient in his music: his keyboards. Synthesizers dated back to the 1940s, but they had first entered popular music through Robert Moog's late-sixties instruments and they swept through popular music, especially soul and disco, in the late seventies. The consumer-electronics revolution of the late seventies and early eighties brought a wave of synthesizers to market; Prince made his earliest albums on Oberheim synthesizers. The Oberheims, especially the OB-Xa (1980 retail price: $5595), gave him brass sounds. They gave him bass sounds. They gave him, on *Dirty Mind*'s "When You Were Mine," a passable approximation of a Farfisa organ. And once he figured out how much more he wanted from them, they gave him that, too. That epiphany came at the same time as his rhythmic epiphany, during the recording of *1999*. "Delirious" had an incessant keyboard figure, almost like a novelty record. "Automatic" was even better, with a segmented earworm of a melody: four notes, then three, then five. Bands like Kraftwerk had bridged the gap between humanity and technology. Prince sprinted across that bridge.

+ + +

When Prince told Dick Clark that he played "thousands" of instruments, the audience laughed. Partly this was because pop-music crowds only cared about a few instruments—and mainly, they cared about guitar. From the start, Prince was intent on bringing rock guitar into disco, soul, and funk. "I'm Yours," from *For You*, showed that he was both fleet and melodic. "Bambi," from *Prince*, was a pyrotechnic display of hammer-ons, pull-offs, and neck slides, and "Let's Go Crazy," an even more powerful rush, belongs on rock's Mount Rushmore. Because of "Let's Go Crazy" and the purple that surrounded it, the most common comparison people made was to Jimi Hendrix, but Carlos Santana was the better one: Prince emulated his long, liquid leads and several times made the debt explicit, most notably with an extended set of Santana covers at Coachella in 2008 (featuring Sheila E., whose father and uncle played in Santana's bands).

It's easy to list Prince's greatest guitars, starting with the Cloud—originally built by Dave Rusan of Knut-Koupee Music in Minneapolis, where Prince shopped as a teen, the model, made distinctive by the squiggly protrusion extending from its body, stayed with him throughout his career and was the basis for more than two dozen additional guitars made by the luthier Andy Beech. But the Cloud was only the most recognizable of a group; there was also the Hohner Mad Cat (which he used on his earliest records, from *Controversy* through *Purple Rain*), the purple acoustic Taylor 612ce (featured prominently on the *Musicology* tour, during which he came forward nightly for an acoustic set), and the symbol-shaped instrument he played at the Super Bowl halftime show in 2007 (also purple, also built by Andy Beech, and more than a little reminiscent of Todd Rundgren's famous Veleno ankh model). Listing Prince's greatest guitar performances, on record and onstage, is more difficult; there are hundreds. Guitar was both how he built the world and how he tore it open, from the syncopated strumming of "Kiss" to the blaring funk of "Batdance" to the gentle sway of "Count the Days" to the tidal solos of "Purple Rain" or "Joy in Repetition" or 3 *Chains o' Gold* or "Man 'O' War." My favorite, partly because it's so obscure, comes in the last thirty seconds of "We Gets Up," a spirited party anthem from *Emancipation*. It's just a knot of power chords, tied and untied and tied again, but its energy rises off it in a corona.

Some of Prince's most intriguing playing came in the service of other artists. In 2011, in Saint-Denis, France, he wandered onstage during a set by his opening act, Sharon Jones and the Dap-Kings, plugged in his guitar, and played a beautifully fleet, jazzy solo on "When I Come Home." It only lasted a minute, but he put his heart into it.* In 2005, he furnished a funky backbone for Stevie Wonder's underrated "So What the Fuss." And in 2004, Prince took on the Beatles. That was the year he was inducted into the Rock and Roll Hall of Fame; one of the other inductees that year was George Harrison, already inducted as a member of the Beatles but re-entering as a solo artist. Harrison had died in 2001, and as a posthumous tribute, the Hall of Fame arranged for an all-star band to close the show with a performance of "While My Guitar Gently Weeps." Tom Petty was on board, as were Jeff Lynne, Steve Winwood, and George's son, Dhani. The show's producer, Joel Gallen, hoped that Prince would join the group to perform the song's famous leads, played by Eric Clapton on the original White Album recording. Prince was interested. He listened to the song. He studied it. The day of the show, he came to the Waldorf Astoria for the run-through. The song actually had two famous solos, one in the middle and one at the end. At the run-through, there was confusion over which of the two would be played by Prince and which would be played by Marc Mann, the lead guitarist in Jeff Lynne's band. When it was time for the first, both musicians stepped forward, and Prince deferred to

---

* Jones, an energetic powerhouse who labored as a session singer in the seventies without much success, went to work as a corrections officer at Rikers Island, and finally became a star in her late forties, was another casualty of 2016: she died on November 18, of complications from pancreatic cancer.

Mann. When it was time for the second, Mann came forward again, and again Prince laid out. As he left rehearsal, Prince told Gallen that Mann should focus on the middle solo. "I'll just step in at the end," Prince said. That night, dressed in a black suit, wearing a red shirt and hat, playing a walnut-grain Hohner Mad Cat with leopard-skin pick guard (a custom-made copy of his early-eighties instrument), he just stepped in at the end. Craig Inciardi, a curator at the Hall, bore witness in the *New York Times*:

> You hear all this sort of harmonics and finger-tapping, sort of like what you'd hear Eddie Van Halen do. He runs through all these different sort of guitar techniques that are sort of astonishing. You hear what sounds like someone cocking a shotgun. There's all these strumming power chords that really, really connected. Then he plays his version of the Eric Clapton solo. He evokes Eric's solo in very sort of truncated fashion. As he ends the song, he plays this flourishing thing that sort of ends up sounding a little bit like Spinal Tap, but in a good way.

Prince saved the best bit of magic for last: he flung his guitar up into the rafters, and it didn't come down. Steve Ferrone, drumming with Petty at the time—he had played on Chaka Khan's cover of Prince's "I Feel for You" twenty years earlier—was unable to solve the mystery: "I was on the stage," he told the *Times*, "and I wonder where it went, too."

✦ ✦ ✦

But Prince wasn't strictly an instrumental artist. Any attempt to account for the singular power of Purple Music has to reckon with his singing. As a vocalist, he wasn't as smooth as Sam Cooke, as powerful as Aretha Franklin, or as insinuating as Smokey

Robinson. It isn't even fair to call him the finest singer of his generation, because his generation included Michael Jackson, and no one survives a comparison to the greatest pop singer in history, not even Prince. (The difference between them is like the difference between a great stage magician and his floating handkerchief. One designs and executes wondrous effects; the other embodies magic itself.)

Any account of Prince's singing has to start with his falsetto. Prince took the same high road as so many before him—as Al Green and Marvin Gaye and Curtis Mayfield and Lou Christie and Frankie Lymon and Frankie Valli and Philip Bailey and Russell Thompkins Jr. The falsetto could be romantic, but just as often it was lustful, using its vulnerable affect as cover for carnal hunger. Miles Davis correctly identified Prince's singing as a way of delivering sexual content without threat:

> He's got that raunchy thing, almost like a pimp and a bitch all wrapped up in one image, that transvestite thing. But when he's singing that funky X-rated shit that he does about sex and women, he's doing it in a high-pitched voice, in almost a girl's voice. If I said "Fuck you" to somebody they would be ready to call the police. But if Prince says it in that girl-like voice that he uses, then everyone says it's cute.

Many of Prince's finest songs harness this falsetto, from the airline fantasy of "International Lover" to the jealous simmer of "The Beautiful Ones" to the undeniable "Kiss," which strikes a perfect balance between sex and love, and throws in jokes to boot. There are lesser songs with even greater vocal performances: "Call My Name," from *Musicology*, for example. But Prince's falsetto was part of a broader palette. He could sing in his relaxed, natural voice, as on "7," or dip into bass, as on the extended "Thieves in the Temple," or go gritty, as on "New Power Generation," in which he mimicked Stevie Wonder's growl. On songs like "Adore," he layered vocals to create synthetic but still persuasive choirs. Moreover, there was no assembly line on which vocal approaches were paired impersonally with songs. Prince treated each composition as a bespoke object for which there was a corresponding strategy. But his insistence on variety meant that records with subpar songwriting (*For You*, say, or later lackluster efforts like *Planet Earth*) could come to seem like buffets of all his styles rather than expertly prepared meals. As with his guitar playing, it's hard to sift through hundreds of songs for one definitive highlight, and the tendency is to avoid the obvious picks. Anyone can admit that "If I Was Your Girlfriend" is wonderfully sung, filled with subtle choices that move along its complex and ever-shifting perspective. Anyone can feel their hair blown back when he lifts into the shrieking overdrive of "The Beautiful Ones." Among obscure but indelible vocals, "Dark," from *Come*, is one of the best. On a somewhat downbeat album with its share of missteps, "Dark" shines. For starters, it's one of his most persuasive arrangements. The drums tumble, like someone going down stairs too quickly. The horns move up and across, like an arch, and Prince's singing passes beneath it. Vocally, the song deploys his full arsenal: his deep, natural voice in the spoken introduction, a slightly serrated falsetto in the verses, backup vocals that dip in under the leads, and a second half that functions as an extended gospel showcase.

If Prince was expert at vocal syntax, he could also punctuate. He screamed in dozens of songs, sometimes climactically ("The Beautiful Ones," "Jack U Off"), sometimes inaugurally ("Gett Off," "Endorphinmachine"). Screams conveyed passion or rage, or verified the ongoing potency of his instrument. They took him one step beyond falsetto: when he screamed, he was no longer cute, and the spirit of James Brown rose up beside him. More complicated, because it is more singular, is the Prince Yelp, a short avian cry: "Aa-owww!"* It appeared first in "Sexuality" and resurfaced repeatedly, with slight variations: in "Baby I'm a Star," in "Eye No." Prince's yelp became a kind of midsong monogram, stamping a bridge or a chorus with his identity. It was a trademark, not to mention the basis for almost every Prince impersonation.

✦ ✦ ✦

Prince's music assembled these ingredients into fully prepared dishes and then served him to his audience. But in 2000, he tried his hand at a kind of recipe book of his own, compiling a seven-CD set called *New Funk Sampling Series*. Based on George Clinton's *Sample Some of Disc—Sample Some of D.A.T.*, the set was designed to give hip-hop acts easy access to samples. The entire project contained seven hundred digital fragments: bass loops, vocal screams, horns, guitars, keyboards, and sound effects. It would cost seven hundred dollars, a one-time payment that would cover all royalties. The set was advertised but never released, though listening to the bits of it that made their way onto the Internet—there's a bass figure from "Come"; there's the keyboard swell from "Little Red Corvette"—is like hanging out with Dr. Frankenstein as he digs up the pieces that will later become his monster.

---

* Other singers had recognizable tics, from Buddy Holly's hiccup to Little Richard's piercing high note. The most direct forebear of Prince's yelp was probably George Clinton's birdcall from Parliament's "Aqua Boogie," which was, in turn, borrowed from old Tarzan movies.

4

MUSICOLOGY

His Music and Its Imitators

TAXONOMIZING PRINCE'S SONGS IS TIME-CONSUMING, BECAUSE THERE are so many of them, but they resolve into a few major groups. There are high-strung electrofunk anthems, starting around "Automatic" and ending around "Chocolate Box." There are jump-blues songs, usually carnal in their concerns: "Delirious," "Horny Toad," and "Courtin' Time." There are love-man appeals like "International Lover," "Scandalous," and "Insatiable"; dipped-hip funk struts like "Kiss" and "Black Sweat"; and state-of-the-world addresses like "Sign O' the Times" and "Dance On." There are curtain-closing ballads like "Purple Rain." And then there are the sprawling, multipart symphonies that move from place to place and state to state, alternating between deep grooves and salvos of innovation. *Dirty Mind*, his first great album, contained exactly none of them: the whole thing is a climax, breathless for its entire half-hour running time. But the title track of *Controversy*, more than seven minutes long, incorporated a recitation of the Lord's Prayer and then Prince's own prayer: "People call me rude, I wish we all were nude / I wish there was no black and white, I wish there were no rules." It echoed the Rude Boy button he wore on the cover.

These extensive Prince epics, which brought so many aspects of his compositions into big tents, came into their own, like so much else about Prince's music, on his best album, *1999*. Songs like "Automatic" and "D.M.S.R." were stretched to their breaking point, but they only became more elastic. While he retreated from epics on the tight, commercial *Purple Rain* (or at least the released version—"Computer Blue" was originally recorded as a fourteen-minute multipart suite), Prince remained determined to prove that he could sustain a composition for eight minutes, or ten, without running out of ideas: "Crystal Ball" ran for more than eleven minutes, as did "Come." Brevity may be the soul of wit, but it's the death of funk—or, as George Clinton said, funk gets stronger as it goes longer. One of the best examples, though hardly a major work, is "Joint 2 Joint," from *Emancipation*. It's a carnal saga, as the sampled female vocals announce right at the beginning: "Sex me." Prince responds by coming on even stronger: "If we're ever naked in the same machine," he sings, "I'm gonna lick it, baby, joint to joint." But once it has set up shop as a relatively straightforward sex song, "Joint 2 Joint" starts to over-top its premise. After the two-minute mark, there's a rap break featuring Ninety-9. After the three-minute mark, there's a tap-dance solo—yes, a tap-dance solo—by Savion Glover. And then it gets weird: the keyboards shift into deep-bass mode, the melody shifts into spooky minor chords, and Prince goes upstairs, both in his falsetto and in the plot of the song. He and his lady friend end up in the bedroom, where he caresses her "nappy hair" and elicits "sweet gypsy moans" (represented by an orgasmic burst of guitar). Then the song jumps ahead to the morning after, and Prince goes downstairs for breakfast, accompanied by sound effects of cereal crunching and a reflection on both that cereal (he recommends using soy milk) and his one-night stand (he worries that she's going to try to get his money). Toward the song's end, Prince enters a car, rides for a while, and then places a phone call. He's calling Mayte to arrange a meeting (and, in a sense, calling ahead to the next song, "The Holy River," which argues in favor of romantic fidelity). With the exception of the rap and the tap, Prince does everything, from the rubbery funk bass to the spacey keyboards to the backing vocals, sometimes massed horizontally like an invading army, sometimes placed high in the spandrels of the mix. "Joint 2 Joint" is digressive, virtuosic, daffy, and thoroughly wonderful.

The only thing holding back these epics from unconditional greatness is their poor aerodynamics. They're like giant whiteboards filled with flowcharts and equations: diagrams of how to make a Prince song work at top speed without actually working at top speed. There's another kind of song that eliminates that problem: Prince's remixes of album tracks, especially those from midcareer, after he stopped using the remix form for extended dance versions and started exploring how remixes could succeed on their own terms, as entirely new compositions. Take "Thieves in the Temple": the original song, added to *Graffiti Bridge* at the last minute, shifted from a hushed Eastern motif to explosive drum machines, incorporating clustered harmonies worthy of Queen and a blaring harmonica solo sampled from the late-sixties LA soul band the Chambers Brothers. The album version of "Thieves in the Temple" moved quickly, like an actual heist, packing everything into a brisk three minutes. The remix was more than double that length, with a section of tumbling drums, an extended funk chant, a swooping falsetto movement, and filigreed funk guitar. It's as if the thieves returned everything that they had stolen to the temple, and brought some new stuff along as well.

✦ ✦ ✦

Sometimes, the best way to understand art is to look at parody. Weird Al Yankovic spent decades taking on (and taking off) top pop stars, from Queen to Coolio, but his most memorable target was Michael Jackson. Yankovic's lampoons of some of Jackson's most canonical songs (he reworked "Beat It" as "Eat It" and "Bad" as "Fat") were not only funny but genuinely analytical. They illuminated some of the main characteristics of Jackson's work—the showmanship, the sound effects, the peculiar mix of triumphalism and victimhood. Jackson's songs, in both their expertise and their excesses, are better understood because of Weird Al. In the eighties, when Prince was at the height of his fame, the Weird Al treatment seemed inevitable. Even Weird Al thought it was. But each time he approached Prince with a parody idea, Prince declined. Weird Al has gone on the record regarding his desire to rewrite "Let's Go Crazy" using the plot of *The Beverly Hillbillies* (the idea later morphed into his massively successful parody of Dire Straits's "Money for Nothing") or create a bargain-retail promotional spot called "$19.99." Fans obsessed with both artists (a narrow but vocal Venn diagram overlap) have also proposed a post–snowball fight lament called "When Gloves Dry" and a slightly risqué Marcel Marceau satire called "Dirty Mime." I personally roughed out a song called "Bris" ("I just want your extra skin in this . . .") and started to write Weird Al a letter.

When Weird Al couldn't get permission for an idea, he recorded what he called a "style parody," an approximate send-up that appropriated an artist's mannerisms (his Beach Boys takeoff "Pancreas" is perhaps the best example). His Prince style parody "Traffic Jam" was indistinct to a fault. Weird Al had more luck on the video front: "UHF," the title song for his first movie, mocked a number of popular MTV clips, from Guns N' Roses's "Paradise City" to George Michael's "Faith." "When Doves Cry" took it on the chin, for a few seconds, as Weird Al coyly stood from a bath.

Prince never came around to Weird Al. It wasn't that he wasn't a fan of comedy: he loved Pee-wee Herman, for example. But he was too obsessed with controlling the movement of his work through the world. Instead, he went the other way, as Weird Al explained in a 2011 interview with *Wired*:

> One of the oddest things to ever happen between me and Prince was the year that he and I were at the American Music Awards at the same time. Apparently I was going to be sitting in the same row as Prince that year and I got a telegram—and I wasn't the only one—from Prince's management company saying that I was not to establish eye contact with him during the show. I just couldn't even believe it. So immediately I sent back a telegram saying that he shouldn't be establishing eye contact with me either.

In addition to rejecting Weird Al's overtures, Prince disliked *Mad* magazine's 1985 parody, "A Fairy Tale We'd Like to See," in which a princess kissed a frog and Prince, in full *Purple Rain* regalia, appeared. The caricature was slightly grotesque, in the way that many caricatures of Prince were at the time—he looked excessively oily.

Prince eventually loosened up: in the late nineties, he performed a version of "Raspberry Beret" titled "Raspberry Sorbet" with the Muppets. In 2004, *Chappelle's Show*—a sketch-comedy television program starring the comedian Dave Chappelle— aired a skit in which Charlie Murphy (Eddie Murphy's brother and a writer on the show) remembered playing basketball against Prince at Paisley Park. Chappelle, a solid six feet tall, played Prince, all ruffled shirts, come-hither expressions, and soft cooing—except on the basketball court, where he turned mad killer. Maybe Prince was older and more mellow. Maybe he was in a better mood, career-wise; he was in the midst of a comeback thanks to *Musicology*. Whatever the reason, Prince accepted the good-natured mockery, to the point where he used a picture of Chappelle in his Prince getup as the cover of the 2014 single "Breakfast Can Wait."

In retrospect, there was only one strong parody of Prince's sound, though it wasn't intended as a parody at all, and it hit the charts. In Flint, Michigan, five hours east of Minneapolis, an R&B group called Ready for the World cut a record for MCA in 1985. Their first two singles, "Tonight" and "Deep Inside Your Love," made a little noise on the charts. Their third, "Oh Sheila," made much more. Released in August 1985, it was top ten by September and number one by October, helped along by the fact that many people thought it was a Prince song. And why not? It had the same falsetto vocals. The beat was reminiscent of (and, as it turned out, derived from) "Lady Cab Driver." And the Sheila in the title had to be Sheila E. right? I remember standing in a record store in Miami early the next year and listening to an extended argument between a woman and a man over "Oh Sheila." "It *is* a Prince song," the man said. "He's using that other band name just to prove that he can. You see that short guy in the cover photo? That's him in disguise."

"That guy's not short," the woman said. "He's just sitting down. You don't know what you're talking about."

"You'll see," the man said, ominously and senselessly.

✦ ✦ ✦

Prince once said that there were only mountains and the sea. But the truth is that there are trenches and valleys, too, and even sinkholes. There's no upside to falsifying a hagiography; any artist who makes as many records as Prince did makes bad ones, too. Bob Dylan released a number of perilously indifferent albums in the late eighties. James Brown responded to disco and New Wave by retreating inside one-dimensional retreads of his hottest grooves. And the less said about David Bowie's lesser records, the better. Prince, always pushing himself forward, could stumble. Sometimes it happened because he had strange ideas about himself. Sometimes it happened because he had strange ideas about his music, or about the music of other artists who were succeeding at the time. Sometimes it happened as a result of distraction, or inertia, or arrogance. But it happened. If consistency is the hobgoblin of little minds, his mind was huge.

Diagnosing the problem is not difficult. For starters, Prince suffered from recurring self-indulgence. It's not an uncommon problem among geniuses, especially ones so driven to demonstrate their genius. That reluctance to establish limits for himself was present in his earliest demos, the ones that Owen Husney encouraged him to trim to a length that could sanely be sent to record companies. His first few records mostly avoided the problem, often because of abbreviated running times—*Dirty Mind* was thirty minutes of sinew and muscle. He could deliver longer records convincingly, as he did on *1999* and *Sign O' the Times*. But as time went on, time went on—improving CD technology kept increasing how much music could be encoded on a single disc, and available running time grew to a previously unthinkable (and largely undesirable) 79.8 minutes. Though the title of *Diamonds and Pearls* suggests glamour through duress (diamonds are forged by pressure and pearls created through irritation), the album just sprawls; it's sixty-five minutes long and largely slack. The stretch on the second side that includes "Walk Don't Walk" and "Jughead" ranks among the most undistinguished music of Prince's career.

But the problems with Prince's quality control weren't only the result of overproduction. There were also gaps in his aesthetics: not exactly blind spots, not deaf spots, but more like dead spots— those areas on the old Boston Garden parquet floor where the basketball just wouldn't bounce. His preoccupation with sweeping ballads comes to mind. "Purple Rain" was the indisputable climax of both its film and its album, a powerful performance of mysterious lyrics set to a beautiful melody. Prince must have felt pressure to reproduce its effect. While many of his early albums led with their title songs and used them as calls to arms ("1999," "Around the World in a Day," "Sign O' the Times"), Prince rounded into the nineties with a new idea—he would close with the title song and make it a midtempo anthem. He did it with "Graffiti Bridge." He did it with "Gold." He did it with "Planet Earth." The results were subpar. The songs meandered, the arrangements were overstuffed, and the uplifting messages were little more than weaponized sentiment.

Prince's shortcomings were perhaps most conspicuous in his use—or, more accurately, his misuse—of hip-hop. Questlove, in the tribute he wrote for *Rolling Stone* a week after Prince's death, made a case that Prince didn't reflect the hip-hop aesthetic so much as originate it: He had his own boutique label. He had a group of hangers-on. He experimented with the same electronic drum machines as pioneers like Afrika Bambaata and Arthur

Baker. None of this changes the fact that Prince's use of actual hip-hop was generally terrible. In 1984, the pairing seemed as if it had potential, largely as the result of Chaka Khan's cover of "I Feel for You," which opened with the immortal stuttering introduction by Grandmaster Melle Mel. As Prince burned brightly through the eighties, hip-hop was enjoying its first golden era, with artists like Run-DMC, Eric B. & Rakim, and NWA. But Prince didn't credit rap as music, and *The Black Album* included an antirap harangue called "Dead on It" in which Prince lambasted "silly rapper[s] talking silly shit."

A few years later, Prince's star was falling slightly, and rap was ascendant. In 1990, Public Enemy's *Fear of a Black Planet* topped many year-end critics' lists, but the louder message came from the charts, where MC Hammer's *Please Hammer Don't Hurt 'Em* held the number one spot for twenty-plus weeks before handing it over to Vanilla Ice's *To the Extreme*. Prince, working on *Graffiti Bridge*, moved quickly to incorporate commercial rap. The album's final track spotlighted T.C. Ellis (the "T.C." stood for "Twin Cities"), a former commercial pilot and juvenile-corrections worker. Ellis's verse was a straightforward story of redemption: he fell into ruin as a result of cocaine but turned his life around. The performance of the verse was also straightforward, without a distinctive style or lyrics, and sometimes the same idea surfaced twice in the same line: "I must tell the truth / I cannot lie."* Prince's next album, *Diamonds and Pearls*, replaced Ellis with Tony M., who had danced in *Purple Rain* and joined Prince's live tours as part of a troupe dubbed the Game Boyz. On songs like "Willing and Able," Mosley didn't do any major damage, but

---

* Nathan Rabin, of the *Onion*'s A.V. Club, was so taken by Ellis's mediocrity that a decade later he did a gag chart comparing T.C. Ellis and T. S. Eliot, at one point setting Ellis's verse from "New Power Generation" against Eliot's "Burnt Norton."

he was purely extraneous—his verse wasn't about anything in particular and detracted just enough from the township slink of the song to be an irritant.

When it comes to Prince's failure to get his head around hip-hop, Michael Jackson furnishes an instructive contrast. He also started his solo career in the disco era and, at the height of his stardom, also created slick pop records that drew heavily on guitar heroics. (He had to hire help, but he hired the best: Eddie Van Halen, Slash, and others.) But beginning in 1991, on *Dangerous*, Jackson began to incorporate elements of hip-hop into his music, mostly by collaborating with established talents. Heavy D appeared on "Jam," Wreckx-N-Effect on "She Drives Me Wild." Jackson wrote two songs that featured the Notorious B.I.G., "This Time Around" and the posthumous (for Biggie, not Michael) "Invincible." The most undistinguished rapper he ever worked with was Shaquille O'Neal, and even he turned in a passable verse on "2 Bad."

Prince didn't reach out that way. He was determined always to exercise control, which limited him to working with people in his camp, and it took him a while to realize that the best rapper in his camp was him. On "Days of Wild," originally intended for *The Gold Experience* but eventually released on *Crystal Ball*, Prince rapped—or at least spoke his lyrics—with a slick wit, taking a swipe at the fashion sense of the hip-hop crowd ("tennis shoes and caps") while reiterating his desire to "dress to make a woman stare."* He returned to this mode repeatedly over time, from "Pope" to "Acknowledge Me" to "S&M Groove," and while he didn't have the flow of a Rakim (or maybe even of an MC Hammer),

---

* "Days of Wild" got an indirect sequel years later, when Prince guest-starred on *Big Train*, a British sketch-comedy show created by Simon Pegg. Prince appeared in a filmed piece that was a parody of nature shows, as a version of himself who stalks and kills jockeys (all the jockeys that were there before him, maybe?) in the wild.

what made his forays into rap successful was exactly what made Tony M. and T.C. Ellis unsuccessful—his performances emphasized personality and idiosyncrasy.

Lesson learned, right? Wrong: even later in his career, Prince couldn't get a clean line on how to use hip-hop. *Rave Un2 the Joy Fantastic*, the 1998 album he designed as a commercial comeback, was festooned with guests, including Chuck D on "Undisputed." But just because Prince allowed other artists on his record didn't mean that he was able to use them properly. Though Chuck D is armed with one of the mightiest voices in hip-hop, Prince employed him primarily as a hype man; until the final stretch of the song, all Chuck did was deliver short exhortations. It was almost a passive-aggressive arrangement, a conclusion supported by Prince's lyrics: "I can give you power, I can take it away."

✦ ✦ ✦

These missteps, rare in the early years, became more common as Prince's career proceeded; some albums punched a higher floor than others. But even the worst had an energy pulsing in them, a sense of surge. In the end, what is most compelling about Prince's sprawling body of work is precisely that: it sprawls. There are plenty of artists who make plenty of songs; nobody says very much about them. Prince, because he explained so many things and yet resisted simple explanation, presents a singular case. Few contemporary pop artists meant more to their fans, but even fewer *meant* more. When Prince made art about sex, he explored the signs and signifiers of sex. When he made art about the self, he explored the signs and signifiers of the self. The same was true of God, of race, of language, of freedom. He crammed substance into every nook and cranny, both musically and lyrically. This could also be the source of his limits: His funk was rarely as earthy or as intuitive as Sly Stone's. He didn't allow himself to be as feral as Little Richard or Jerry Lee Lewis. His music almost always had production sheen, a polish that could feel slick and hermetic. Still, what he wasn't paled in comparison to what he was—gifted, restless, virtuosic, relentless, airborne. Prince suggested so many contradictions that it seemed that he must also be the source of their resolution; he created the impression that anyone who followed him into the heart of his puzzle was capable of the same range and depth. And he did it in a wild rush, taking risks continually, almost obsessively. Science-fiction authors have played around with the idea of extreme longevity and what effect it might have on the human psyche, speculating that if humans lived to be a thousand years old, they'd be so preoccupied with protecting that lifespan that they would never even cross the street. Prince took the opposite tack, and then some.

Section Two

MEANING

5

GIRLS AND BOYS

Sex in His Music

THE FIRST HIT PRINCE SANG, "SOFT AND WET," GOT RIGHT TO IT: "HEY, lover, I got a sugarcane / that I wanna lose in you." The rest of the song stayed sugary: the ingratiating funk-lite melody, the creamy falsetto, the two cutesy images that paid off the title ("soft as a lion tamed" and "wet as the evening rain"). The whole thing was confectionary, and though Prince didn't write the lyrics—Chris Moon did—he put them across.

The first hit Prince wrote himself, "I Wanna Be Your Lover," drove its point home even more aggressively. In the first verse, Prince worried about the other men circling around his girl-friend. But that vulnerability lasted only until the chorus, when he opted for the hard sell ("I want to turn you on, turn you out, / all night long, make you shout"). In the song, Prince wasn't a player. He wasn't catting around; he wanted an exclusive relationship, though maybe not in the way his girlfriend expected. "I want to be the only one that makes you come," he sang, cleaning up his meaning with an extraneous final word: "running." The end of the chorus reiterated the point: "I want to be the only one you come for," he sang, pulling the line out for an extra half second before rolling right into the second verse, same as the first.

As Miles Davis noted, Prince's presentation—the doe eyes and coquettish falsetto—helped him sell sex without menace. The songs on his early albums, even when they were filthy, were innocently filthy, all tugged-at zippers and hastily rearranged sweaters. They could have come from some alternate-universe production of *Grease*. But with Prince's third album, *Dirty Mind*, subtext became text. On the title track, Prince sang about sitting in his "daddy's car" with his girl and being inflamed by her beauty. But his girl was a good girl who never "[went] too far." Before he could get in her pants, he had to get in her head. His solution? He would buy her a dirty mind. This abstract approach to the problem reveals the secret of early Prince: the dirty happens in the mind rather than in the car.

The rest of the album's songs found that mind unchanged. "Do It All Night," with a pinging keyboard line, was Prince's funniest early song, a wonderful bait and switch in which he promised love and affection, hugging and kissing and anything else his girl wanted. At the end, almost as an afterthought, he got back to the business at hand: "I wanna do it / Do it all night." Elsewhere, taboos were explored and then exploded: "When You Were Mine" sketched out a ménage à trois, and "Sister" sang the praises of incest, along the way remarking both on fashion choices ("she don't wear no underwear") and sexual technique ("blow job doesn't mean blow"). But Prince's narrative powers were strongest on the four-minute "Head," which plays like a mix of a *Penthouse Forum* letter and one of the racier Canterbury tales.

In the song, Prince is out for a walk when he encounters a young woman "on her way to be wed." She is also, as she quickly establishes, a virgin. In a fit of something (adventuresomeness? last-hurrah fervor? overheated fantasy on the part of the man narrating?), she offers him a blow job. It still doesn't mean blow, and she works him over: till he's burning up, till he gets enough, till his love is red. Finally, romantically, thrillingly, she delivers the coup de grâce: "love you till you're dead."

The second half of the song engineers a neat reversal. After Prince sullies her wedding gown, the virgin (and she still is, technically, a virgin) abandons her impending nuptials and marries Prince instead, at which point he returns the titular favor— till she gets enough, till her love is red. "Head" remains one of Prince's most daring and successful early songs, thanks to its outlandish conceit and to the contributions of others, including Lisa Coleman's affectless backing vocals and Dr. Fink's sizzling synthesizer solo. Robert Christgau's review of the album, delivered in 140 hilariously compressed words, noted that Prince "stops a wedding by gamahuching the bride on her way to church" and ended by saying, "Mick Jagger should fold up his penis and go home."

Controversy retreated somewhat in amatory matters. It wasn't that there weren't sex songs, only that they weren't especially risqué. "Do Me, Baby" was a pro forma ballad written by André Cymone (though Prince took credit); "Sexuality" concerned itself more with the political dimensions of the act; and "Jack U Off," while it had energy to spare, was his most juvenile lyric yet. Only the propulsive "Private Joy" got into the same position as "I Wanna Be Your Lover" ("You're my little lover, Orgasmatron / Only I know, only I know, baby, what turns you on"). Prince was also getting some on the side: the debut album by the Time, a project for which he wrote all the songs (and played all of the instruments) was released a few months before *Controversy* and ended with "The Stick," written by Prince and Lisa Coleman. From the first line, it makes its intentions clear: Morris Day sings about his "stick" and "get[ing] some stimulation anywhere." It's a manual transmission, if you know what he means. And everyone does—the song is so insistent that it's almost a single entendre. At the end, there's a unexpected conclusion, possibly courtesy of Lisa. The woman is satisfied too soon, leaving the man to finish himself off. Morris, a former drummer, is stuck with his stick.

✦ ✦ ✦

All this, even *Dirty Mind*, was only foreplay. In 1982, Prince released *1999*, still his most outré album in both sonics and themes. Sex is all over *1999*; the record is an object lesson in how to load up a pop song with sex. Excitement, anticipation, recreation, procreation—it's all there.

The album's title song ended with a boom, possibly the sound of one of the bombs going off. Prince, deep in the mix, wailed soulfully, and there was a rustling of percussion, the first sound of "Little Red Corvette." In Prince's large catalog, there are hundreds of good songs, dozens of great ones, and a handful that are absolutely perfect. "Little Red Corvette" is one of the perfect few, joining a motorcade of car songs driving through the history of rock and roll: "Don't Worry Baby," "Mustang Sally," "Paradise by the Dashboard Light," even Grace Jones's "Pull Up to the Bumper," released just the year before. With the very first line— "I guess I should have known / by the way you parked your car sideways / that it wouldn't last"—Prince displayed a mastery of detail and compression worthy of Bruce Springsteen, or Raymond Carver for that matter. The rest of the song was about sex, but in ways that avoided common pitfalls. In many songs, sex represents the end of productive artistic tension, and it's why songs about sex tend to divide into insinuation and pornography. Here, Prince kept tension in the rope by writing not just about pleasure but about all the other things that sex is about—being valued by another person, social mores, logistics, pressuring, and being pressured.

"You had a pocket full of horses," Prince says, "Trojans, and some of them used." At first blush, this seems to suggest that the song is written from the perspective of a woman reflecting on a guy who goes on the prowl, stocked with condoms, certain that he's going to get laid. But the rest of the song clarified the matter: Prince is singing to a woman who packs her own protection. Her sexually forward ways were intimidating—his ardor flagged when he thought of "all the jockeys that were there before" him, and he even felt a little ill. Still, it was Saturday night; that made it all right. "And you say, 'Baby, have you got enough gas?' " Here, gas was both a literal and metaphorical reference, but all roads led to the same conclusion. If gas meant libido, the answer should be yes, so they could get on with the loving (and leaving fast). If gas meant gas, the answer should be no, in which case the narrator could pretend they were stranded up near Makeout Point.*

The image of the little red Corvette itself in the song deserves a brief inspection. Cars are often figured as phallic, but a phallic

---

* The line also surfaces in the eternal fifth-set tiebreaker between Prince and Michael Jackson. Jackson released *Thriller* in November of 1982, a month after *1999*. The following summer, after the dominant performance of the first set of singles—"The Girl Is Mine" (number two), "Billie Jean" (number one), "Beat It" (number one), and "Wanna Be Startin' Somethin'" (number five)—*Thriller* had started to fall off a bit. Jackson called Walter Yetnikoff, the president of CBS, to express his alarm, and Jackson's manager, Frank DiLeo, proposed a video for the title song. The John Landis–directed video, which came out at the end of December 1983, found Michael and Ola Ray out in the woods, their car—not a Corvette—unwilling to start. "Honestly," Michael says, coding masculine, "we're out of gas!"

metaphor wouldn't emphasize smallness. Maybe it's something else: a photo of a Corvette from the time, seen from the front, looks almost labial. That would explain the color, not to mention Prince's determination to tame her "little red love machine." Or maybe the car's curves are a more general stand-in for a female body, like the hourglass shape of a violin. "Girl," Prince sings in the vocal breakdown, "you got an ass like I never seen," before straining the metaphor to its breaking point: "And the ride / I say the ride is so smooth / you must be a limousine." (The ad that Chevrolet took out after Prince's death, which showed a red Corvette under the caption, "Baby, That Was Much Too Fast" ably demonstrated what a seductive-looking machine it is, and the fact that it is not a limousine at all.) But even here, in the most libidinal of songs, there's consequence: "You got to slow down," Prince says, "or you're gonna run that body right into the ground." In romance, as in a road race, speed kills.

Right behind "Little Red Corvette" came "Delirious," with squeaky keyboards that sounded like air being let out of the pinched neck of a balloon. It was one of the jump-blues-cum-rockabilly songs that Prince liked to return to now and again, a cousin of "Jack U Off," from *Controversy*, and of "Courtin' Time," from *Emancipation*. It was also his second-best car song. Once again, he found himself powerless in the presence of female sexuality. He lost his self-control; his wheels got locked in place. The look on his face? Stupid. He found himself incapable of making a pass (automotive pun alert). Eventually, he resorted to begging: "Girl, you gotta take me for a little ride up and down / in and out and around your lake." As in "The Stick," it's eminently clear what Prince meant, and it wasn't Lake Minnetonka he had in mind.

The fourth song, "Let's Pretend We're Married," was a fantastically perverse look at flat-out balling in which Prince agreed to feign wedded bliss in order to experience bedded bliss. During the second half of the song, he abandoned innuendo entirely, declaring, "I sincerely want to fuck the taste out of your mouth." Even then, he worried about mutual enjoyment ("Can you relate?") and about sustaining his pretend marriage when he was already pledged to a higher power. The salacious stretch on *1999* ends with "D.M.S.R." (for "dance, music, sex, romance"), the only song that mentions sex (almost) overtly in its title. But it's the least explicit of any of them, a sequel to "Sexuality," in which getting off is just another form of getting free. Burbling and sinuous, it's all liberation, except for Lisa Coleman's frightening scream at the end: "Help me! Somebody please help me!" Side two of the album found Prince in a mostly transportational mind-set where sex was concerned. "Lady Cab Driver" included a scene of a sadistic (and possibly not consensual) tryst in a taxi, and "International Lover," breathily glossy, welcomed us all aboard Prince International Airlines with some of Prince's most mordant lyrics: try not to laugh when he says "Extinguish all clothing materials."

✦ ✦ ✦

In 1984, an eleven-year-old girl in Washington, DC, bought *Purple Rain*. On the face of it, that's not news; millions of kids did. But this girl had a mother who heard the lyrics, especially those toward the end of side one that recounted a meeting between Prince and a woman in a hotel lobby, masturbating with a magazine. (She was using it to masturbate? Holding it while she was masturbating? He was holding the magazine while she masturbated? Sometimes poetic compression just creates unclear pictures.) This particular mother also had a husband who was a congressman from Tennessee. And so Tipper Gore, the girl's mother and the wife of Representative Al Gore (D-Tenn.), went with her friend Susan Baker, the wife of the secretary of the treasury, to Capitol Hill, where they set about protecting children from objectionable content in pop music. The group—they called themselves the Parents' Music Resource Center (PMRC)—compiled a hit list of their most hated songs, the "Filthy Fifteen," to illustrate their point. "Darling Nikki" was number one. Number two was another song written by Prince, Sheena Easton's "Sugar Walls." The rest of the list was largely composed of other sex offenders (Vanity's "Strap On 'Robbie Baby,'" a love song to a vibrator from her solo debut, not written by Prince; AC/DC's "Let Me Put My Love into You," a straightforwardly lunkheaded double entendre; and Madonna's "Dress You Up," which could not possibly have offended anyone), though Twisted Sister's "We're Not Gonna Take It" was nicked for violence and Venom's "Possessed" for occult themes.

Hearings were convened to investigate the issue, and a motley crew of artists (though none from Mötley Crüe, whose "Bastard" made the Filthy Fifteen) came before the United States Senate: Frank Zappa, Dee Snider of Twisted Sister, Jello Biafra of the Dead Kennedys, and even soft-rock stalwart John Denver. All of them challenged the PMRC, both on premise and execution. Denver opposed censorship in any form, noting that his song "Rocky Mountain High" had been the subject of misguided antidrug crusades for years. Zappa was more caustic: he called the group's proposal "an ill-conceived piece of nonsense which fails to deliver any real benefits to children [but] infringes the civil liberties of people who are not children," and compared the suggested remedies to "the equivalent of treating dandruff by decapitation." In the end, the Recording Industry Association of America agreed to a generic warning label that would be affixed to the covers of albums considered offensive. Since the remedy was not retroactive, *Purple Rain* never carried any advisory.

Tipper Gore's comstockery was not only politically misguided but critically limited. "Darling Nikki," the song that inspired the Parental Advisory label, may be about sex on its surface, but beneath that it's a metaphor for popular entertainment. Prince signed his name on the dotted line, watched as the lights went out, and then witnessed a performance. What did Nikki owe him when the lights came back on? Was he telling his audience something about what he did or did not owe them?

But other songs were sneakily voluptuous, the equivalent of a lace teddy underneath a pantsuit. "Raspberry Beret" is one of his sweetest and most innocent love songs (unless, as some suggest, it refers to—and proceed with caution here, because once this mental picture has been seen, it cannot be unseen—the foreskin of an uncircumcised penis). Of all of Prince's sex songs, "Erotic City" is perhaps the purest. Though the song was written after Prince saw the P-Funk All-Stars at the Beverly Theatre in April 1983, it draws on other influences as well; the synth line was inspired by, if not borrowed from, the European dance hit "White Horse," by the Danish duo Laid Back. Working with these loanwords, Prince conceived a deceptively childlike whistling riff, added Sheila E. as a duet partner, and charted their course through a lyric that was at times brilliantly self-referential ("All of my purple life / I've been looking for a dame") and at times just flat-out brilliant ("Every time I comb my hair / thoughts of you get in my eyes"). The song also unyoked sex from procreation ("If we cannot make babies, maybe we can make some time") and matched Prince's dirty mind with straightforwardly dirty language ("We can fuck until the dawn"). In many live performances from around that time, the riff is played on guitar instead, which sacrifices the plastic quality that is among the song's greatest charms.

A few years later, Prince booked a return engagement to Erotic City for "Sex," a *Batman* B side with a similar staccato keyboard part. Times had changed, and now he argued for monogamy and trust, so long as the sex still "[made] him shout." Preoccupied with the dangers of promiscuity, "Sex" included perhaps the least catchy call-and-response in Prince's entire catalog: "One lover? Sex! Two lovers? Death!" Like most sequels, it fell short of the original, though a cover of the song made for a bright spot on the debut album of a Dutch band with the unlikely name of Lois Lane.

+ + +

The sex wouldn't matter as much if it wasn't laced with love. Think of "The Beautiful Ones," on *Purple Rain*, which follows the defibrillator start of "Let's Go Crazy" and the relatively low-impact "Take Me with U." A rubbery rhythm opened the song, followed by a distorted bass note and then Prince crooning: "Baby, baby, baby." He was pleading with an unseen lover: that she should stay the night, that she shouldn't make him lose his mind. He was suspicious of her beauty, because "the beautiful ones" consistently hurt you (or, as he explains in a spoken interlude, they "always smash the picture, always, every time"). As the song progressed, it became clear that his romantic proclamations (including the immortal "If we got married / would that be cool?") weren't being made in a vacuum; rather, he was in competition with another lover (which, as he would explain a few albums later, you need like you need a hole in the head). A little more than three minutes in, he emptied himself of everything other than his central concern: "What's it going to be, baby?" he demanded. "Do you want him, or do you want me? 'Cause I want you."

The power of the song, tremendous on record, was multiplied a hundredfold in the movie, in which the song was performed at a moment when the Kid (Prince's character) saw Apollonia sitting in the club with Morris Day, getting light-headed on the champagne he had ordered for her. During the Kid's performance, the camera pushed in on Apollonia's face, alternating accusatory shots of her with shots of him onstage, writhing and scream-singing. The strength of his feeling for her was shocking, almost unbearable. She had only one choice, which was to accept his offer—but also only one other choice, which was to save herself before she was destroyed by his intensity. The song closed on an electronic burbling that sounded like everything was dissolving in molten metal.

In a sense, it was. Prince would rarely express his love that vehemently again. "Condition of the Heart," from *Around the World in a Day*, was Prince's next great love song, and the first of his historical fictions—he'd revisit the same romantic, debauched Jazz Age territory, with slight variations, in the movie *Under the Cherry Moon* and on songs like "The Ballad of Dorothy Parker" and (more cynically) "Illusion, Coma, Pimp and Circumstance." Singing gently, he sketched out a fragile long-distance romance that started with a letter to a girl in Paris. There are many things to love about "Condition of the Heart," including the slow build through piano and synths, the crash of drums and organ like waves on a shore (all, according to the liner notes, by Prince), its reemergence as a swirling ballad. But one of its best qualities is the way the lines of the verses topple into each other, hyphens carrying them across: "Now wasn't that a fool- / hardy notion on the part of a some- / times lonely musician." Love, once started, is hard to stop.

Around the World in a Day concluded with a trial. "Temptation," a song that alternately celebrated and condemned "animal lust," featured a dialogue between Prince and a deep-voiced God (presumably also played by Prince) in which Prince was upbraided for not understanding that love was more than important sex. "I do," Prince protested. "You don't," God snapped back. "Now die." For a while after that, there was a real attempt on Prince's part to do penance. Valentino was always present as a romantic archetype, but there was a big difference between the possessive "Private Joy" in 1981 ("I strangled Valentino / You've been mine ever since / If anybody asks / You belong to Prince") and the dreamy "Manic Monday" in 1985 ("kissing Valentino / by a crystal blue Italian stream").

The peak of this kind of thinking, like so many other peaks, came on *Sign O' the Times*, on "Adore," a six-minute ballad where the only other credited musicians were the brass section—Eric Leeds on saxophone and Atlanta Bliss on trumpet. Prince declares eternal love, promising that if God struck him blind, he'd still see his lover's beauty. He recounts the beginning of the romance, especially their first meeting, after which he feels compelled to call her and make his case to her all night long. Quickly enough, love becomes indistinguishable from sex, sex becomes indistinguishable from spirit, and spirit demands that love be revalued. In the end, Prince pledges his body, his mind, and even his car (though he thinks better of it immediately, and puckishly withdraws the offer: "Well, maybe not the ride"). There are limits to Prince's achievement: as poetry, the song doesn't approach the beauty of, say, Smokey Robinson and the Miracles' "I'll Try Something New" ("I will bring you a flower from the floor of the sea / to wear in your hair"), or even "Condition of the Heart." But he gets off some marvelously compressed lines ("I've got to have your face / all up in the place"), and the way that love creates a harmony of mind, body, and soul is perfectly articulated in the vocals: choired, climbing over one another on the way up to worship, they express devotion as well as any poem ever could.

+ + +

Other songwriters had written about sex before. Other singers had sung about it. Marvin Gaye had. Millie Jackson had. Donna Summer shuddered her way through an extended orgasm in "Love to Love You Baby"; Rod Stewart invited his lady friend to spread her wings and let him come on inside. But no one pursued the project with as much enthusiasm and imagination as Prince. In the years that followed the release of *Sign O' the Times,* any artist who addressed any aspect of the sexual experience was invariably compared to Prince, whether it was Janet Jackson or George Michael, Rihanna or R. Kelly. When Beyoncé released "Blow," an explicitly pro-cunnilingus song, all people seemed to be able to say was that she was channeling her inner Prince. It was vaguely insulting to Beyoncé, a fully formed artist in her own right, but also an illustration of how deeply Prince penetrated our understanding of the role of sex in popular music.

Sexuality was connected, of course, to questions of sexual orientation. Not Prince's own sexual orientation; he seems to have been straight. But like David Bowie before him, he made a point of designing an image that moved across the full spectrum of sexuality. He struck poses and hit notes that were traditionally feminine. He wore makeup and kept his hair long and sometimes went out onstage in nothing but black underwear and thigh-high socks. He urged his fans to let their bodies be free, in "Sexuality," and, more memorably and charmingly, in "Controversy" he wished three things in quick succession: that we all were nude, that there was no black and white, and that there were no rules. At a time when most African-American male superstars were either sleazily lickerish (Rick James), relentlessly inoffensive (Lionel Richie), or entirely alien (Michael Jackson), Prince not only sang frankly about sex but sang freakily about sexuality. His view of pleasure took in all comers.

By switching perspectives and points of view, by discouraging easy answers, Prince benefitted many people, but he benefitted gay Americans in particular. In the eighties, gay America was in crisis, suffering the ravages of AIDS, and antisodomy laws—which had been rolled back during the seventies—received a temporary reprieve in 1986, when the Supreme Court upheld such statutes in *Bowers v. Hardwick*. Prince marched proudly into the spotlight, refusing to answer any questions about his sexuality, and if he couldn't change any laws, he could (and did) blow the roof off of existing attitudes. Simply by existing as an indisputable force and an indecipherable enigma, he encouraged people to ask more questions. It was especially liberating for gay African-Americans, who commonly suffered from even more restrictive ideas of masculinity. After Prince's death, the singer Frank Ocean explained how Prince helped him come to terms with his own sexuality: "He was a straight black man who played his first televised set in bikini bottoms and knee high heeled boots, epic. He made me feel more comfortable with how I identify sexually simply by his display of freedom from and irreverence for obviously archaic ideas like gender conformity etc. He moved me to be more daring and intuitive with my own work by his demonstration."

✦ ✦ ✦

Prince didn't always evade gender conformity. Some songs confronted simple obsession (on "It," from *Sign O' the Times*, he confessed that he "thinks about it, baby, all the time"), and others made up for their lack of freedom and irreverence with straightforward energy ("Tick, Tick, Bang," on *Graffiti Bridge*, was a no-nonsense nut-buster in which Prince warned a potential lover that "there's no telling how long I'd last / before I tick, tick, bang all over you").

His last great sex song was like a furtive assignation in an alley, coming when his back was against the wall. After the mixed reaction to *Under the Cherry Moon*, Prince charged ahead with his third film, *Graffiti Bridge*. It was a kind of sequel to *Purple Rain* that reentered the lives of the main characters some years later: the Kid (Prince) has a club named Glam Slam; he co-owns it with Morris Day (still played by Morris Day), who also owns a club named Pandemonium. Morris is trying to force out all the other club owners, who include Mavis Staples and George Clinton. Madonna was involved in the project at an early stage, but exited prior to shooting. The entire film was an exercise in Sardoodle-dom. "As a film director," wrote John Ferguson of *Radio Times*, "Prince remains a brilliant musician." Much of the problem came from the film's sense of place, or lack of it; *Graffiti Bridge* existed in a world only slightly more realistic than the one depicted in Vanilla Ice's *Cool as Ice*. Rather than set it in Minneapolis and benefit from the city's actual texture, Prince invented a garish, lifeless soundstage city named Seven Corners. Seven Corners was nowhere, which is exactly where the film went.

When it stiffed, Prince was spooked. Rather than spend any more time exploring internal conflict, he set out to dazzle. A casting call went out for two tall dancers, ideally twins. Two women who were not twins, Lori Elle and Robia LaMorte, were selected and cast as the titular spokespeople for his new album, *Diamonds and Pearls*. Diamond and Pearl accompanied Prince, sentineling him, at public appearances. The album that accompanied these publicity stunts was flashy even from a distance. The cover was a hologram; the music dipped in and out of hip-hop styles. The songs were subpar, but they were delivered with tremendous energy. Everything was in place for Prince's confident return to the top, and he got it. "Cream," an exercise in ersatz T. Rex, shot back up the charts. (The cream he was talking about wasn't dairy.) But the real highlight on the record was added at the last minute, as Lenny Waronker later recounted to the *Star Tribune*:

> The urban department didn't think there was a song on the album that they could get played on radio. So I get him on the phone, and he said, "Maybe I could take so-and-so and turn it around." Then he stopped and said, "It's a marketing problem. You guys deal with it." And he hung up. That was on a Friday. On Monday, I get a call from him, and he says, "You've got yourself a new baby." It was an amazing new track.

That new track, "Gett Off," was an upjut of *jouissance* that brought together several scattered sources—one of the many "Glam Slam" remixes, the Time/Elisa Fiorillo workout "Love Machine," an earlier song called "Get Off"—but it was its own thing. It opened with a bloodcurdling scream. It thumped. It thundered. It name-checked James Brown, joked and jived, and even contained a credible rap break. Dirty-minded ("twenty-three positions in a one-night stand") but also respectful of female desire and choice ("I'll only call you after if you say I can"), it was the thematic opposite of "Purple Rain": here, he always wanted to be your weekend lover. The song helped Prince recapture the imagination of the nation when he performed it at the MTV Video Music Awards in September 1991 in a yellow suit, its backside cut out. The B side, "Horny Pony," was a strong dance number and a good joke, Prince's version of Rufus Thomas's "Do the Funky

Chicken" but randier ("it's the sex dance, it's the love dance, and it's rocking from coast to coast"). But "Gett Off" was the monument, not only a collection of all of Prince's sexual signs, signifiers, and symbols up until that time but a summation of them: a fully satisfying climax.

6

WALK BY THE MIRROR

Self in His Music

ROCK AND ROLL IS FULL OF ICONIC LOGOS: THE ROLLING STONES' tongue, the Grateful Dead's skull, Boston's spaceship. Early on, Prince didn't have a logo, exactly—his image was too fluid for that—but he had a trademark (if not trademarked) phrase: "Produced, Arranged, Composed, and Performed by Prince." If you bought a Prince album and ran your finger down the last stretch of the liner notes, you'd find it there. It was talismanic, promoting an idea of creative self-sufficiency that separated Prince from almost every other pop artist on earth. Lennon became Lennon partly because of McCartney, and vice versa. The Glimmer Twins had each other. Michael Jackson needed song-writers to supply him with material.

The idea of Prince as a one-man band was a collective illusion shared by both his adherents and his detractors. Even casual fans knew that Prince didn't actually write every word and play every note. There were acknowledged examples, from Dez Dickerson's guitar solo on "Little Red Corvette" to Susannah Melvoin's co-writing credit on "Starfish and Coffee." There were also cases in which Prince strategically concealed the contributions of others: Morris Day wrote "Partyup" and then donated it to *Dirty Mind* in return for an album's worth of songs by the Time, the group Prince set up as a side project. André Cymone wrote "Do Me, Baby" but wasn't credited for it. And near the beginning of the *Parade* sessions, Prince gave a new song to Mazarati, a Minneapolis band working with his bassist, Brown Mark, and his engineer, David Z. The song was slow and soft, almost a folk-blues composition, with lyrics inspired by Joni Mitchell's "Jericho." Mazarati wasn't sure what to do with it, other than smile politely and thank Prince, but David Z. went into the studio on a rescue mission. He lifted a hi-hat sound from a drum machine, delayed it slightly, and alternated between the original and the delayed version; he then tied some acoustic guitar chords to the off-kilter rhythm. The next morning, before anyone else was even awake, Prince returned to the studio to find his country-folk song reborn. He transformed it further, stripping out the bass and replaying the guitar part. When Mazarati showed up, they were greeted with the news that Prince was reclaiming the track. The song, of course, was "Kiss," which remains central to Prince's canon. When the record that contained it, *Parade*, came out, David Z.'s credit was reduced to "arranged by."*

---

* As it made its way through the world, "Kiss," fittingly, remained a song about collaboration. A few months after Prince released his version, it was covered by the British industrial band Age of Chance, who opened their version with the superb couplet "You don't have to be Prince if you want to dance / you just have to get down with the Age of Chance." They also released a remix called "Kisspower" that was one of the first pop songs to be built around samples from other songs: it incorporated Prince's original, as well as Run-DMC's "Walk This Way," Xavier's "Work That Sucker to Death," the MC5's "Ramblin' Rose," and Bruce Springsteen's "Born in the

Prince's habit of absorbing the contributions of others echoed the practices of Duke Ellington, memorably outlined in Terry Teachout's excellent 2013 biography, *Duke: A Life of Duke Ellington*:

> Not only was Ellington inspired by the sounds and styles of his musicians, but he plucked bits and pieces from their solos and wove them into his compositions. Some of his most popular songs were spun out of melodic fragments that he gleaned from his close listening on the bandstand each night.

Ellington, Teachout explains, borrowed partly because he didn't have a natural capacity for creating catchy pop songs. That wasn't Prince's issue. But Teachout suggests another equally important motive:

> It was as much a matter of vanity as money, for Ellington preferred for the public to think that he did it all by himself.

The illusion of full artistic independence, the reality of collaboration: that tension informed much of Prince's early career. The most conspicuous, and most sustained, example of Prince working with other artists was, of course, his relationship with Wendy Melvoin and Lisa Coleman in the Revolution. The Revolution was, and still is, his most famous band. Eagle-eyed fans had already

---

USA." The band's label, Virgin, hedged on its release over copyright concerns, putting it out in a limited-edition run of five hundred copies. Two years later, another British group with a similar name, the Art of Noise, saw the Welsh sex god Tom Jones performing "Kiss" in his Las Vegas act and contacted him with the idea of turning it into a recording. They did. In Britain, it charted higher than Prince's original.

spotted the group's name on the cover of *1999*, mirror-written in the multicolored football hanging on the "I" in Prince. The core of the group—bassist Brown Mark, drummer Bobby Z., keyboardists Matt Fink and Lisa Coleman—had been with him for years. But in the wake of *1999*, his longtime lead guitarist Dez Dickerson (he of the solo on "Little Red Corvette") left for reasons that, depending on who and when you asked, were either religious (he went on to record for a Christian label) or financial (Prince demanded a three-year commitment at the same rate, and Dickerson balked). Dickerson was replaced by Lisa Coleman's friend Wendy Melvoin. Both women were the daughters of players in the famous 1960s session-musician group known as the Wrecking Crew: Lisa's father, Gary L. Coleman, was a percussionist; Wendy's father, Mike Melvoin, was a keyboard player. The two women had been friends since childhood. Lisa, who had had some success as a teen musician—she and her siblings formed a bubblegum pop band called Waldorf Salad that signed to A&M and released a single—came to Prince's attention in the late seventies, through a mutual friend, and joined his band in 1980, when she replaced Gayle Chapman on keyboards. In 1983, she brought Wendy into the fold. One of the highlights of *Purple Rain* was the mysterious, erotic dialogue between Wendy and Lisa at the beginning of "Computer Blue." Wendy got only one line, repeated three times—"Yes, Lisa," she answered any time Lisa asked her anything, about the water, about beginning—but she made the most of it.

Wendy and Lisa became Prince's most important creative foils. Take "Strange Relationship," a loping look inside a sadistic love affair that is one of Prince's slowest songs—not in tempo, but in the time required for its development. Originally recorded during the *1999* sessions, "Strange Relationship" didn't make the final cut. Three years later, Wendy and Lisa took a crack at rearranging it, adding significant overdubs that gave the song an Indian feel, including a prominent wood flute and synthesized sitar. At that point, the song was slated for inclusion on an album; unfortunately, it was the ill-fated double album *Dream Factory*. After the project grew (to the triple album *Crystal Ball*), shrank (back to a double album that was finalized in summer 1986), and finally disappeared (to be reborn as *Sign O' the Times*), Prince went back to the drawing board with "Strange Relationship," rerecording the vocals and de-emphasizing the work that Wendy and Lisa had done, though he mentioned them in the liner notes.

A strange relationship, indeed—and it continued. Wendy and Lisa contributed string arrangements for "Raspberry Beret," and cowrote songs like "17 Days," "America," "Mountains," and "Sometimes It Snows in April." (Sometimes the women's work was outright writing that became cowriting when Prince claimed an after-the-fact credit.) Those songs proceeded from *Purple Rain*, both chronologically and thematically: the film was a feature-length exploration of the perils of solitary genius. In the early going, the Kid is a loner who tears around town on his motorcycle and treats Wendy and Lisa like hired help. The songs he performs, especially tortured ballads like "The Beautiful Ones" and "Darling Nikki," are cast almost as pure projections of his psychic state. When Wendy gives the Kid a cassette, asking him to listen to the music they've recorded, he shrugs and then sets it aside. He's not interested in ideas that originate with others. But after his father, driven by self-hatred and despair, shoots himself in the head, the Kid discovers a box of his compositions in the basement and pops Wendy's cassette in the player. It's an instrumental called "Slow Groove," and he transforms it into "Purple Rain." The song allows him not only to connect with the nightclub audience that has soured on his hermetic talent but also to confront his own feelings about his family drama and his father's musical achievement. What is *Purple Rain*, the movie, but an argument for collaboration?

Within two years, the terms of the argument had shifted, and the Revolution was over. There were warning signs: At the beginning of the *Parade* tour, Prince hired a new set of musicians to help re-create the album's complex sound onstage. Miko Weaver joined up as an additional guitarist; Eric Leeds and Atlanta Bliss came aboard as a permanent horn section. Susannah Melvoin, Prince's fiancée and Wendy's twin sister, started singing backup vocals. The time and energy devoted to integrating the new members increased discontent within the Revolution. Wendy and Lisa, in particular, felt their contribution was being minimized. In September of 1986, Prince met with Wendy and Lisa and informed them that he was making some changes. They were out.

The following September, Wendy and Lisa spoke to the *Los Angeles Times* about the circumstances surrounding their departure from the Revolution. Neither betrayed any resentment. Both discussed the move in what the writer, Dennis Hunt, called "very vague and strangely positive terms." Asked if they had noticed any warning signs before Prince dissolved the band, Lisa said she had. The article described her as the quieter of the two, but here she had plenty to relate:

> He had been working more on his own than usual. We weren't with him in the studio as much. We worked with him more than anyone else. For a while we were just about the only people he worked with. We were Prince's embellishers. We embellished his musical vision.

The two women stayed together as a musical (and, for a time, romantic) duo and released several albums—all adventurous, all interesting, but none with the magical spark that marked their work with their former boss. For years, rumors circulated of a reunion with the Revolution, or at least with Wendy and Lisa, around *Roadhouse Garden*, an album that the band had started before it dissolved in 1986. There was talk in 1998—the same year that Wendy and Lisa put out their fifth duo record under the Warner-tweaking name Girl Bros.—that the Revolution would be releasing a new record, and there was even an announcement on Prince's website, though it was accompanied by a cryptic message that "the group needn't b 2gether 2 release an album." A second message explained that Prince (or rather, ♀, at the time) "can and will finish the album alone unless the tide turns otherwise."

He didn't. But almost a decade later, Wendy and Lisa rejoined the Prince camp for *Planet Earth*. "Lion of Judah" opened with a chord that was a dead ringer for "Purple Rain," and while "The One U Wanna C" was slight, it was also sprightly and winning, largely as a result of Wendy and Lisa's backup vocals. The final track, "Resolution" (it's a freighted title, though "Revelation," which is how the song was mislabeled on early copies of the album, is equally laden), offered a jazz-funk position paper on the equivocal benefits of burying the hatchet, noting that "making amends / is a difficult pill to swallow."

Pills could also be coughed up. In 2012, when the Revolution reunited at First Avenue to play a tribute show for Bobby Z.—he was recovering from a near-fatal heart attack a year before—Prince's gear was all set up onstage in case he decided to join the rest of the band. He never showed; Wendy sang lead. The next Revolution reunion, in the summer of 2016, was also a tribute, though a far more disorienting one: a posthumous celebration of Prince at First Avenue. It was well attended. André Cymone and Dez Dickerson rejoined the band onstage, which made it a full count of the early-eighties group, and both of Prince's ex-wives were in the crowd, along with Susannah Melvoin and Apollonia Kotero. "I encourage every one of you to take every one of these songs and make them your own," Wendy said, but every single one of them was Prince's.

+ + +

Whether he was with or without Wendy and Lisa, Prince was always, in a sense, working with women. Prince may have wanted the idea of his solitary genius to be highly visible, but he also went to great lengths to make it highly divisible. From the first, he made a point of aggressively expressing his own duality. "Am I black or white?" he sang in "Controversy," and then "Am I straight or gay?" His songs followed suit: they comprised organic and electronic elements, juxtaposed overheated melodrama and robotic coldness. In a sense, he was collaborating with himself, with all the creative tension that implied. Even the plot of "Head," in which he was serviced by a bride on the way to her wedding only to end up, a verse later, servicing her (and married to her), asked a series of questions about assertiveness, reciprocation, and the pleasure of complicating both. But as "Head" suggests, Prince's understanding of creative duality is inseparable from sex, or at the very least from gender. From the start, Prince was interested not only in giving agency to the female characters in his songs—think of the sexually liberated women of "Little Red Corvette" or "Delirious"—but in giving voice to the female experience. It wasn't simply a matter of sharing the microphone with women, though he did plenty of that: "Head" is a duet with Lisa, whose spoken parts are central to the song's concept, and she returned to deliver the first line of "1999" (well, the first sung line—Prince, in a robotic voice, opens the album). Even when Prince was the only vocalist on a song, he often represented the point of view of female characters. "Darling Nikki" was about a dominatrix, but a dominatrix with dialogue: "How'd you like to waste some time?" and then "Sign your name on the dotted line." In "Raspberry Beret," his memory of his sylvan summer includes a quip (if not exactly a quote) from the girl in the title: "Built like she was / she had the nerve to ask me / if I planned to do her any harm." And *Sign O' the Times*, his most sustained accomplishment, includes "I Could Never Take the Place of Your Man," which reads almost like a TV drama that includes numerous speaking parts for its female lead.

One of the results of this interest in female perspective, of course, was that Prince's songs were easy for female singers to interpret without significant changes to the lyrics. "When You Were Mine" was already about a threesome when Cyndi Lauper got hold of it; she could complete the picture just as easily as a male singer. "I Feel for You" required no reupholstery for Chaka Khan, save one "girl" hovering in the background at the end of the second verse. And Sinéad O'Connor only switched out a few pronouns for her devastatingly intimate take on "Nothing Compares 2 U." Both men and women forget love affairs by eating dinners in fancy restaurants; both men and women go to the doctor.*

Acknowledging female perspectives in his lyrics was only the beginning. Prince's songs subverted traditional male structures. The musicologist Nancy Holland has claimed that "When Doves Cry" represented a female model of desire in the sense that it did

---

* The one switch O'Connor didn't make turned out to be an emotional mainspring. Prince's original included the lyric "All the flowers that you planted, mama / in the backyard / all died when you went away." In his version, "mama" referred to his ex-girlfriend. O'Connor left it intact because it reminded her of her mother, who had died a few years before. During the filming of the song's famous video, which consisted largely of an intense close-up of O'Connor's face as she sang, the emotional power of the lyric overwhelmed her, and tears welled up in her eyes and ran down her face. It's the most powerful moment in the performance.

not build traditionally toward a sonic climax but rather remained on a steady plateau; it also lacked bass and depended heavily on call-and-response within the vocals.

Once Prince was onto an idea, he wasn't the kind to stop half-way. In late 1981, while he was finishing up *Controversy*, Prince recorded "Feel U Up," a lubricious trifle that must have sounded somewhat undistinguished among its more visionary company. It didn't make *Controversy* or *1999*, or even sneak out as a B side. A half decade later, during the fertile period surrounding *Sign O' the Times*, Prince revisited the song with a new idea: it would be sung not by him but by a character, and he would mark the difference by altering his vocals. As his recording engineer, Susan Rogers, explained, Prince discovered "that if you put the tape machine down to half speed, you can sing in your normal voice and play guitar, and when you put the tape machine back to regular speed, it's going to be higher and thinner." The technique wasn't only a tech trick; it had its roots in canonical funk, most notably in the various characters that George Clinton developed for Parliament records in the 1970s: the Lollipop Man, Starchild, Sir Nose. Like these alter egos, Prince's new voice had a critical function. On *Mothership Connection*, in 1975, Clinton used the Lollipop Man as a high-pitched DJ who dramatized the way in which P-Funk's music was excluded from traditional radio programming. Sir Nose sketched out a can't-dance policy that reached back into Ishmael Reed's Jes Grew. Prince's high-pitched voice served his own purposes, in the sense that it interrogated and deconstructed the way that gender functioned in his songs. This pitch-shifted version of Prince hovered between male and female and, in the process, cracked open previously conventional issues of power, sexuality, ego, and id. Who exactly was singing "Let me touch your body, baby"? A man? A woman?

Something you could never understand? Did it matter? Did the answer change when the lyrics were "I'm sweating, girl, and it's all because of you"?

Prince began to conceive of an entire album for this character: it would include not only "Feel U Up" but songs like "Housequake," "Good Love," the mighty "Rebirth of the Flesh," and the even mightier "Shockadelica." The last of these has one of the best backstories of any song in Prince's catalog: In 1985, Jesse Johnson, the lead guitarist for the Time, struck out on his own with the help of Prince's former manager, Owen Husney. Johnson's second album, which he titled *Shockadelica*, included a duet with Sly Stone on "Crazay." When Prince heard about the record, he fixated on the fact that it had no title track, and—in a particularly canny bit of psychological warfare—rushed into the studio to record one. Prince didn't just get one over on Johnson; he rolled him up and smoked him. "Shockadelica" was one of Prince's finest mid-eighties efforts, a witchy bit of funk that also named the voice. "You're so tired," Prince sang, "and the reason is Camille."

Camille was a name with a long tradition, stretching back to mid-nineteenth-century France, at least, and to the strange, sad case of a young Parisian named Herculine Barbin. When Herculine fell in love with another woman, she was forced by a judge to undergo a sex change so that the love affair was not immoral. Trapped midway between two sexes, Barbin abandoned her original name and instead went by Abel—or Camille. Barbin's memoir of the ordeal was rediscovered and published, with a new introduction, by Michel Foucault, as *Herculine Barbin: Being the Recently Discovered Memoirs of a Nineteenth-Century French Hermaphrodite*. While there's no way to know for sure if Prince was familiar with the book, it's certainly possible—the first English edition came out in 1980, from Pantheon.

The Camille album came and went in the watershed year of

1986, while Prince was culling tracks from the massive triple album *Dream Factory* and then refashioning the culled set into the double album *Crystal Ball*. Intended for release without a mention of Prince, the Camille project was shelved relatively quickly, though a copy resurfaced at auction after Prince's death, where it fetched five thousand dollars. The officially released album bore traces of its origins: The "Sign O' the Times" single was released in February of 1987, a month before the album; the cover art showed Cat Glover holding a giant black heart over her face. Many people argued that it was Prince in drag. (I may have known some of those people. I may have briefly been one of those people.)

Sign O' the Times retained four of the Camille songs, though neither "Shockadelica" nor "Feel U Up" was among them (they would resurface as B sides). "Strange Relationship" was, as was "Housequake." The Sheena Easton duet "U Got the Look" featured sped-up vocals, though it was not technically a Camille song. The most outlandish deployment of the Camille persona was a song from a few years earlier, when Prince was engaged to Susannah Melvoin and observed with interest (and no small measure of jealousy) that she and her sister Wendy had a bond that he couldn't replicate. The result was a bit of speculative psychology in which Prince (as Camille) wondered what life would be like if he was his girl's girlfriend. In "If I Was Your Girlfriend," wires crossed immediately, throwing off a shower of sparks. Was Camille a (somewhat) male character musing on the ways in which his gender limited his access? Was Camille a (somewhat) female character hoping that platonic intimacy would bloom into sexual involvement? Was this Prince as Tiresias, engaged in a taste test that compared the sexual pleasures experienced by men and women? To get a sense of the subversive power of the song, compare TLC's cover on *CrazySexyCool* in 1994. It has energy and sexiness to spare, but it also simplifies the perspective; here it is women imagining being girlfriends. When the gender is no longer bent, the site of resistance is erased, and with it much of the song's allure.

Within two years, *Camille* was more or less mothballed. Still, Prince would retain the same interest in erasing the boundaries between male and female. One of the most pointed examples came on *Lovesexy*, during the spoken-word seduction toward the end of the title track. "Okay," Prince starts, "so like first I'll start by telling you / how intelligent a curve your behind has." As the song moves through increasingly lurid come-ons ("And then I can tell you that I can just smell you," he says, "and race cars burn rubber in my pants"), the vocal undergoes a kind of sex change of its own: it starts as a woman's voice, is pitched down into false bass, rises back up until it has Camille-like properties, and then rises further, into the rafters, before settling into Prince's natural singing voice, with which he paints an almost pornographic picture of sexual excitement, male but with female attributes (and aspirations). "You got me dripping," he sings, "dripping all over the floor / If I come back as a woman, I want a body like yours."

The relevant precursor here isn't only Herculine Barbin but also William Blake, the visionary poet, painter, and mystic of the late eighteenth and early nineteenth centuries. (It may seem like something of a stretch, but remember—Blake thought of his poems as songs, even called them that, and sang his work to friends at social gatherings.) In his poetry, Blake developed an elaborate private mythology around his own spiritual crises and epiphanies. His cosmology spanned across four realms, from the fallen (Ulro) to the Utopian (Eden); for a true Utopia to emerge, Blake argued, opposing forces would have to be brought into harmony with one another. Beulah, the realm just beneath Eden, was described in *Milton: A Poem* as a "place where Contraries are equally true," where stubborn oppositions like those between the living and the dead, or imagination and the real, were dissolved. One of the most entrenched polarities, of course, was the distinction between male and female. Blake distinguished between two kinds of beings that defied traditional gender: there were hermaphrodites, who are neither entirely male nor entirely female and consequently cannot profitably struggle with duality, and there were androgynes, who accept the presence of sexual difference and conflict within themselves. Albion, Blake's embodiment of both mankind and Britain in his last and most ambitious poem, *Jerusalem: The Emanation of the Giant Albion*, is the highest evolution of androgyny, and he helps to unify Blake's universe. Prince can't be mapped exactly into Blake, but he leans toward the androgynous end of this spectrum. It's in the falsetto; it's in Camille; it's in that verse of "Lovesexy." It's in "Arrogance," a rumbling miniature from the Love Symbol album: "What makes a man want to rule the world? / Make him man enough to say he's 50-50 girl." For that matter, it's in Prince's name itself—not his birth name but the symbol he used in the nineties, which efficiently combined both male and female iconography.

7

WHAT TIME IS IT?

Others in His Music

THE MAN'S ONSTAGE. HE'S SINGING. THEN HE'S NOT SINGING. THE BAND behind him is still playing, but he's just standing there. He's considering the room. And the longer he considers the room, the more it becomes clear that he's considering the way the room is considering him. He knows that everyone is looking at him, and he has a sudden urge to do the same. "Somebody bring me a mirror," he says. Another man appears from the wings, mirror under his arm. He holds it up to the first man, who considers his reflection. He likes what he sees.

The man looking at himself in the mirror is Morris Day, the lead singer of the Time, the side band that Prince launched in 1981. Morris Day was a real person, but also a persona: a slick-but-also-clumsy loverman so louche he made Billy Dee Williams look like W. E. B. Du Bois. But Morris Day was also Prince, observing a fun-house reflection of himself and achieving genuine self-reflection.

+ + +

The contract with Warner Bros. that Owen Husney negotiated for Prince in the late seventies not only gave him full creative control over his own recordings but also included a clause that let him develop other talent. Prince was a flamboyant star with a penchant for intellectual exploration, but he was also a sly comedian, a critic of existing soul-music stereotypes, and a massive egomaniac. As his own albums grew more complex and introspective, he wanted an outlet for his straightforward dance-funk material.

He didn't have to look far. His old high school rivals, Flyte Tyme, were in flux. The band's original lead vocalist, Cynthia Johnson, had left for a new project, Lipps Inc., which surrounded her with a rotating cast of session musicians and promptly had a huge hit with "Funkytown" (produced by future Prince associate David Z.). Flyte Tyme soldiered on with a new vocalist named Alexander O'Neal, and in 1980, Prince hired what remained of the group, adding Jesse Johnson as lead guitarist. At first, he retained O'Neal as lead vocalist, but after a disagreement over work habits (though some remembered it as a disagreement over weed habits), he replaced him with Day, who had been working with Johnson in a band called Enterprise. The new band was called the Time, partly as a contraction of Flyte Tyme and partly as a gimmick; the name gave Day an easy catch phrase ("What time is it?") and photos included plenty of clocks and watches.

In the spring of 1981, Prince and Day recorded the Time's debut album—Prince did most of it, billing himself as Jamie Starr, and Day focused mostly on rerecording Prince's guide vocals. The songs were largely new compositions, though Prince reused "Oh, Baby," a track he had left off his second album. Two singles, "Get It Up" and "Cool," were released, and together they established the template for the band's early work: lean synth-funk played at great length (both songs were in the ten-minute range) and concerned primarily with sex. "Get It Up" would have been at home on *Dirty Mind*, except that Morris, less intense as a vocalist, turned it into something lighter and more palatable, an appealing combination of sticky funk rhythms and shticky Casanova posing. Call it *Flirty Mind*. "Cool" was practically a speech act—when they said it, they were it. Self-awareness or self-doubt weren't on the menu; Morris was on the menu, and he was serving up generous helpings of himself. There was also a gleeful artificiality to the album. When Morris called for the band, he got a pulsing synthesizer line that sounded like anything but live musicians, and when Prince's backup vocals were occasionally audible, their sophistication only underscored Morris's studied artlessness.

The second time around, with *What Time Is It?*, a little over a year later, the band not only continued in the vein of the first album, with songs like "Wild and Loose" and "777-9311," but consolidated its gains. The Time was leaner and meaner than Prince's own band, less at risk of becoming tangled up in their ideas because they had only a few ideas—dress sharply, get girls, occasionally moon about the difficulties of dressing sharply and getting girls. The band's appeal was even more evident in concert. In 1982, the Time opened for Prince on what was called the Triple Threat tour (the third threat was Vanity 6, Prince's new girl group). Onstage, the Time made the most of Day's preening, thanks in large part to Jerome Benton, who acted as a kind of comic-relief valet for Day, carrying the mirror onstage and performing other sidekick business. "The Time became such a force as a live band that there was this onstage competition—they pushed us to the limit," said Dez Dickerson. "Which was a good thing. We were out to blow one another off the stage every night." That rivalry furnished one of the main subplots of *Purple Rain*. It also allowed Prince to be onstage, in a sense, whether he was or not; the Time, singing Prince's songs, trying to outdo the Revolution, satisfied both his desire to show himself (or at least his work) and his need for behind-the-scenes manipulation.

If Prince welcomed the competition (which was really more a form of extension), he also welcomed the chance to assert his authority. Jimmy Jam and Terry Lewis had embarked upon a side career as a production duo. One night, a snowstorm prevented them from returning from Milwaukee, where they were working with the S.O.S. Band, and Prince cashiered them.* Without them, the Time soldiered on—the band's third album, *Ice Cream Castle*, was at once its least representative and most successful. Released the same summer as *Purple Rain*, it spawned two dance-funk favorites—"Jungle Love" and "The Bird," both of which were featured in the film—but also branched out with "Ice Cream Castles," a hippie-tinged message song urging tolerance for interracial romance, and the explicitly sexual "If the Kid Can't Make You Come" (the Kid, confusingly, was the name of Prince's character in *Purple Rain*). Prince's stranglehold on the group was loosening somewhat: Jesse Johnson contributed guitar to the recording of "Jungle Love," and the version of "The Bird" on *Ice Cream Castle* was the live version from the film, which featured the whole band and no Prince.

The Time broke up in the wake of *Ice Cream Castle*—Morris Day and Jesse Johnson left for solo careers—but regrouped in the late eighties to begin work on a fourth album with Prince, tentatively titled *Corporate World*. But after they appeared as themselves

---

* Their story, of course, had the happiest of endings. The song they were producing, "Just Be Good to Me," charted, and by the late eighties they were working steadily with Janet Jackson, helping shepherd her to superstardom. They also lent their talents to artists such as Mariah Carey ("Thank God I Found You"), Boyz II Men ("On Bended Knee"), George Michael ("Monkey"), and more.

in *Graffiti Bridge*, *Corporate World* was shelved, and when the Time (now with Jam and Lewis back in the fold) finally released *Pandemonium* in 1993, they were a different kind of band. *Pandemonium* was a far more diverse and sprawling record than any of the others. It had fifteen songs, rather than the tight six that had been the band's formula through its first three albums, and only five of them were Prince compositions. One was the prescient "Donald Trump (Black Version)." Another was "Jerk Out," a slick Morris-on-the-town narrative with a classic opening line ("I got real bored on a Friday night / I couldn't find a damn thing to do / So I pulled out a suit about the same color as my BMW." It was the band's first and only top ten hit, and the final time that Prince successfully used the Time as a creative outlet. Like the Revolution, the Time eventually came around again; the full band performed together in 2008 in Las Vegas and began work on an album without any involvement from Prince. That may have been liberating, but it was also limiting—Prince's absence meant that they couldn't use the Time name, and so they took a new one: the Original 7ven. The album was written and produced by Jam and Lewis. Its first single, "#Trendin," did not trend.

The band may have been minor, but the loss was major. In the introduction to *The Second Sex*, Simone de Beauvoir discusses how human identity is based on difference and contrast:

> The category of the *Other* is as primordial as consciousness itself. In the most primitive societies, in the most ancient mythologies, one finds the expression of a duality—that of the Self and the Other.

The Time was an external projection of Prince's id, as well as an especially efficient case of defining Self through Other. With it, he could stand on the crossroads of myth, self, and society. He could play freely with others' expectations that he be a cad, a ladies' man, a sensitive artist, all of the above, or none of the above. Without the Time, there were parts of his psyche that couldn't find full expression—or that had to find that expression in such a straightforward manner that they could not profitably see around corners. And yet, even when there was no more Time, Prince forced the issue. "Movie Star," an oft-bootlegged song that eventually appeared on *Crystal Ball*, opened with Prince about to go out for the night, running through a little ritual: "Let's see, body oil, check, incense, check / Environmental records, double check / I'ma get some serious drawers tonight." It's a Time song in every sense. Prince plans to trick his friends by getting to the club an hour early, which will give him time to scope out the girls (he hopefully anticipates "mo' drawers"). While he manages to pick up a young lady and take her back to his place ("You like my crib? It's not mine, it's rented"), she falls asleep before there are any drawers at all, let alone mo' of them.

But the key lyric comes earlier in the song, when Prince arrives at the club and steps out of his limousine: "They said, 'Ooh, it's good to see you' / I said, 'Oh, it's good to be seen / You know what I mean?'" Prince gradually reclaimed the original Time material. At a 2009 aftershow at the Avalon Hollywood, he burned through a set list that was mostly covers—Allen Toussaint's "Yes We Can Can," the Cars' "Let's Go," the Beatles' "Come Together," Jimmy Eat World's "The Middle" (?!). He ended on a medley of "The Bird" and "Jungle Love" and, after the final squawk, looked out over the audience. "Who wrote that song?" he said. It's good to be seen.

✦ ✦ ✦

If the Time was Prince's first attempt to export aspects of his creative personality, it was hardly his last. The band he created from the ashes of the Time, the Family, put out an album that prefigured

Prince's exploration of jazz-funk and included the original version of "Nothing Compares 2 U." Mazarati, a group founded by his bassist, Brown Mark, helped him shape "Kiss" on its way to becoming a megahit. But most of his protégés, both during the era of the Time and after, were women. In this sense, his outward creativity with these groups returned him to his most inward concerns with identity, sexuality, and the dual nature of the self.

In pop music, female artists are often controlled by male artists—they are given songs to sing, costumes to wear, sometimes even new names to replace their real names. There's a long tradition of this, or rather, two of them: the Pygmalion tradition on one hand and the Svengali tradition on the other. Pygmalion stories, which began in Ovid and crystallized into their modern formulation in George Bernard Shaw's 1913 comedy of the same name, usually end with the older male figure falling in love with his protégée. Svengali stories, rooted in George du Maurier's 1895 novel *Trilby*, tended to be more exploitative and predatory: du Maurier's own illustrations depicted the character as a spider in a web, trapping and devouring his prey. Historically, the music industry has lent itself more to the latter model. Rebecca Haithcoat, writing in Vice Media's *Broadly* just a few weeks before Prince died, explored the history of the male Svengali in pop music, from Phil Spector to Kim Fowley, with a special emphasis on the economics of the arrangement. Women were permitted to write and perform songs, while men tended to occupy producer roles, in large part because production was needed (and compensated) whether or not songs were released. Similarly, upward mobility was distributed unevenly among the sexes; women had plenty of male mentors (older industry figures who helped them find their way to more work) but not nearly as many male sponsors (older industry figures who taught those younger women how to create work themselves). In these terms, Prince was a Svengali, though his special relationship with female identity ensured that he was just as snared in the web.

Backstage at the American Music Awards in 1980, he met a young model and actress named Denise Matthews. Matthews, who had just turned twenty-one, had been born on the Canadian side of Niagara Falls, the product of an ethnic crazy quilt that included Afro-Canadian, Native American, Hawaiian, Polish, German, and Jewish blood. She had gone to New York to model, but she was too short, and an agent suggested Los Angeles and acting roles instead. She found some, including a small part in *Terror Train* (a slasher film set aboard a moving train that starred Jamie Lee Curtis) and a larger one in *Tanya's Island* (a romantic adventure, of a sort, about a castaway juggling relationships with both her brother and an ape-man). In both films, Matthews was billed as "D. D. Winters." In neither film was she especially memorable.

But she made an impression on Prince. The two of them began a relationship, and when he returned to Minneapolis, he invited her to come stay with him. Once she arrived, he began to involve her in a new idea he had—a highly sexualized girl group performing songs he would create especially for them. The initial incarnation of the group, called the Hookers, was built around Susan Moonsie, a friend of Prince's from high school. The Hookers petered out around the time of *Controversy*, but Prince revisited the concept with Denise, who he felt would be a perfect front woman for the band. He tried to convince her to change her name to Vagina. She refused, understandably. They compromised on Vanity.

The name had at least two meanings, both perfect: Prince liked to think of Vanity as his female mirror image, and she was also about to become the center of his first true vanity project (though you could make the argument that Morris Day, with his actual mirror, was also all about vanity). Vanity, Susan Moonsie, and a third singer, Brenda Bennett, entered the recording studio in March of 1982 to add vocals to a set of tracks that Prince had already prepared. Five months later, Vanity 6 released its debut. "Nasty Girl," the opening song, established the formula: spare synth-pop with salacious lyrics and vocals that were more coy than powerful. "Do you think I'm a nasty girl?" Vanity asked, and answered a few lines later: "I need seven inches or more / Get it up, get it up—I can't wait anymore."* Elsewhere on the record, Prince gave the band more outré electronics ("Drive Me Wild," "Make-Up"), risqué songs ("Bite the Beat," a celebration of oral sex which could have been handed off to Blondie or the Go-Go's), and relatively innocent songs with risqué titles ("Wet Dream"). The ballad "$3 \times 2 = 6$" had an attractive melody, but it exposed Vanity's limitations as a vocalist. The funkiest, funniest moment was the Time-like "If a Girl Answers (Don't Hang Up)," a skit-song combo in which Vanity tangled with the new girlfriend of an ex (played, hilariously and unconvincingly, by Prince).

Vanity 6 ran its course—or rather, ran off course. Vanity was cast as the romantic lead in *Purple Rain* but departed before shooting started. Replacement auditions for the film were hastily arranged. The part went to Patricia Kotero, a Mexican-American model and actress who had had appeared in various television shows and a few music videos, including Ray Parker Jr.'s "The Other Woman." Prince renamed her Apollonia—this time, he only had to look as far as her middle name—and cast her in both the film and a new version of Vanity 6. Apollonia 6 featured

---

* During the third debate of the 2016 US presidential campaign, when Donald Trump derided Hillary Clinton as "such a nasty woman," the song that got the bounce (and became the center of the resulting meme) was Janet Jackson's "Nasty," produced by Jimmy Jam and Terry Lewis, rather than "Nasty Girl," which was a better fit but not as big a hit.

mostly Kotero and Brenda Bennett, along with backing vocals by Lisa Coleman and Jill Jones. Though Apollonia was a better singer than Vanity, the music had little of the punkish insistence of its antecedent. The songs were more fully realized, which ironically worked to their disadvantage—mostly they just sounded like less energetic Prince songs, and in fact several tracks demoed by Apollonia 6 and left off the album ultimately entered the Prince canon via other routes: "Manic Monday" (which ended up with the Bangles), "The Glamorous Life" (which found a home with Sheila E.), and "17 Days" (which became the B side of "When Doves Cry"). The two keepers were "Sex Shooter," a close cousin of "17 Days" that the band performed on-screen in *Purple Rain*, and "Happy Birthday, Mr. Christian," which reversed the plot of the Police's "Don't Stand So Close to Me" and added a deadbeat-dad twist: Mr. Christian, the high school principal, impregnated a student but wouldn't support her and her child. Apollonia left after the band's sole album.

+++

Over the years, Prince contributed material to a series of female acts. Not all qualified as protégées. The list ran the gamut from artists who received donations from Prince in the early eighties, as he was getting his footing as a songwriter (Renn Woods), to those who were sent one-offs that seemed designed solely to prove his versatility across the spectrum of pop music (Paula Abdul, Deborah Allen, Dale Bozzio), to those he worked with more closely, writing and producing multiple tracks and controlling their career trajectory to some degree (Martika, Elisa Fiorillo, Taja Sevelle). Then there were the female stars who either preempted his creative advances (Stevie Nicks invited him to contribute uncredited keyboards to "Stand Back," a song that she wrote after hearing "Little Red Corvette") or resisted them (Bonnie Raitt recorded with him in 1987 and considered signing with Paisley Park, but the project fell through).

The most successful protégées, generally, existed at an optimal distance from Prince: they were famous enough in their own right, with enough of a musical personality to ensure that his input yielded interesting output. Sheila E. came from a musical family—her father and uncle were percussionists with Santana—and made the most of expansive mid-eighties anthems like "The Glamorous Life" and "A Love Bizarre" with style and grace. (It didn't hurt that she also looked great in the Victorian fashions the Prince camp favored at the time.) Sheena Easton afforded Prince an opportunity to remake a peppy pop ingenue as something sleeker and more sexual, with the anatomically unequivocal "Sugar Walls" and the undeniable "U Got the Look." But many of Prince's Trilbys were no credit to his reputation as a Svengali: Ingrid Chavez's "Elephant Box" was dreamy poetry that floated away over electric piano improvisation by Prince; Carmen Electra's take on hip-hop was more like *Hop on Pop*; and the less said about his unreleased sessions with Kim Basinger, the better.

In the end, only one of the female acts in the Prince camp produced an album that could stand proudly alongside his own body of work. Jill Jones grew up in a musical family, singing backup for her cousin Teena Marie, whom her mother managed. In 1980, when Teena Marie was the opening act for the *Dirty Mind* tour, Jones and Prince struck up a friendship and later a relationship. She joined him in 1982 for the *1999* sessions, during which she contributed to several songs, including "Lady Cab Driver" and "1999" (she's probably most memorable from the video, in which she wears a short nightgown and an airline pilot's hat); played a small but important role in *Purple Rain* (she was the waitress who wouldn't let Apollonia into First Avenue); and then recorded her own excellent solo record. The self-titled album, which she and Prince worked on periodically through the mid-eighties and eventually released in 1987, offers a nearly perfect distillation of the Minneapolis aesthetic: synth-heavy funk loaded with double entendre, heartfelt ballads, and layered vocal arrangements. The lead single, "G-Spot," anatomizes desire using consistently clever lyrics: "I'm listening to the voice beneath my hair," "I am a clock / the time is 9:15." The album is elevated throughout by Jones's superb vocals. She sings the hell out of Prince's 1980 album track "With You," saunters through "Violet Blue," and delivers a bravura performance of the liquid, lovely "Baby, You're a Trip." Though Prince and Jones recorded a handful of singles toward a second album, the magic proved impossible to recapture. Prince moved on from her, but he never moved up.

He was still trying to launch female stars late in his career. *Milk & Honey*, a Támar Davis record that included at least a pair of significant additions to the Prince-protégée canon—"Holla & Shout" (sprightly sex brag) and "Beautiful, Loved & Blessed" (retro soul duet)—was scheduled to be bundled with the 2006 album *3121* before a last-minute shelving.* He put out Bria Valente's *Elixer* as part of his *LotusFlow3r* package, contributing everything but what the album desperately needed: charisma and personality. He worked with Andy Allo, a talented Cameroon-born singer and guitarist, collaborating on three songs on her 2012 album *Superconductor* and casting her in an important supporting role on *Art Official Age* in 2014. A year before his death, he

---

* Támar Davis grew up in Houston, where she was a member of Girl's Tyme, a six-piece all-female rap and soul group that also included two young singers named Kelly Rowland and Beyoncé Knowles. After Támar's departure, Girl's Tyme evolved into Destiny's Child—and into superstars. During the final Destiny's Child tour in 2005, Prince went to see the group in Las Vegas and went backstage afterward. "We were all excited," Michelle Williams, who had joined the group long after the Girl's Tyme era, told *Entertainment Weekly*. "He came in like a beast in the night . . . I'm telling you he was so swift. He was so encouraging. He said, 'You gave me goosebumps.'"

recorded an album with Judith Hill, who had been a backup singer for Michael Jackson and a contestant on *The Voice*. Prince wrote new songs for Hill, produced them, and sent out a free download link to the resulting album, *Back in Time*, only to be sued by Hill's former label for poaching. Scrambled eggs, so boring.

+ + +

One of the most captivating works of world literature is Benjamin Jowett's lucid, hallucinatory translation of Plato's collected works. Especially noteworthy is the passage in the *Symposium* in which Aristophanes, one of the guests at the drunken dinner party that gives the work its name, relates how Zeus halved primeval men. It's a bit of a stretch, perhaps, to call them "men": the creatures Aristophanes proposes were, by human standards, monsters, spherical beings with four hands, four feet, and two faces, each of which looked in the opposite direction from the other. Some were male on both sides, some female on both sides, and some a mix. They possessed great powers and threatened the gods, which didn't sit well with Zeus. He got out his instruments and went to work:

> He spoke and cut men in two, like a sorb-apple which is halved for pickling, or as you might divide an egg with a hair; and as he cut them one after another, he bade Apollo give the face and the half of the neck a turn in order that man might contemplate the section of himself: he would thus learn a lesson of humility.

The split resulted in beings that felt forever incomplete and were compelled to roam the earth until they found their complement. "Each of us when separated, having one side only, like a flat fish, is but the tally-half of a man," Aristophanes says, "and he is always looking for his other half." Aristophanes was known as the "prince of ancient comedy." Prince took the idea seriously in the modern world. His idea of the relationship between the sexes, especially in the matter of his female protégées, cannily combined androgyny (as imagined by Blake) and the eternal search for the other that would complete the self (as imagined by Plato). When he found a tally-half that was a good fit, he got a care package of songs ready to go.

✦ ✦ ✦

Work could, at length, spill into Prince's life. During the summer of 1979, he and his band holed up in Mountain Ears, a studio in Boulder, Colorado, suffering the pun and working on new music. Prince had just finished his second album and had an idea for a side project called the Rebels in which he would operate on a more democratic basis with the rest of his band, sharing songwriting and vocal duties. Since only Dez Dickerson, the band's guitarist, and André Cymone, the bassist, were songwriters of any appreciable talent, Dickerson wrote two songs, "Too Long" and "Disco Away" while Cymone contributed "Thrill You or Kill You." The rest of the Rebels material was written by Prince.

The Rebels album never emerged; in later years, the band discussed it as if it was merely a strategy on Prince's part to placate the rest of them. But one of Prince's compositions lived to see another day: "If I Love You Tonight." Sung by Gayle Chapman in the Rebels sessions, the song was a slow, circumspect ballad in which a woman explains why she is holding off on consummating her relationship ("If I love you tonight / promise me that you'll stay with me till the morning light"). Prince returned to the song during the annus mirabilis of 1987. He had just opened his Paisley Park studio, and "If I Love You Tonight" was one of the first songs he tackled. He sent the track to a young British singer named Mica Paris, who had appeared with Prince onstage at Camden Palace in London in July, singing the Temptations' "Just My Imagination." She recorded a new vocal with the British producer Nellee Hooper. The track, now brought into compliance with Prince spelling as "If I Love U 2 Nite," ended up on her second album, *Contribution*, where Hooper slowed down the instrumental track so that it slotted in nicely with other British neosoul of the period. (The twelve-inch single is a rarity, since it was accidentally released with Prince's original guide-vocal performance.)*

But Prince wasn't done with "If I Love You Tonight." The same year that *Contribution* came out, he received a video of a young dancer named Mayte Garcia, an Alabama-born army brat living in Germany. Garcia, still in her teens, had earned some fame for her belly dancing, including an appearance on *That's Incredible* as an eight-year-old back in 1981. Her mother filmed an audition tape and sent it to Prince's management; when the Nude Tour came to Germany in the summer of 1990, Prince met with the Garcias, and late the next year he hired her as a dancer for his Diamonds and Pearls Tour. She was central to his next album, the Love Symbol album, contributing backup vocals, dancing in videos, and serving as an all-around muse. The album was accompanied by a straight-to-video movie, *3 Chains o' Gold*, that starred Mayte as an Egyptian princess who enlisted Prince's help to protect the sacred chains of the title. Romance ensued.

3 Chains o' Gold (the contracted "o" hearkened back to *Sign O' the Times*, with misplaced optimism) was terrible. But it was also

---

* Hooper would also work with Sinéad O'Connor on her version of "Nothing Compares 2 U."

WHAT TIME IS IT? 115

telling—Prince and Mayte were now dating in real life as well. In 1993, one of the rare years in which Prince released no material of his own, he worked on an album for Mayte. Initially titled *Latino Barbie Doll* (the title wasn't quite as gratuitous as it sounds; there was a song of that name as well), the project included songs cowritten by Mayte ("Children of the Sun," "Ain't No Place Like U"), new or relatively new Prince compositions ("Mo' Better," "The Rhythm of Your Heart"), reclamations from other protégée projects ("Love's No Fun," which had appeared on the Elisa Fiorillo album *I Am* in 1990; "Baby Don't Care," which had been sketched out for Tevin Campbell's sophomore album *I'm Ready*), and a cover of the Commodores' funk classic "Brick House." It also included a new version of "If I Love You Tonight." Two new versions, in fact: Mayte recorded it both in English (the title had been further Princified to "If 👁 ♥ U 2 Nite") and in Spanish (as "Si Te Amo Esta Noche").

Mayte's album, now titled *Child of the Sun*, was released in Europe on NPG Records in late 1995. Warner Bros., heels dug in, refused to release the album in North America. If Prince's relationship with the label had deteriorated, his relationship with Mayte had solidified. The following Valentine's Day, they married. Prince was thirty-seven; she was twenty-two.

✦ ✦ ✦

The Love Symbol album charted Prince's courtship of Mayte, but the clearest snapshots of their relationship were folded inside *Emancipation*, the triple album that he released in 1996 after severing his ties with Warner Bros. In serving no masters, *Emancipation* served many: it declared Prince's independence from corporate servitude, demonstrated the breadth of his talent for fans new and old, and covered songs by artists who had inspired him (from the Delfonics to Bonnie Raitt). It also found Prince speaking more frankly about his personal life than ever before. "Friend, Lover, Sister, Mother/Wife" made the case that any previous dalliance had in fact led him to Mayte ("If I ever held a hand / It was only because I'd never held your hand"). The vocals were as confident and soulful as any he had ever sung. "Saviour," spelled in the British fashion (maybe to include the *u*), pledged his devotion to his new bride in elegant botanical terms ("We're like two petals from the same flower, baby / We're like two branches from the same tree"). Most intimate, and most heartbreaking, was "Let's Have a Baby," a let's-get-it-on song as ardent as anything Marvin Gaye or R. Kelly ever recorded, but with purely procreative motives. He told Mayte that he had spent hours gazing into her eyes "wondering what they'd look like on a newborn child," and confessed that when his hand is on her thigh, he thinks mostly about the miracle of life. The thought even got to him in the car: "I can't even go for a ride . . . without thinking about a little baby . . . sittin' right by my side." The song wasn't perfect: the melody cloyed a bit; the piano dripped with wet notes that dried like watermarks. But there was no irony at all in its tone. The song came off as utterly unguarded, the equivalent of a proud father-to-be who keeps rubbing his wife's pregnant belly at family gatherings.

And Mayte's belly was, in fact, pregnant. She gave birth in October of 1996, a month early. The baby, Boy Gregory, was born with Pfeiffer syndrome, a congenital condition marked by craniosynostosis, or early fusion of the skull bones. There are three types: Type 1 sufferers can live a normal life span, but often with facial deformity. More severe variations are fatal. Boy Gregory died a month later. His death eerily echoed a lyric from almost a decade earlier, on *Lovesexy*'s "Anna Stesia": "Gregory looks just like a ghost / then a beautiful girl (the most) / wets her lips to say / 'We could live for a little while / If you could just learn to smile / you and I could fly away.' "*

Prince dealt with his grief with what was, for him, an unusual degree of public visibility. As part of the promotion for *Emancipation*, he toured daytime TV shows for the first time ever. Mayte came along with him to *Oprah* just before Thanksgiving, where they spoke about their son as if he was still alive. Just before Christmas, Prince appeared on the *Today* show, where he was interviewed by Bryant Gumbel. The segment was largely devoted to reviewing Prince's credentials ("he's a musical genius who plays more than twenty instruments") and explaining his break with Warner. Prince, wearing a brunch outfit (salmon turtleneck, sable vest), answered questions slowly and quietly. After the first commercial break, Gumbel turned to the matter of Prince's marriage. Prince, laughing, said that Mayte was trying to get him to work less. "She's got me in studio rehab," he said.

Gumbel looked past the camera and called for Mayte to join them. She came onto the set and perched on the back of Prince's chair. "What do you want him to do instead?" Bryant asked. "Mow the lawn?"

"Dishes," Mayte said. Prince cataloged the many ways in which Mayte had changed his life. Most were extremely abstract (she had made it possible for him "to focus on the earth" and easier for him to "talk to God" by teaching him "a new language"). Both of them agreed that they had met in a previous life, probably in Egypt. ("Do the two of you believe in reincarnation?" Gumbel asked. "I do!" Prince said.)

---

* Of course, plenty of people read "Anna Stesia" as "Anastasia," the youngest daughter of Tsar Nicholas II, and "Gregory" as "Grigory," as in Rasputin, a historical pair that also featured in the lyrics of the Rolling Stones' "Sympathy for the Devil."

At the end, Gumbel turned to the issue of their child. There had been rumors in the news following the birth, but the Prince camp had not yet released a statement. "The two of you had a baby in October. Is the baby well?"

Prince answered, mostly looking away from Gumbel. "My obliqueness when people ask questions about that particular situation is that we both believe that thoughts and words can breed reality. How we look at the situation is very important. What we say about the situation is very important. All I can say is that we're both enlightened individuals that know that if you leave things in God's hands, you'll find out everything, the answer to the plan. So anything that happens, we accept."

"That sounds like there's been a problem but you're of the belief that whatever has happened has happened for the best," Gumbel said. Both Prince and Mayte nodded. Silence filled the set.

Bryant shifted to lighter matters, with a series of fashion questions. "Do you own a blazer?"

"No."

"Do you own a pair of pleated khakis?"

"No."

"Would you ever wear my shoes?"

Prince leaned over to get a look. "Hell, no."* The interview ended in laughter. The following year, when Gumbel retired, Prince wandered on set dressed exactly like him.

Prince didn't go into studio rehab for long; in 1997, he was

---

* This was right after O. J. Simpson's famous "ugly-ass shoes" scandal. During a deposition for the civil trial that followed his criminal case, Simpson claimed that he would never wear Bruno Magli Lorenzo boots, which matched shoe prints found near the spot near where Nicole Brown Simpson and Ron Goldman were murdered. The *National Enquirer* promptly unearthed a photo of Simpson wearing the shoes at a Buffalo Bills game nine months before the murder.

back at work on a pair of albums for NPG Records, Chaka Khan's *Come 2 My House* and Graham Central Station's *GCS 2000*. He went into marriage rehab instead, filing for divorce in 1998. It was all over by 2000. A year after divorcing Mayte, Prince married again, to Manuela Testolini, a Canadian-born business-woman and philanthropist who was employed as an adminis-trator at one of Prince's charities. Their marriage lasted six years. There were no children.

8

I WISH U HEAVEN

Virtue and Sin in His Music

"**A**T SOME POINT, FUN'S NO FUN." I WAS IN CHICAGO, LIMPING THROUGH grad school, listening to a friend tell me why she didn't like Prince. She thought he was a heedless hedonist, that all his songs were about ass-grabbing and gamahuching and going uptown and getting down. "Watch," she said. "I'll just pick one at random." This was in the age of cassettes, so that meant sliding one of the cases out of the wall-mounted rack and opening it. If you were especially deft, you could do it all with one hand. She was. "'Head'?" she said. "I told you. It's all below the belt with this guy." She waved the other hand around angrily.

"That's *Dirty Mind*," I said. "That's exactly what that album is. You know."

"I don't know," she said. "And I don't like it."

"Try a different record," I said.

"Yeah," she said. But about a week later, I noticed her in the library, wearing headphones, the *Lovesexy* cassette on the table beside her. "What gives?" I said.

She looked up at me. Her eyes were wet. "He's trying so hard to understand the idea of God," she said. "How can you not admire that?"

I didn't, at least not early on. As a young man, I liked Prince most for his flamboyant lewdness. Other people judged it taboo. But in those days, when I was just learning to use music as a form of self-expression, I was attracted to the artists who were as transgressive as possible. I was pretty certain that shattering convention was the main job of art. Ironically, then, what I found most offensive about the early Prince was his faith. Both of his parents were devout Seventh Day Adventists—his mother believed that Prince's epileptic seizures, which afflicted him until he was seven, stopped because an angel touched him—as was André Cymone's mother, Bernadette, who helped raise him when he left home. On his first records, he wore his deep connection to God on his sleeve. On his sleeves, in fact. In the liner notes to *Controversy*, he gave "Special thanks to God and U." For *1999*, he wrote "Thank U—God." As a suburban Jewish kid, these devotionals unnerved me. It wasn't just that I felt excluded by his Christian faith. It was that I was in a constant state of excitement regarding pop culture, and I believed in a separation of church and that state. Pop culture, to me, needed to be wilder and freer, and I thought that those impulses—which were already blooming in Prince's music—should take precedence. If there was to be religion, I wanted it to be handled subversively, the way Prince incorporated the Lord's Prayer into "Controversy." (I wouldn't have thought of it in these terms at the time, but it was like the split in Ishmael Reed's *Mumbo Jumbo* between the Wallflower Order, a secret society devoted to monotheism and control—Reed called them Atonists—and more unregulated animist forces like Jes

Grew, a black-music-based dance craze that authorities treated like a virus that needed to be eliminated. Prince thanking God so much had too much Atonism, and not enough dance, music, sex, or romance.)

In 1984, I assumed (with, I'll admit, a little relief) that Prince would retreat from his faith a bit. I assumed that his plans for mainstream domination required moderation. An overtly religious artist might have trouble selling into secular America. But *Purple Rain* was dedicated upward, just like the other records ("All thanks 2 God—The Light"), and the songwriting followed suit. "Darling Nikki" ended with a backmasked choir that people said hid a message about all the nasty things that Prince wanted to do to Nikki ("It says he's going to use a whip," one girl said, breathlessly). But in fact, it was angelic as it sounded. When played forward, it put a messianic spin on the rest of the record: "Hello! How are you? I'm fine, 'cause I know that the Lord is coming soon . . . coming, coming soon!" I knew that someone would be coming in "Darling Nikki," but I didn't figure it would be the Lord. And "Let's Go Crazy" sketches out an eschatology in its opening monologue: life, death, afterworld.

In other songs from the period, Prince got even more explicit about his faith: cross-rated, you could say. He recorded a track called "God" that was subtitled "Love Theme from *Purple Rain*" and relegated it to an instrumental B side, at least in America and the United Kingdom—elsewhere in the world, fans got a vocal version. What that meant, at least for the first minute of the song, was cooing and screeching and gurgling and keening. The vocalizing was followed by actual vocals, with lyrics about creation and the necessity of dancing in the face of the impending apocalypse. "Wake up, children," Prince sang. "Dance the dance electric. There isn't much time. Who screamed? Was it you?"

+ + +

It wasn't the first time there wasn't much time. A year and a half earlier, *1999* had opened with a computer voice, pitched downward. "Don't worry," it said, "I won't hurt you. I only want you to have some fun." That wasn't an uncommon sentiment for an entertainer. What was uncommon was *why* he wanted you to have fun.

The voice gave way to drums, then synthesizers that blared brightly, like trumpets heralding the end of the world. In fact, that's exactly what they were doing. Like so many other Prince songs, "1999" began in a dream ("I was dreaming when I wrote this / forgive me if it goes astray").* The dreamer soon woke, though, into an apocalyptic tableau ("When I woke up this morning / could have sworn it was Judgment Day"). The vocals were separated— Lisa Coleman first, then Dez Dickerson, then Prince—and the vision was one of panic: "The sky was all purple / There were people running everywhere." The image evoked the Book of Revelation in the New Testament, in which the sky wasn't exactly purple, but rather darkened "by smoke from the Abyss." (A competing scriptural interpretation suggests that the association of purple with Revelation comes from mixing together red blood and blue sky in the final moments of human existence on earth.) It wasn't a good scene—or rather, it was a great scene of a terrible scene.

---

* This and "When Doves Cry" are the two most famous, but there are dozens of others. He invoked dreams in "When You Were Mine" ("It was just like a dream"), in "U Got the Look" ("Here we are, folks / The dream we all dream of"), in "Glam Slam" ("Must be a dream, it's so magical"), in "Lovesexy" (the skidding, bass-modulated "Sweet dreams" that ends the song). His 1980s magnum opus, never released, was titled *Dream Factory*. The William Blinn script that evolved into *Purple Rain* was called *Dreams*.

But "1999" took a stance on how to brace for the curtain coming down, suggesting that the only reasonable preparation was celebration. Don DeLillo's *Zero K*, published just days after Prince's death, opened with a variation on that idea: "Everybody wants to own the end of the world." Prince didn't want to own it, but he didn't want it to own him, either. If the world was going to end, he suggested, the only recourse was to live in the moment. Start in the Wallflower Order, but move quickly to Jes Grew. Assiduously seek pleasure in the face of annihilation. Listen to your body tonight.

In "1999," Prince seems to be following the chronology proposed by James Ussher, the seventeenth-century archbishop of Armagh. Ussher dated the earth's creation at roughly 4000 BC, and, drawing on the then-popular belief that the planet's life span was six thousand years—each day of Biblical creation was figured as a millennium, citing 2 Peter 3:8: "with the Lord one day is as a thousand years, and a thousand years as one day"—to place the party-over-oops-out-of-time date right around 2000. David Bowie's "Let's Dance," released about six months later, pulled on the same thread: its video showed an Aboriginal Australian girl finding a pair of red shoes and dancing in them before watching a flash over a distant range and then the swell of a mushroom cloud.

Prince would return to the same territory himself soon enough, with *Purple Rain*, whose very title was an apocalyptic weather report. "Let's Go Crazy" asked a highly rhetorical question ("What's it all for?") and furnished a highly familiar answer: "You better live now / before the Grim Reaper comes knocking at your door." A half decade later, R.E.M. recorded their own apocalyptic anthem, "It's the End of the World as We Know It (And I Feel Fine)." They opted for meditation: in the chorus, Michael Stipe's title line was followed by Mike Mills's relatively antisocial counter (and countermelody): "It's time I had some time alone." Prince preferred to spend his time with others, feeling even finer.

✦ ✦ ✦

Prince didn't always practice what he preached. As he outwardly advised hedonism, he was increasingly drawing inward toward a kind of spiritual stoicism. The final stop on the *Purple Rain* tour brought the Revolution to the Orange Bowl in Miami, which was affectionately renamed the Purple Bowl for the night. Prior to the show, Prince's manager, Steve Fargnoli, issued a statement: according to Fargnoli, the Orange Bowl concert would be Prince's last live performance for an "indeterminate number of years." Fargnoli added that when he asked Prince what he planned to do, Prince answered that he was "going to look for the ladder."

What did that mean? People speculated. Did he need to clear out storm gutters or change a lightbulb, or was it something more empyrean? Prince offered a clue as he opened the show. "Happy Easter," he said. "My name is Prince, and I've come to play with you." In sequined pants and a matching shirt over a white ruffled shirt, he launched into "Let's Go Crazy." The show went at a breakneck pace. Prince reproduced the first stretch of *1999*, slightly out of order ("Delirious" to "1999" to "Little Red Corvette"); blazed through a James Brown–style miniset that included the unreleased "Possessed" and the B side "Irresistible Bitch"; debuted a song that he said was "Temptation," from the new album *Around the World in a Day* (it featured a jaunty piano melody and scattershot lyrics about a lascivious prince). He even played "God," pairing it with "Father's Song," which made it seem as if he was auditioning for the third spot in the Trinity. He closed out the concert with a sustained climax composed of side two of *Purple Rain*: "When Doves Cry," "I Would Die 4 U," a thirteen-minute "Baby I'm A Star," and a twenty-minute "Purple Rain."

People left, thoroughly satisfied, if still perplexed about the ladder. Two weeks later, when the new Prince and the Revolution album, *Around the World in a Day*, appeared in stores without so much as a lead single, the question was answered, to some degree. The album, the first on Prince's boutique label, Paisley Park—the label's logo was more cephalic than phallic, a brain shape rendered in a psychedelic font—conjured up the spirit of the sixties, a little Haight-Ashbury, a little Beatles. The cover was a painting by Doug Henders, the artist who had worked on the *Purple Rain* movie; he was responsible for the faces that adorned the wall of the Kid's bedroom. When Prince started work on the new album, he gave Henders a list of fifteen elements that he wanted incorporated into the cover art, including a tearful old woman, a clown juggling the earth, and a ladder ascending to heaven. Henders debated doing the cover as a collage but settled on painting it instead. Working in a highly illustrative, highly trippy style, he incorporated the items from Prince's list, adding in an airplane, a baby waving the American flag, several figures meant to represent the band, and a flock of doves. During the arduous *Purple Rain* tour, working in hotel rooms whenever he could get a moment of peace, Henders completed the painting and, unwilling to trust it to baggage handlers, had it flown back to Los Angeles in its own seat. Along the left edge of the cover—centered if the album was opened to full gatefold—was the ladder, rising from a swimming pool to the sky.

The ladder was mentioned prominently in the opening song and title track, which dramatized the process of Prince building on (and away from) the immense success of *Purple Rain*, explaining that "the little one will escort you to places within your mind," and that "the ladder is purple, come on and climb." "The Ladder" was also the name of the penultimate song on the album, a mid-tempo ballad which was cocredited to Prince's father (as with a few of the *Purple Rain* compositions, he had incorporated elements of his father's music). The arrangement featured a full string section, and the lyrics were gentler and more abstract than anything he had yet released, an explicitly spiritual parable of a king and his realm and the difficulty of finding inner peace. "Temptation," the record's final song, was not the frolicsome piano fragment he had played in Miami but an eruption of guitar accompanied by a morality play that detailed how Prince's carnal concerns had caused him to drift away from the divine. It ended with a descent into hell, sentineled by free-form saxophone squeaking courtesy of Eddie M., and then a reiteration of Fargnoli's pre–Purple Bowl remarks. "I have to go," Prince said. "I don't know when I'll return. Good-bye." He stayed offstage for the rest of the year.

+ + +

Prince's retreat was his version of the motorcycle accident that Bob Dylan suffered (or exaggerated, or invented) in 1966. It gave him a break from popping flashbulbs and swarming crowds; it also allowed him to reconsider his approach to deploying his faith in his music. *Parade* handled the matter more obliquely, with lyrics like "let's go fishing in the river, the river of life" in "New Position," which alluded to the Book of Revelation, and the entirety of "Sometimes It Snows in April," which presented Christopher Tracy as a Christ figure: dead, awaiting resurrection. (Years later, parts of the song would turn out to be remarkably prophetic.) *Sign O' the Times* sounded at times like a secular gospel album: songs like "Play in the Sunshine" could have been about either faith or fun, just as songs like "Forever in My Life" could have been about either God or a girl. Toward the end of the record was "The Cross," a muscular cluster of power chords that was Prince's most explicitly Christian song to date. But even here he tied faith back into social policy—and, it could be argued, socialist policy ("there'll be bread for all of us"). And even if you accepted its spiritual argument, it was only a few songs away from "Hot Thing" or "It." Not everyone could reconcile the two. I remember an argument in a college dorm room between two women: "Prince is nasty," the second one said, proudly. "But he loves God," the first one said. "He loves God while he's being nasty," the second one said, even more proudly. "That's just wrong," the first one said. Both of them were right.*

+ + +

In college, after *Sign O' the Times*, our antennas were extended. We had heard the best album of our young lives and we wanted more. There were rumors all through the fall that Prince had already completed his next record, *The Black Album*, which was scheduled to come out on December 8. Suddenly, the record was withdrawn: it would not be released December 8, or December 15, or ever. Various explanations circulated. Some said that Prince worried that it represented a dark vision of the world— that the black in the title wasn't just black music, but a pessimistic and even demonic mind-set that had to be exorcised. Some said that Prince had dabbled in Ecstasy and had a bad trip that

---

* At the time of this argument, John Updike had just published his novel *Roger's Version*, in which a complacent theology professor has his faith challenged by the appearance of a young computer programmer who claims to be able to prove the existence of God. The theology professor—that's Roger—does not want this. He insists that the persistence of faith despite proof is the strongest proof of faith. One of the examples he uses is a prince: "the way the Mahdi's or the Aga Khan's turning into obese sybarites failed to affect their alleged divinity." By that light, Prince's lewdness not only failed to disqualify him but in fact qualified him. Aga Khan, let me rock you, let me rock you, Aga Khan.

soured him on the record's message. Some said he was playing games with his record label. Some said that he was cracking up.

Fans mourning *The Black Album* made for the black market, where bootlegs were already circulating. I skipped class to ride the train into New York City and drop a hundred dollars on a cassette version that looked like it had been quickly put together in someone's basement, and probably was. *The Black Album*, despite the rumors, was not a devil album, but it was a defensive one. Prince had grown concerned that his rise as a pop star was jeopardizing his bona fides as an African-American artist. *The Black Album* solved this problem to some degree, rolling back to the hard funk of *1999*. "Le Grind," the opener, set its dance in France (though a very pidgin-dominated France: "Nouveau grind, come on," Prince called out, and then, elsewhere, "Ce soir, la chantez"), surrounding it with various keyboard borborygmi and a wafer of funk guitar. "Cindy C" made a specific appeal to the supermodel Cindy Crawford ("Oh, Cindy C, will you play with me?" and, "Maybe you and I should be undressing"), and the blazing "Superfunkycalifragisexy" illuminated the deepest, freakiest corners of Prince's mind and mythology (its inventory, which included a bucket of squirrel meat, neon lights, masturbation, and a bondage chair, was like a whole new list for Doug Henders). But the album was padded out with filler and experiment, some of which couldn't have gladdened the hearts of Warner Bros. Of particular concern was "Bob George," a violent fantasy in which Prince, voice lowered electronically, played an abusive man threatening his girlfriend, whom he suspected of cheating on him with Prince's manager: "What's he do, manage rock stars? Who? Prince? That skinny motherfucker with the high voice? Who do I look like, baby, yesterday's fool?" This was comedy, and psychology, too—a commentary on Prince's divided psyche—but it was also profanity, and it had only been a half decade since the

PMRC charged in, pistols drawn and pointing at "Darling Nikki."

If *The Black Album* made Tipper Gore nervous, it had a similar effect on a nation of Prince fans, but for different reasons. Without it, who knew how long we'd have to wait for new Prince music? As it turned out, not very long: a new song, "Good Love," came out on the *Bright Lights, Big City* soundtrack in April of 1988, and by May there was a whole new record, *Lovesexy*.

The cover photo of *Lovesexy* showed Prince, entirely nude, sitting inside a giant flower—or possibly Prince shrunk down to fit inside an ordinary-size flower. His left leg was angled up for purposes of strategic concealment, though right behind him the flower was letting it all hang out: shaft of stamen, bulge of anther, a botanical representation of the Blakean androgyny he had been circling for years. The cassette itself was transparent plastic, as Prince's cassettes had been since the mid-eighties*, and the music on it opened with a soft wash of synths, and then the trademark yelp. The opening song, "Eye No" (rendered as " 👁 No" on the track list), was lavishly spare—on the one hand skeletally polyrhythmic, on the other filled with sparkling detail.

The record's lead single, and biggest hit, came next: "Alphabet St." Pairing its syncopated rhythm track with a strummed acoustic guitar, the song had a warm, organic feel that was new for Prince. (The song would later be sampled by the alternative rap group Arrested Development for their huge 1992 hit "Tennessee"; they didn't seek permission for the sample and ended up paying a hundred thousand dollars for it.) And what was Alphabet

---

* It is possible that *Around the World in a Day* was not only Paisley Park's first release but the first major album to be distributed on a clear cassette. They weren't in wide circulation until 1985, certainly. There is a rumor, somewhat plausible, that they were invented for prison mail-order catalogs, so that files and other small weapons couldn't be concealed inside opaque cassette shells and smuggled behind bars.

Street? Maybe it was like *Sesame Street*: Cat Glover counted down—or spelled down—at the end, semiorgasmically, getting from A to I (as in "I love you") before rolling over to go to sleep. The rest of the album expanded Prince's musical horizons in all directions at once. "Glam Slam," a paean to sex so good it put Prince in mind of God, seemed always to be reaching up: guitars streaked heavenward alongside massed falsetto vocals. "Anna Stesia" started off as a piano ballad about abject loneliness (a guy in my dorm in college swore that it was a slowed-down version of Billy Joel's "All For Leyna") before thickening into anguished soul-metal. And the title track—loaded up with vroom-vroom guitars, at least four different percussion tracks, and electronically treated vocals that traveled from male to female and back again—traced a perimeter around the idea that sex and spirit might be profitably fused. Throughout, Sheila E. drummed as if possessed, Miko Weaver played pointillistic funk guitar, and Prince did the rest: the liner notes credited him with "Whatever."* There was lots of whatever. Even the space between compositions—and really, there wasn't any, since the whole album was sequenced as one long track—was stuffed full of music, as if the songs themselves couldn't contain all of his ideas. To eighteen-year-old ears, the album sounded miraculous, and more than twenty-five years later, it has not lost its luster.

The lyrics could be preposterous, of course. In "Glam Slam," there was a couplet that pulled together kinky sex, procreation, and nature in the silliest way possible: "Heavy feather, flicka nipple / Baby scam, water ripple." But the frivolity was undergirded by seriousness. The end of "Anna Stesia" was both an apology and

---

* "Whatever" was the same exact credit that one of Prince's primary inspirations, Sly Stone, had taken on one of the weakest Sly and the Family Stone albums, *Heard Ya Missed Me, Well I'm Back*, from 1976. The cover of that album showed Sly as a true one-man band, drums strapped to back, top hat in hand.

a pledge, promising God that "I shall be wild, I shall be quick, I shall be strong—I'll tell your story no matter how long."

No matter how long: the extended remixes that Prince snuck out on the B sides of singles were even braver and bolder. The "I Wish U Heaven" remix (subtitled Parts 1, 2, & 3) incorporated a Morris Day–like vocal and James Brown exhortation, turning the empyrean earthly fast. One of the "Glam Slam" remixes, now titled "(Escape) Free Yo Mind from This Rat Race," was a jumble sale of sounds, adding in a chunky bass, sudden violent outbursts of guitar, and sci-fi sound effects, not to mention lyrics that successfully melded the spiritual awareness of *Lovesexy* with the street smarts of *The Black Album* ("Don't get on the scale if you can't stand the weight"). Prince had made better albums, more consistent albums, and more intelligent albums, but he was never as joyfully inventive as he was on *Lovesexy*.

✦ ✦ ✦

In trading scatology for eschatology, Prince made his agenda clear—he was a spiritual pilgrim, aware of his own dark side and afraid of it, not just for what it might mean for his soul but for what it might mean for those who followed him. Questlove, writing after Prince's death, remembered visiting Paisley Park in the nineties and being made aware of Prince's swear jar—if visitors used profanity, they had to contribute a dollar. Questlove slipped up and swore, and after calling for a dollar, Prince thought better of it. "You're rich," he said. "Give me twenty." Questlove protested: "You're the one who taught me to swear when I was little." Prince laughed, but with a little hitch. Questlove wondered to what degree Prince remained preoccupied by the idea that he had corrupted a generation of young fans with his lewdness.

In the late eighties, he seemed to be spending much of his energy apologizing for that aspect of his art. Prince didn't plan on an "Alphabet St." video. But then it was a snowy day in March, and everyone was bored. He called for a video crew, and Alan Leeds, his tour manager, found one at a local cable station. The production values were modest and the concept was rudimentary: Prince sang the song against a computer-generated background swimming with random letters, and in front of a Thunderbird (owned by his father, as the lyrics say, but a 1964, not a 1967).* At the moment when Prince sang "She'll want me from my head to my feet," the letters arranged into a vertical message: "Don't buy *The Black Album*—I'm sorry."

From a distance of almost thirty years, Prince's disavowal of *The Black Album* in favor of *Lovesexy* seems like a calculation that incorporated both financial and creative motives. He sacrificed a record that had limited commercial prospects to placate his record company and assuage his own sense of unease. But in some ways, it was the whole game. In matters of gender, Prince had addressed the contraries of male and female by acknowledging that each contained the other, and he had designed complex, creative strategies to illustrate that interdependence. When it came to good and evil, though, he took a different approach. Here, he went to great lengths to separate them—and, moreover, to ensure that he was firmly on the side of good. There was even a Satanic figure, Spooky Electric, who appeared on both "Eye No" and "Positivity" but failed to lead Prince into error.

Again, the poetic precedent is relevant. William Blake had criticized Milton for a certain disingenuousness: Milton wrote

---

* People love to talk about all the different automotive makes and models mentioned in Bruce Springsteen's music, but has anyone ever done a comprehensive study of cars in Prince's music? Thunderbird in "Dead on It." Thunderbird in "Alphabet St." Corvette, of course, in "Little Red Corvette." Honda in "Sex in the Summer." Cadillac in "Jack U Off" and also in "Chaos and Disorder," where there's also a Mercedes-Benz.

about paradise, but his attempt to portray (let alone achieve) spiritual innocence was doomed to fray at the edges as a result of his own fallen state. Blake, writing in Milton's wake (and in his debt), wove those contradictions into the fabric of his work. His *Songs of Innocence and Experience* complemented each other, between them they offered a complete account of humanity's equivocal relationship to sin and divinity. Prince, in *Lovesexy*, opted for a more Miltonian approach. He proposed himself as a messenger of paradise, as a privileged observer capable of leading others out of error. The attitude is clearest in "Positivity," the closing track of *Lovesexy*, on which he describes a world of "plus signs" presided over by "new kings of the world" and urges his listeners to steer clear of evil: "Don't kiss the beast / Be superior at least." This, the culmination of *Lovesexy*, is undone by the same falsely elevated notion of self that, in Blake's view, tripped up Milton.

The idea of staging the tension between contraries overtook the idea of resolving that tension on Prince's next album, the *Batman* soundtrack. The original comic-book series trafficked in explicit moral duality. Batman was at war not only with a cast of villains but with himself: on the one hand, he was the wealthy and philanthropic Bruce Wayne; on the other, he was a tortured vigilante driven by revenge for the murder of his parents. He tried, often vainly, to reconcile these two parts of his personality. Prince not only wrote a set of songs for *Batman* but inserted himself into its universe. He created Gemini, a divided being whose face was painted half green and half purple (the colors evoked Prince but also the Joker, Batman's most dangerous nemesis and a character who regularly explored the possibilities of evil). Gemini juxtaposed those two sides without integrating them; in Blakean terms, he was more hermaphrodite than androgyne. And yet, that coexistence was also a kind of symbiosis: so long as one lived, the other would live, too. At the end of the "Batdance" video, he triggered a detonator, in an echo of the album's strongest song, "Electric Chair," and that was that for Gemini (though he would return briefly in an early-nineties comic-book series titled *Alter Ego*, which revolved around a disturbance in the moral fabric of the universe and ended with a fight between Prince and Gemini). The split between good and evil was dealt with most directly in an outtake from the *Batman* sessions, "Dance with the Devil," where Prince leaned on the low notes of the piano: "Dance with the devil in the pale moonlight / Put your arms around him and hold him tight." Glacially paced, "Dance with the Devil" dragged along for eight grim minutes, disappearing deeper and deeper into its own vortex before a synth-horn blared and the whole thing just shut off, doubling the darkness.*

✦ ✦ ✦

Unlike sixties and seventies soul stars like Sam Cooke and Al Green, Prince didn't traffic much in traditional gospel. He worked extensively with Mavis Staples, both in *Graffiti Bridge* and on a pair of solo albums, and their creative relationship always felt like a bit of a missed opportunity. There are a few exceptions, like the secular gospel "Adore" and the spiritual gospel "Still Would Stand All Time." "Still Would Stand All Time" dated back to a solo demo from the *Lovesexy* sessions; Prince added backup vocals by the Steeles, a Minneapolis quartet, and put the song on *Graffiti Bridge*. The melody wandered around at first but then found its

---

* The *Batman* soundtrack became a kind of stepchild in Prince's discography—due to licensing conflicts with the comic-book franchise, he was not allowed to use any of the material on compilations or in merchandising. When he sold tour shirts that listed his entire discography, *Batman* was replaced by "Scandalous"—the big sex ballad on the record, but neither representative of its contents nor particularly interesting in its own right.

feet, and the lyrics figured salvation not as something abstract but rather "just around the corner . . . just around the block."

Diamonds and Pearls, calculated as a commercial comeback, mostly backed off on the spiritual material, but the Love Symbol album returned to it forcefully. A concept album with an overarching plot about Prince, a princess, and some magical chains stolen by a phalanx of assassins, the Love Symbol album also retold the Gospels from Prince's perspective. Biblical scholars have written about the *ego eimi*, or "I am," a rhetorical (and ontological) strategy favored by Jesus in the Gospels. The Love Symbol album opened with its own *ego eimi*, "My Name Is Prince": "My name is Prince, and I am funky / My name is Prince, the one and only." (This was an equivocal claim, since very soon after the album's release his name was not, in fact, Prince but the symbol that gave the album its title.) The album's hit single, "7," both echoed the seven incidences of the *ego eimi* and invoked the seven trumpets of the apocalypse. And the closer, "The Sacrifice of Victor," was a semiautobiographical narrative that opened with a graphic scene of birth (bloodstained table, cord wrapped around his neck). The song's title allied it with the idea of the Christus Victor, a view of Jesus's death set forth and promoted by the Swedish theologian and author Gustaf Aulén. While traditional theology saw Jesus's death as a kind of ransom or bail payment for man's evil, Aulén saw it as a kind of emancipation from (and exposure of) the bondage of sin. The Christus Victor theory, for many years espoused only by Orthodox Christians, became increasingly influential in the twentieth century among liberal Christians and peace churches.

In the theological narrative Prince was developing, all the action was rising toward one key moment: the dawn. The idea had been with Prince as early as *Purple Rain*, in which the end credits included a message: "May You Live to See the Dawn."

(It was explicitly spiritual even then, though there's a far earthier use of it in "Erotic City": "We can fuck until the dawn.") *The Dawn* was briefly a title for a film and then a title for a massive album along the lines of *Dream Factory*. Prince tried to submit it to Warner Bros. during the early nineties, when his contract situation was becoming untenable. They refused to accept the record in its original form, and it became a fountainhead for a series of records: *Come*, *The Gold Experience*, parts of *Crystal Ball*. It also became what it should have been in the first place: less a title for a specific work and more an overarching symbol of Prince's abiding faith in a time of reawakening that would follow the end of days. The clearest articulation of what it meant and what it promised was the sweet ballad "Welcome 2 the Dawn," from *The Truth*, in which he laid it all out clearly: "When the light of God / is the only thing in life that will redeem / Welcome, welcome to the dawn."

✦ ✦ ✦

Dawn or no, Prince was heading toward an explicit reckoning with his own faith. In the late nineties, Prince married into funk history by forging a relationship with Sly and the Family Stone's old bassist, Larry Graham. Graham had parted ways with Sly in the early seventies and founded a new band, Graham Central Station—not to be confused with Prince's first band, Grand Central—that specialized in showcasing Graham's slap-bass mastery ("Hair") and, with increasing frequency, his way with an oily ballad ("One in a Million You"). During that time, Graham Central Station was signed to Warner Bros., where they were one of the label's top soul properties. Graham joined Prince's band in 1997 as his touring bassist and, with a new version of Graham Central Station, released his NPG Records debut, the prematurely titled *GCS 2000*, in 1998.

But Graham's creative contributions paled beside his spiritual influence. Since the mid-seventies, he had been a Jehovah's Witness, a member of the millenarian form of Christianity founded by the Pennsylvania businessman Charles Russell in 1869 and centered around the belief that the Witnesses represented God's only voice on earth. Soon after Graham entered the Prince camp, he brought Prince into the Jehovah's Witness fold, and Prince officially converted in 2001, after two years of study with Graham. Prince's newfound devotion to his faith changed his relationship to his work. He did away with his most outrageous outfits and onstage antics. When he sang old songs, he bowdlerized them, replacing the profanity with tamer language. "When you use those words," he said, "you call up all the anger, all the negative times the word has been used before—you bring it toward yourself. Why would you want that?" He even indulged in some revisionist religious history. Jehovah's Witnesses didn't believe in the Biblical story of the cross; rather, they read the Greek word *stauros* as referring to a single stake. Prince accepted this tenet and then went back through his own catalog, editing accordingly. The main target was "The Cross," from *Sign O' the Times*, which became "The Christ" when he performed it live.

Then, in 2000, he made an entire record about his faith. *The Rainbow Children* was historically important if for no other reason than that it marked the point at which Prince decided to mothball the glyph he had used since 1993 and return to his birth name. It was a rebirth in other ways, too. The album had listed tracks, fourteen of them, but it was, like *Lovesexy*, more properly thought of as a continuous composition that kaleidoscopically combined airy soul, contemplative jazz, and slinky funk. Nearly every song began with a spoken interlude, delivered in an electronic basso profundo, that zeroed in on the spiritual issues that were foremost in Prince's mind. The title track again invoked the *ego eimi*

("The one who commands your mama / with the simple phrase 'I am' ") but moved quickly to a recitation about humanity's place in the heavenly hierachy:

> With the accurate understanding of God and His law they went about the work of building a new nation: The Rainbow Children. The Wise One who understood the law that was handed down from God long ago reflected the true meaning to his woman every day and she surrendered her discerning of it in2 his care and keeping 4 she trusted he would lead in the right way. Her children in subjection 2 her, she in subjection 2 the Wise One, and the Wise One in subjection 2 the only begotten one, all 4ever in subjection 2 God.

The wise one, male, must maintain the subjection of "his woman" or else risking violating "accurate understanding." The rest of the album reiterates this hierarchy. Many songs were written for, or to, Manuela Testolini, who became Prince's second wife, and they were structured as tests of her fitness as a wife, much of which depended upon her willingness to accept her secondary station. In "1 + 1 + 1 Is 3," Prince repeatedly reiterated the presence of "a theocratic order," which expressly lays out the chain of command: God over man, man over woman. On top of the album's considerable sexism, there is also a devotion to faith so comprehensive it can border on incoherence. In another song, Prince notes that "the opposite of NATO is OTAN," which is true, but difficult to parse: Does he mean Odin, the Norse deity? Or is it Aten, the ancient Egyptian disk of the sun that was an aspect of the great god Ra? At times, it doesn't seem to matter, because the music behind the lyrics is magical. Other than John Blackwell on drums, Najee on sax and flute, and Milenia on backing vocals, Prince acts mostly a one-man band on the record, and while there are plenty of moments in his catalog at which this is hard to believe, here it is impossible to believe. As a guitarist, he goes at all genres from all angles and sometimes from multiple angles at once, pulling together surging rock chords, subtle acoustic shadings, reticulated jazz.

The record peaked with a pair of funk songs, "Family Name" and "The Everlasting Now," each more than eight minutes long, both explicitly political. "Family Name" provided a full account of Prince's struggle to reclaim his own identity. After opening with a coy reference to the Akashic record (an occult idea, popularized by the theosophists, that held that a full account of all past and future experiences was located in the astral plane), Prince suggested that faith can erase difference:

> When a minority realizes its similarities on a higher level—not just "black"—but "PEOPLE OF COLOR," and higher still "INDIGENOUS," and even higher still, "FROM THE TRIBE OF," and yet higher—the "RAINBOW CHILDREN." When this understanding comes, the so-called minority becomes a majority in the wink of an eye.

It was an admirable idea. Unfortunately, it was also mired in division. Throughout the song, Prince waged spiritual war against the oppressors who robbed him of his rightful identity. When they wondered why he was angry, he threw the question right back at them: "You might say, 'what you mad about?' / But you still got your family name." And though he professed civility, his own lyrics betrayed him—when he sang, "Pleased to meet you," it was impossible not to hear echoes of "Sympathy for the Devil." His concept of the devil was especially problematic here. The lyrics weren't afraid to name names—and the names were

Rosenblum, Pearlman, and Goldstruck. If that doesn't sound at least a little anti-Semitic, then you're not listening closely enough. "Family Name" also furnished yet another example of Prince's devotion to duality, this time on the issue of race: "First of all," he said, "the term 'black and white' is a fallacy / It simply is another way of saying 'this or that.'" Better, in the end, to be the other thing. "The Everlasting Now," hot on the heels of "Family Name," sang the praises of funk, God, and self-determination, not necessarily in that order. It also provided some much-needed levity. Prince was certainly speaking from the heart, but he also knew that proselytes don't always keep an audience's ear. "You know," he said, mimicking the pinched tones of an unconverted fan, "this is funky, but I wish he'd play like he used to, old scragglyhead." The response was the sharp report of a slap.

That concern didn't dissuade him in real life. Tavis Smiley, a close friend and confidant to Prince throughout his life, wrote a remembrance for *USA Today* in which he recalled hanging out at Paisley Park, in the upstairs "Knowledge Room," where Prince studied Bible. Prince tried to convert Smiley, selling him on the eternal wisdom of his newfound faith; Smiley, who had been raised Pentecostal, resisted. Prince left the room for a little while, not because he had given up on Smiley but because he was reloading.

> Thirty minutes later Larry Graham walks in, and Prince starts strutting around the room like, "Uh huh! Uh huh! What you gon' say NOW!" I laughed out loud, and Prince, Larry and I talked into the wee hours of the morning about our respective pathways to deeper spiritual truths. Afterwards, we went downstairs for a jam session where I got to play drums. What a night, the spiritual and the secular were conjoined!

He continued to testify on record: the slinky sermon "The Word" was buried toward the back of *3121*. Prince also took his faith to the streets. Witnesses are perhaps best known for their door-to-door preaching. On a Sunday afternoon in 2003, a couple in Eden Prairie, a southwestern suburb of Minneapolis, heard a knock on the door. It was Prince and Larry Graham, both of them holding Bibles. The conversion didn't take: the couple was Jewish, for starters, and it happened to be Yom Kippur, the holiest holiday in the Jewish calendar. On top of that, the Vikings were playing on TV. Prince and Graham stayed for about twenty-five minutes, politely presented their opinion, handed out pamphlets, and left in a big black truck.

✦ ✦ ✦

Prince had always been a free thinker, even at the expense of internal consistency. That didn't seem like a drawback, and often it seemed like an advantage. William Blake, the great annihilator of polarities, warned against letting ideas grow stale: "The man who never alters his opinion is like standing water, and breeds reptiles of the mind." When Prince's beliefs hardened around the doctrine of the Witnesses, reptiles of the mind began to appear, and they had teeth. Even before his conversion, Prince joked about homosexuality in a way that could seem prejudicial. In 1997, he explained to Chris Rock why Michael Jackson's "Bad," intended as a duet between the two superstars, never happened: "The first line of that song is 'Your butt is mine.' Now I said, who's gonna sing that to who? Cause you sure ain't singing it to me, and I sure ain't singing it to you."* The Witness faith intensified his

---

* The comment was homophobic, or at least insensitive, but it was probably more properly a measure of the tension between the two men. Jackson found Prince rude and told confidants that he was worried—or was it hopeful?—that Prince would harm

discomfort. It was explicit in its rejection of homosexuality; in 2015, a former Jehovah's Witness named Misha Anouk detailed his break with the church over its strong and persistent homophobia, noting that gay behavior was labeled "unnatural sexual perversion," "perverted desire," and "abhorrent" and even compared to the sexual abuse of children. In 2008, asked for his opinion of gay marriage by Claire Hoffman of the *New Yorker*, Prince seemed to condemn it. He tapped his Bible and said, "God came to earth and saw people sticking it wherever and doing it with whatever, and he just cleared it all out. He was, like, 'Enough.'" Representatives from his camp quickly reached out to the blogger Perez Hilton to clarify: "What His Purpleness actually did was gesture to the Bible and said he follows what it teaches, referring mainly to the parts about loving everyone and refraining from judgment." But the clarification may not have been necessary. What His Purpleness actually did was even more nuanced. In the *New Yorker* piece, a paragraph before, he pointed at the Bible instead of tapping and made his view clear.

> Here's how it is: you've got the Republicans, and basically they want to live according to *this*. . . . But there's the problem of interpretation, and you've got some churches, some people, basically doing things and saying it comes from here, but it doesn't. And then on the opposite end of the spectrum you've got blue, you've got the Democrats, and they're, like, "You can do whatever you want." Gay marriage, whatever. But neither of them is right.

---

himself. And in "Invincible," in 2001, Jackson imagines wresting a woman away from a man who buys her "diamonds and pearls."

Here, Prince echoed the aphorist E. M. Cioran, who identified the paradox at the heart of any religion, or for that matter any other system of programmatic thought: "My mission is to see things as they are. Exactly the contrary of a mission." Prince dreamed of synthesis and saw a world that fed off antithesis. Here's how it isn't.

9

AMERICA

Race and Politics in His Music

THE NEW-RELEASES KIOSK OF THE RECORD STORE IS A MOSAIC ASSEM-
bled by several different artists, foot-square squares stacked five
high and facing in all four directions, the entire assembly occu-
pying a prime spot at the head of the cash-register line, near the
door—the hub of the place. "Excuse me." It's 1980 in suburban
Miami. I'm eleven years old. I'm trying to get past the woman in
front of me to the kiosk. The covers show heavy-metal bands
playing out medieval myth. They show New Wavers arranged
amiably, often photographed at a slant. Stevie Nicks is on the
cover of *Bella Donna*, hair a healthy size, cockatoo perched on her
hand; Kim Carnes, equally flaxen, stares out like a hostage from
Mistaken Identity. "Excuse me, please." I'm trying to get to the
records off to the right. I'm in seventh grade, interested mostly in
Styx's *Paradise Theatre* (vintage theater marquee) and Journey's
Escape (beetle-shaped spaceship). "I just need to get by. Excuse

me." The third time's the charm—the woman in front of me turns. It's not a woman; it's a girl. She's slightly older than me, which means much older. There's blooming and blossoming, a body making the most of faded black jeans and a ripped red T-shirt. When she reaches up, I can see into the armhole of the shirt: no bra. Her hand travels to one of the covers—high on the rack, thankfully. It shows a young black man in a light purple suit. He has a mustache, or maybe it's more accurate to say that the mustache has him. This is the first time I see a Prince cover. I know that because it says his name, and also the title, *Controversy*. I'm intrigued by it, but only briefly. I don't even notice the Rude Boy button on his lapel. The T-shirt repossesses my attention. The girl looks at the cover, laughs, and takes Prince with her to the cash register.

It would be a year before I returned to buy my own copy of the record. By that time, I had come around to the mustache, and what attracted my attention was the headlines. Arrayed around Prince on the cover of *Controversy* are a number of fake newspaper front pages that touch on both spiritual and political themes: "Annie Christian Sentenced to Die!" "Love Thy Neighbor," "Do You Believe in God," "President Signs Gun Control Act." The first of these pointed toward one of the record's most explicitly political songs, "Annie Christian," which relied on a second-grade-level pun (going from "Annie Christian" to "Annie Christ" is confusing for several reasons, including that it's not how nicknames work) to remark upon recent tragedies and scandals such as the so-called Atlanta Child Murders, Abscam, the murder of John Lennon, and even the attempted assassination of Ronald Reagan. The final headline emphasized one of Prince's early preoccupations. In "The Second Coming," a *Controversy*-era rarity, Prince preached that "all of God's children must learn to love" and then, in the next breath, wondered "how many more good men must die before there's gun control?"

Larger weapons worried him even more. "Ronnie, Talk to Russia" urged President Reagan to negotiate with the Soviets "before it's too late / before they blow up the world." In the summer of 1982, about a month after Prince began work on "1999," the funk outfit the Gap Band had a radio hit with "You Dropped a Bomb on Me." Prince was less cool with the prospect, and for the rest of his career, he would worry about America and about what might happen if a screaming came across the sky. On December 24, 1998—only a week before the arrival of calendar-year 1999—Prince played an aftershow at the Tivoli in Utrecht, Netherlands. The set list included an extended jam in which he extemporized about international affairs, eventually incorporating a topical rap: "Osama bin Laden getting ready to bomb," he said, and then called out a date: "2001 . . . America, you better watch out." The mention of bin Laden makes sense—a few months earlier, he had organized the US embassy bombings in Dar es Salaam and Nairobi, but singling out a specific year verges on the prophetic.

✦ ✦ ✦

It wasn't only weapons that worried Prince. He fretted about income inequality, about the environment, about social justice, about the hubristic deployment of new technologies. While he would return to these issues again and again over the course of his career, any consideration of his political conscience and the way he integrated it into mature art should start with *Sign O' the Times*.

I remember hearing the title song in my dorm room in college, back in the first months of 1987. "New music from Prince," the DJ said. "Sounds like he's been down in the basement with Apollonia, listening to those old records." I wasn't sure what he meant. Did he mean the basement from *Purple Rain*? Did he mean that

Prince was listening to his own old records, or old records from other artists?

When the song started, it obliterated all those questions. A synthesizer line appeared first, spare and menacing. At the ten-second mark, a drumbeat struck, and Prince came in behind it: "Oh, yeah!" But there was no jubilation in this "Oh, yeah!" or in the synth-bass that followed, which sounded like a tensed muscle, and the lyrics were grim from the jump. "In France, a skinny man died with a big disease with a little name." As the song went on, it traced the consequences of the skinny man's behavior—"By chance his girlfriend came across a needle and soon she did the same"—and then traveled from France back to America, where the lens widened to take in gang violence, drugs, even the hubris of space travel (the *Challenger* disaster was only a few months old when the song was recorded). The song was set far from the late-night party land of "Uptown," or for that matter from the eschatological dreamworld of "1999." Prince had been here before (in "Mountains," there's a line that gets lost in the surging funk: "Africa divided, hijack in the air / It's enough to make you want to lose your mind"), but never with such sustained purpose. And what was the purpose? It seemed as though it was dual: both to allow Prince to process the terrible afflictions of the world and to make the rest of us take comfort in the fact that they could inspire great art. Julian Barnes sketched out the process in an essay on Théodore Géricault's *The Raft of the Medusa*:

> We have to understand it, of course, this catastrophe; to understand it, we have to imagine it, so we need the imaginative arts. But we also need to justify it and forgive it, this catastrophe, however minimally. Why did it happen, this mad act of Nature, this crazed human moment?

Well, at least it produced art. Perhaps, in the end, that's
what catastrophe is *for*.

In producing art, "Sign O' the Times" also produced a powerful
sense of the artist at work. Earlier on, Prince's one-man-band
ambitions had led him to layer his arrangements, both instru-
mentally and vocally, for the purpose of enlarging his songs.
"Sign O' the Times" was a one-man-band song that sounded like
it: wise, defiant, alone in the world. The Revolution was no longer
a going concern, but the revolution was going on, and Prince
was concerned. He made the song on the Fairlight synthesizer,
but the creativity was all in the lyrics and the arrangement. In
part, in fact, the creativity was in the lack of creativity—rather
than program new effects for the synthesizer, Prince used some
of the stock sounds built into the machine. It's a nice match of
subject and style: just as the lyrics used found materials in the form
of his observations about the surrounding culture, the music used
the found sounds already loaded into the instrument. What he
layered over it was some of his most minimal and effective guitar-
playing. If there had been a party, it was over.

In ensuing years, Prince went back to the well, though he used
different vessels to carry water. *Lovesexy* had "Dance On," which
opened with rattlesnake percussion and skittered along on its
minimalism, but its list of social infractions left something to be
desired ("Nuclear ban never stays in tune" was redundant to past
concerns, and "stealing ladies' purses and setting them aflame"
seemed like maybe not as much a problem as Prince thought it
was). *Batman* had "The Future," an anthem of cool despair and
economic privation that sarcastically quotes Lincoln Steffens's
famous assessment of the USSR: "I've seen the future, and it
works." But iterations of the theme became either more superfi-
cial (the title track of *Chaos and Disorder*) or more enervated

("United States of Division," a listlessly pessimistic download from 2004). In 2005, when Hurricane Katrina devastated New Orleans, Prince rushed into the studio and rushed out a song called "S.S.T." The title was oblique—it referred to "sea surface tempera- ture," a meteorological metric for forecasting hurricanes—and the song was not particularly memorable. And "Planet Earth," the title track from his 2007 album, couldn't measure up to simi- lar endeavors like Michael Jackson's "Earth Song," a loony burst of empathic rage from 1995 in which Jackson wails about our responsibility to other living things ("What about elephants? / Have we lost their trust?").

The most satisfying articulation of Prince's social conscience was buried on one of his least satisfying albums: "Money Don't Matter 2 Night," from *Diamonds and Pearls*. A modest, tuneful work that explicitly reached back to early-seventies social- conscience songs by artists like Curtis Mayfield, "Money Don't Matter 2 Night" emphasized the value of ethical living in a world dominated by greed and power. It eschewed flash and technol- ogy; the only vocal effect, a flattening out when his voice increased in volume, was a recording-booth error that Prince liked enough to leave uncorrected.

On the album version of "Money Don't Matter 2 Night," Prince didn't identify the race of his characters. "Make certain that your soul's all right," he sang, specifying nothing about the body that encased that soul. In the video that Spike Lee made for the song, however, the family in crisis was figured as African-American. The video was only an interpretation, but it explicitly raised the issue of race, which was a complex and contradictory one through- out Prince's career.

Ten years earlier, at the beginning of "Lady Cab Driver," Prince tries to hail a cab, only to have several (from the sound of it) pass him by. It was a canny joke about the difficulty for a black man in hailing a cab in New York City, but also a rare early admission that he was a black artist. More commonly, he refused to answer the question he raised on "Controversy": "Am I black or white?" In interviews, he promoted confusion about his background, telling Bill Adler of *Rolling Stone* that he was "the son of a half-black father and an Italian mother." *Purple Rain*, which cast the Greek actress Olga Karlatos as the Kid's mother, reinforced this notion, and for years even devoted fans insisted that it was the case. (The story persisted until after his death— prominent newspapers, including the *New York Times* and the British *Independent*, referred to him incorrectly as "biracial.")

His obfuscation on matters of race may have been a way of toying with interviewers or a strategy for broadening his audience base ("Don't make me black," he had told Lenny Waronker). It may also have been a more meaningful fiction, a nod to one of his inspirations. In a number of songs ("Private Joy," "Manic Monday"), not to mention in his portrayal of Christopher Tracy in the movie *Under the Cherry Moon*, he linked himself to Rudolph Valentino, the Italian-born American actor who rose to fame in the 1920s playing roles like the Sheik. Valentino was not only a romantic icon, he was a trailblazer when it came to dissolving racial stereotypes in American movies. He played the Sheik as a fully formed character, and when he was asked if it was plausible for a woman to fall in love with a savage, he attacked the premise. "The Arabian civilization is one of the oldest in the world," Valentino said. "The Moors are closely akin to the Arabs. I know them. The Arabians are dignified and keen-brained. People are not savages because they have dark skin."

Racial identity was connected, of course, to cultural identity. Classic soul music, most prominent in the sixties and early seventies, drew on the rawness of blues and the spirituality of gospel to take a measure of the human condition. But when soul music promoted social advancement, it did so primarily with an eye toward upward mobility. Soul singers placed a high value on conventional markers of social success like marriage, income, and home ownership. Prince could sound those notes, certainly, and there were periods where he foregrounded them—the "let's fall in love, get married, have a baby" line in "Sign O' the Times," or for that matter the *Emancipation* era, where he sketched out precisely that life in a series of songs. But Prince was also a rock-and-roll star and a funk subversive with a penchant for behaviors that would have shocked most of those soul artists.

Through the middle of his career, he struggled to reconcile these two approaches to social change, traveling between respectable aspiration and radical affect. "Sign O' the Times" was a soul song at heart—it located the solution to the world's problems in falling in love and having a baby. *The Black Album* not only restored his funk bona fides but also turned away from the very idea of reasonable solutions and toward outlaw sex and violence: it was beautiful, dark, and twisted a quarter century before Kanye West. Much of his late work seemed more conventional in its aims, especially after he became a Jehovah's Witness. But as late as "Lavaux," in 2010, on the album *20Ten* (it was, as the critic Parke Puterbaugh once said of Toto's *Toto IV*, "cleverly titled"), he was still flashing that subversive spirit: "Revolution time has come today."

✦ ✦ ✦

As he got older, Prince increasingly demonstrated a willingness to engage with issues that affected the African-American community. Tavis Smiley told *USA Today* that after he hosted the State of the Black Union—televised panel discussions that included prominent academics, activists, thinkers, and geniuses—Prince would sometimes call up and request a private audience.

> He'd taken copious notes and wanted me to continue the conversation over at his house. He wanted in. And, he wanted me to bring certain panelists over to the house with me for a sort of academic after party. I'd always oblige, and everybody from Cornel West to Dick Gregory would sit around his table dissecting the political, economic, social and cultural issues confronting the black community in particular, the nation and the world. I've never met a more curious mind.

His inquisitiveness ranged far and wide, into ideas that were, depending on your perspective, either trenchant or conspiratorial. In a 2009 interview with Smiley, he showed a predisposition for dissident thinking, in particular referencing remarks made by the comedian and activist Dick Gregory on the prevalence of chemtrails in African-American neighborhoods. "You know, when I was a kid, I used to see these trails in the sky all the time," he said. "A jet just went over. And then you started to see a whole bunch of them. And the next thing you know, everybody in your neighborhood was fighting and arguing and you didn't know why." It was not his first exposure to that way of thinking. In the late eighties, Prince signed the funk forefather George Clinton to Paisley Park for a pair of records, including the sneakily titled *The Cinderella Theory* (someday my Prince will come). During sessions, Clinton read aloud to Prince from Milton William Cooper's *Behold a Pale Horse*, which proposed a far-flung conspiracy that twined together UFOs, the Kennedy assassination, the Trilateral Commission, AIDS, and more. Clinton wrote in his memoir that his motives in reading from the book were "more silly serious than straightforwardly earnest," but that "Prince listened, some-times asked questions, sometimes joked."*

Toward the end of his life, Prince wrote more overtly about the way America dealt with race. In April of 2015, after Freddie Gray was killed in Baltimore, Prince announced plans for a concert in Baltimore to promote peace, along with a new single: "Baltimore." Recorded first with his 3RDEYEGIRL band and then rerecorded as a solo performance, the song was sweetened with vocals by the young vocalist Eryn Allen Kane and released online on May 9, the day before the concert. Prince meant for it to harmonize overtly with the aims of the growing Black Lives Matter move-ment; he felt acutely the way that racial attitudes were limiting opportunities for young African-Americans. And tucked near the back of HITnRUN Phase Two, the collection he put out on the streaming service Tidal in 2015, was "Black Muse," an explicit statement of African-American heritage that touched on every-thing from the painful legacy of slavery to the joyful legacy of musical invention ("rhythm and blues, rock and roll and jazz, so you know we're built to last"). The song is breezily organic and exuberantly hopeful. "A new day is dawning," he sang, too close to dusk.

✦ ✦ ✦

Prince's embrace of African-American identity was reflected in the evolution of his musical tastes. From the first, he had an en-cyclopedic knowledge of funk and soul, and kaleidoscopic ideas about how to use them. He was more mixed on other genres.

---

* In the book, which I cowrote, Clinton also corroborated the accounts of many others regarding Prince's drug use—or rather, the absence of it. "He has always claimed that he didn't do any drugs," Clinton write, "and I never saw him do any, but he must have at least done coffee, because I don't know any other motherfucker who could go to sleep at five thirty in the morning and be back at eight daisy fresh."

Early on in his career, on "All the Critics Love U in New York," in 1982, Prince took a direct swipe at jazz. "It's time for a new direction," he sang. "It's time for jazz to die." Still interested in being seen as a punkish provocateur, Prince was determined to dismantle the conventional tastes of his parents—and specifically *his* parents, who had sung and played with jazz groups around Minneapolis in the 1950s. But in the time when Prince was coming into his own as a recording artist, jazz changed significantly. In the 1970s, it absorbed aspects of rock and funk, interpenetrating with black pop to the point where it was unrecognizable to its most conservative gatekeepers. Greg Tate, in an essay titled "Black Jazz in the Digital Age," sketched out the climate of cultural exchange that characterized the era:

> Equally peculiar to this era was a sense of unified Black community that didn't require the worlds of Black jazz and Black pop to play by the rules of intracultural segregation that prevail today. In the fusion moment you could go to venues like Howard University's Cramton Auditorium and see Weather Report open for the afro-funk band Osibisa, or witness Billy Cobham's Stratus unit on tour with P-Funk or strangely enough, Bob Marley and the Wailers warming up the stage for Chick Corea's Return To Forever while future members of DC's Rasta-punk pioneers Bad Brains sat taking notes on both.

Jazz was no longer a traditional form watched over by nervous conservators. Rather, it was a music that admitted other musics, a living organism that adapted to its surroundings. It was also implicitly individualistic. Unlike the canonical soul music of the 1960s, jazz was not preoccupied with middle-class respectability. To return to the terms sketched out by Ishmael Reed in *Mumbo*

Jumbo, jazz could be radically animist, a vehicle for virtuosity and freedom and a useful weapon against the Atonist program. In the mid-eighties, Prince began to explore jazz more deeply, first through an unsuccessful side project called the Flesh, and then through a successful one called Madhouse. Madhouse released two albums in quick succession, with covers showing a young model in cutesy shots designed to look like 1940s pinup pictures, and Prince incorporated jazz into his concerts as well, especially during the *Sign O' the Times* tour, when his band would play Charlie Parker's "Now's the Time" while Prince changed costumes. But Prince's closest connection to jazz came through Miles Davis. Miles had been aware of Prince since the release of *1999.* "His shit was the most exciting music I was hearing in 1982," Miles wrote in his autobiography. Word reached Prince, and he signaled back: the second Madhouse album was subtitled "New Directions in Garage Music," in reference to Miles's practice of labeling some of his landmark albums as "Directions in Music." There was a philosophical affinity between the two men as well. Davis, of course, was intense and protean, an uncompromising artist who continually redefined genre. As Greg Tate puts it, Miles "made a forced hybridity of free jazz, soul, and funk ideas seem not only hip, but inevitable and inexorable." Moreover, he was a black artist, fiercely so. In March of 1978, a month before the release of *For You,* Miles came out of retirement with a session at Columbia Studio B. The universe is filled with pointless coincidences, but pointing to them can at least illuminate a path. It is like the process of teasing out a shape from a grouping of stars and calling it a constellation.

The affinity between the two men wasn't musically productive in the traditional sense. In 1985, Warner Bros. signed Davis and cast around for songwriters and players to contribute to his debut for the label. Prince sprang to mind immediately. Late that year, Prince recorded a song called "Can I Play with U?" and sent it to Miles, along with a modest handwritten note:

> Miles, even though we have never met, I can tell just from listening to your music that you and I are so exactly alike that I know whatever you play would be what I'd do. So if this tape is of any use to you, please go ahead and play whatever you feel over it because I trust what you hear and play.

That trust bore no fruit; the track was scrapped. Miles went on to work with Marcus Miller, and their collaboration, *Tutu*, released in 1986, was considered the high point of Miles's final electronic phase. The album's final song, "Full Nelson," was not about Prince but rather Nelson Mandela. (It also referenced Davis's earlier composition, "Half Nelson," which was named for the bassist Nelson Boyd, a former bandmate of Davis's who earned his nickname as a result of his diminutive stature. Closer, but still not Prince.)

The failed collaboration doesn't seem to have engendered any animosity between the two men. There's a 1987 New Year's Eve performance at Paisley Park that ends with a version of "It's Gonna Be a Beautiful Night" that runs for more than thirty-five minutes, incorporating "Housequake," "Mother Popcorn," "Land of 1000 Dances," "Chain of Fools," and "Cold Sweat," and featuring an extended section during which Davis solos over the band. Prince doesn't lie back and watch. He scats Davis's melody lines immediately afterwards, like an echo.

The two of them eventually teamed up on "Sticky Wicked," the story of an addled addict that ended up on Chaka Khan's 1988 album, *CK*. At the end, Miles blows a note and then adds, hoarsely: "Don't that sound like one of them crows or something?" Prince kept trying to place material with Miles. In early 1991, he sent Miles three songs he had recorded with Madhouse, titled, like all Madhouse compositions, with numbers (though they had alternate titles as well): "17" ("Penetration"), "19" ("Jailbait"), and "20" (the slightly less debauched "A Girl and Her Puppy"). Miles took all three songs into the studio with his band and also played them on tour throughout the year. That September, Miles died of complications from a stroke and pneumonia. The *Los Angeles Times*, in the fourth paragraph of its obituary, noted that Davis was called "the 'Black Prince' for the distant elegance that was his persona." Warner Bros. asked the actual Prince to do postproduction work on the studio tracks, but he felt that they did not show Davis at his best, and he refused. The circle of his relationship with Davis closed without him the following year, when Chaka Khan worked with Marcus Miller on *The Woman I Am*, an album dedicated to Davis. Prince did not appear on that album.

Prince's affinity for jazz has a fascinating countermovement in his reluctance to fully embrace blues. Prince dipped into the blues less frequently, and with less success, than might be expected. It wasn't that he couldn't play it—one of his concert staples in the late eighties, "If I Had a Harem," was a showcase for his blues guitar, and he covered Jimi Hendrix's "Red House" as "Purple House." But his blues-inflected songs tend to be uninteresting, playing down to the genre rather than using it as fuel for elevating. That's not to say that Prince never began in blues, only to say that he rarely ended there. The first pass at "Kiss" was acoustic blues, as was the first pass at "Alphabet St." But by the time he was done working his magic (or, in the case of "Kiss," letting David Z. work his magic so that he could work his magic on top of it) they were polyrhythmic, pyrotechnic pop songs that bore little trace of their origins.

There's one interesting footnote to Prince's relationship with the blues. In the fall of 1989, right after the summer of *Batman*, newspapers reported that Prince was planning to star in two new movies. One was *Graffiti Bridge*, the quasi sequel to *Purple Rain*. The other one was a biopic of the famous Delta bluesman Robert Johnson. Johnson, who died in 1938, at age twenty-seven, under mysterious circumstances, was one of the sources of the original crossroads legend, in which a musician traded his soul to the devil for a supernatural talent. Details of the project trickled out over the next year or so: there was a title, *Love in Vain*, after another famous Johnson song; Martin Scorsese was briefly attached as a director. *Love in Vain* was ultimately in vain itself: it was shelved within the year. It's just as well. Prince could have played profitably off the spiritual aspects of the story—he had already, on songs like "Temptation" and "Dance with the Devil"—but the music he would have been expected to make while in character would have been restrictive. Prince's creative impulses accorded more with a famous passage by W. E. B. Du Bois from *Black Reconstruction*:

> A great song arose, the loveliest thing born this side the seas. It was a new song. It did not come from Africa, though the dark throb and beat of that Ancient of Days was in it and through it. It did not come from white America—never from so pale and hard and thin a thing, however deep these vulgar and surrounding tones had driven. Not the indies nor the hot South, the cold East or heavy West made that music. It was a new song and its deep and plaintive beauty, its great cadences and wild appeal wailed, throbbed and thundered on the world's ears with a message seldom voiced by man. It swelled and blossomed like incense, improvised and born anew out of an age long past, and weaving into its texture the old and new melodies in word and in thought.

The African-American culture that leaped into existence, "the loveliest thing born," would share its DNA with jazz, America's own native classical music, and also with Prince. W. C. Handy, who would become the most important composer in the development of early jazz music, died in March 1958, just a few months before Prince was born. The universe is filled with constellations.

✦ ✦ ✦

Self-actualization, self-empowerment, self-determination: these principles not only accorded with the aesthetics of jazz but also informed Prince's political ideas. Prince could be stubbornly traditionalist when it came to issues like gay marriage. He was a Luddite. He held regressive notions regarding intellectual property. On the other hand, he was an avowed rebel: as he said in "Partyman," from *Batman*, "rules and regulations [had] no place in his nation." To the degree that he had a consistent philosophy, it revolved around the importance of thinking for yourself and the equal importance of taking responsibility for those thoughts. In "Sexuality," one of Prince's sharpest early manifestos, he blamed groupthink for most of society's ills. "No child is bad from the beginning," he sang, "they only imitate their atmosphere." That tendency could be overcome, but it took some effort. It took, above all else, self-control. "P Control," one of the strongest Prince songs of the nineties, laid out the case. Originally titled "Pussy Control" and bowdlerized for its inclusion on *The Gold Experience* in 1994, it was an empowerment anthem so straightforward that it could, indelicate language aside, be part of a public service campaign. In the song, "Pussy" wasn't an anatomical reference.*

---

* It had been before, and also hadn't. In the *Sign O' the Times* era, Prince released a pair of B sides, "Scarlet Pussy" and "La La La, Hee Hee Hee" that introduced a feline character, sort of his equivalent of George Clinton's Atomic Dog.

Rather, it was the name of the song's main character, who learned through a series of encounters that she didn't need to use overt sexuality to get ahead in the world but could get by on education and business acumen. That strain of self-actualization remained prominent in Prince's work, taking on a new centrality in the years after he broke away from Warner Bros. "Style," from *Emancipation*, was Prince's version of Baldassare Castiglione's *The Book of the Courtier*, offering business advice ("Style ain't sitting courtside with the owner of the team / Style is owning the court and charging them all a fee") and relationship advice ("Style don't get married then break the vow in a year / Style is keeping a promise"). That was followed by a more impressionistic, scattershot extended definition of what style is: growing your own food, a nonviolent march, an accurate account of what's inside every heart, not a lie, a man that cries, the glow in a pregnant woman's eyes.

Style was also giving, and giving a damn. In the mid-seventies, Stevie Wonder recorded a song called "Black Man" that included, in its second half, a long roll call of America's racially diverse visionaries and inventors. Stevie would throw out a name and describe that person's achievements, and a group of children would respond with the appropriate label: white man, black woman, and so on. (The other color-coding in the song, which used yellow for people of Asian descent and red for Native Americans, probably wouldn't pass contemporary political-correctness tests.) The children backing Wonder were fourth-grade students from a Marva Collins school in Chicago. Collins, a pioneer in inner-city education in America, became close to Prince in the late eighties and nineties. He featured her in the video to his 1994 ballad "The Most Beautiful Girl in the World," donated a half million dollars to her cause, and served as cofounder and honorary chairman of Collins's National Teacher Training Institute. Black man.

Prince's generosity to the Collins schools was only the tip of the iceberg. In 1985, he explained his view on charitable giving to *Rolling Stone*: "I was never rich, so I have very little regard for money now. I only respect it inasmuch as it can feed somebody. I give a lot of things away, a lot of presents and money. Money is best spent on someone who needs it. That's all I'm going to say. I don't like to make a big deal about the things I do that way." That same year, he released "Pop Life," one of his most direct expressions of the importance of education, the role of charity, and the pointlessness of materialism. The song was subtle enough that some fans missed its message entirely, and matters were made worse when Prince declined to participate in Michael Jackson and Quincy Jones's USA for Africa sing-along "We Are the World," though he did contribute a new song "4 the Tears in Your Eyes," to the album. (The B side of the "Pop Life" single, "Hello," explained the situation with almost documentary straightforwardness: "I tried to tell them that I didn't want to sing / But I'd gladly write a song instead.")

Prince tried to keep his charitable contributions quiet. Misty Copeland, a principal dancer with the American Ballet Theatre who performed with Prince on his Welcome 2 America tour, was one of the beneficiaries of his generosity: "He gave money to a school that I was close with," she said, "this small ballet school in Harlem. They were about to lose their school, and he's the reason that the school is still standing."

In the weeks after Prince's death, the political activist and broadcaster Van Jones revealed that Prince had been active in several other causes, including #YesWeCode, an organization that encouraged computer programming skills for inner-city kids, and Green For All, which promoted ecological responsibility. "There are people who have solar panels on their houses right now in Oakland, California, that they don't know Prince paid

s's mind, these initiatives were not side
rince's understanding of the world: "He
into people. If he wanted to be a politi-
en king of the earth." Prince would
the characterization—in fact, he had,
Whom It May Concern," a B side on
single: "There are no kings on this

Section Three

METHOD, MADNESS

10

WHAT'S MY NAME

Why He Changed His Name,
and What That Wrought

ANY DISCUSSION OF FREEDOM AND PRINCE HAS TO CONTEND WITH THE extended period in which he sought freedom from Prince. On June 7, 1993, his thirty-fifth birthday, Prince announced that he no longer wished to be referred to by his birth name. Instead, he asked that others call him by his new name, the squiggly glyph that had appeared the previous fall on the cover of the Love Symbol album.

He had always had a penchant for unconventional typography. *Controversy* had newspaper-like headlines and a normal Gothic font for the title of the fake paper, the *Controversy Daily*, but in the top right corner there was Prince's name, with superfluous floating slits (or were they pupils?) inside the "P" and the "R" and an oddly curved top on the "E." *Dirty Mind* was even stranger. At first, the letters seemed normal, but a closer inspection revealed that they were decoratively edged, like they had been cut out with special scissors. Most people associated Prince with the *Purple Rain* logotype, originally commissioned by Warner Bros. and adapted by Jay Vigon for the record cover and all associated singles. But there were dedicated fonts for every album—for *Lovesexy*, for *Batman*, for *Graffiti Bridge*. And then, of course, there was the famed Prince shorthand. In 1980, on *Dirty Mind*, he recorded a surprisingly nuanced assessment of a three-some called "When You Were Mine." A year later, on *Controversy*, he recorded a silly but entirely enjoyable guitar rave-up about masturbation called "Jack U Off." The stylized spelling took hold: The next album, *1999*, had "All the Critics Love U in New York." *Purple Rain* had "Take Me with U" and "I Would Die 4 U." As he released more records, he began using more abbreviations in addition to "4" and "U" (his debut, "For You," stuck out like the sorest of sore thumbs): "to" became "2" and "are" became "R."*

The Love Symbol was a clean break, and a messy one as well. All lines, swirls, and loops, the symbol mystified people at first. Was it a doodle that had come to Prince in a dream? A pilcrow clambering up an ampersand? Reporters quickly sussed out the meaning: it was a glyph that combined the astrological symbols for Venus and Mars and added in a kind of royal trumpet (alarum!). Oh, why describe when you can show? It looks like this: ⚥.

---

* Prince's shorthand had a funny afterlife. When artists wanted to borrow a little of his vibe, they adopted the spelling (Swamp Dogg's "Love Song 4 U," for example). And in the twenty-first century, text messaging adopted these abbreviations as standard language. It was to save time, mostly, to save space, a little, and to eliminate unnecessary typos, but it became a kind of joke to say that Prince invented texting. George Lopez raised the issue of texting shorthand to him on *Lopez Tonight* in 2011. "Will you take credit?" Lopez asked, and Prince answered immediately: "There is so much craziness on the Internet now, I don't want to take no credit for nothing." Note the double negative. Was he saying that he did want 2 take credit 4 everything?

And why just show when you can show while quoting from an official document? In late December 1992, Prince's lawyers filed four trademark applications for the use of $\male$, which they referred to as "Love Symbol #2."

—U.S. Reg. No. 1,849,644 for entertainment services
—U.S. Reg. No. 1,871,900 for posters, publications, bumper stickers, and stickers
—U.S. Reg. No. 1,860,429 for clothing
—U.S. Reg. No. 1,822,461 for sound recordings and videotapes featuring music and entertainment

Down in the search fields, the trademark office tried to describe the symbol: "Brass instruments, including trumpets, bugles, tubas, trombones, hunting horns and post horns; Bugles; Trombones; Trumpets; Tubas." The clerks, apparently, had read *The Crying of Lot 49*, but they weren't hip to androgyny.

Since Prince would now be releasing music only as $\male$, he furnished the glyph to whatever publications were unable to produce it from their current fonts—in other words, to every publication. And since this was the days before widespread e-mail, he was forced to mail out hundreds of floppy discs containing the symbol in multiple resolutions and variations.

Some journalists used them. Others opted for the ASCII equivalent: 0-+->. Others referred to him as Symbol Man, or The Artist Formerly Known as Prince, or The Artist, or, infelicitously, TAFKAP. Fans were equally conflicted. Many continued to call him Prince. A few looked more closely at the previous winter's Love Symbol album, and particularly its final song, "The Sacrifice of Victor." Maybe that held a clue to his new name, in the sense that it seemed to be a disassembly of the various parts of Love Symbol #2—the V from the arrow of the Mars symbol, the

I from the shaft, and so on. A friend and I invented our own name for him, Zimpimgat, which was an acronym formed from the ASCII approximation of the symbol: Zero Minus Plus Minus Greater Than.

✦✦✦

What was Zimpimgat up to? Many entertainers set aside their birth names for stage names, but not many make the switch at the height of their fame, after establishing an audience and creating a body of work. From the start, Prince made it clear that his new identity was not simply a stage name.

To some degree, of course, it was a flight from the corrosive force of fame. Prince had tried to turn away from it at least once before, when he went to find the ladder after *Purple Rain*, but celebrity had closed over him again. The results were a mixed bag at best—fame created the illusion of connection with millions of fans when in fact it was deeply disorienting and isolating. "Two Bears," by the fourteenth-century Persian poet Hafiz, distills the problem nicely:

> *One bear said,*
> *"Did you hear about Rustam?*
> *He has become famous*
> *And travels from city to city*
> *In a golden cage;*
>
> *He performs to hundreds of people*
> *Who laugh and applaud*
> *His carnival*
> *Stunts."*
>
> *The other bear thought for*

A few seconds
Then started
Weeping.

But there was a business rationale as well. For a time in the eighties, the marriage between Prince and Warner Bros. was all honeymoon. Prince was a commercial juggernaut, selling fifteen million copies of *Purple Rain* in the United States alone. Warner rewarded him with a boutique label, Paisley Park, and a large measure of creative control. But they wanted their golden goose to make good with the eggs. *Around the World in a Day* and *Parade*, both of which departed significantly from the formula of their predecessor, sold around four million each, and *Sign O' the Times* managed almost two million, more than respectable for a double album. But *Lovesexy*, in 1988, lagged: it was the first album since his debut a decade earlier to stall at gold and the first since *Controversy* to miss the top ten. After that, the best albums sold fewer and fewer copies, and the albums that sold best came more and more to resemble commercial product. And his output came to compete with itself—there was just so much of it, so many of his own albums, so many mentored artists, so many acts signed to Paisley Park, so many costly tours. Indulgences.

His film career experienced a similar trajectory. When Prince announced plans to make a second movie in the mid-eighties, hands in boardrooms rubbed together with glee, expecting another *Purple Rain*. Instead, they got *Under the Cherry Moon*, a black-and-white Jazz Age fantasy. Prince, puckish and brilliantined, skinny as a shadow, played Christopher Tracy, a nightclub performer and gigolo who set his sights on seducing a wealthy heiress named Mary (Kristin Scott Thomas) over the objections of her father (Steven Berkoff). At Christopher's side, always, was his campy valet, Tricky (Jerome Benton, proving that Time travel was possible). Tonally, the film was a drastic about-face from its predecessor. Where *Purple Rain* was heartfelt and earnest, almost an after-school special about family discord, *Under the Cherry Moon* was a paisley lark, filled with knockabout comedy, inexplicable costume changes, and inside jokes. Critics generally found it trivial, foolish, and irritating. Even at a brisk one hundred minutes, it struck them as interminable. In the *New York Times*, Walter Goodman questioned the plausibility of the attraction between Mary and Christopher, managing in the process (possibly with the help of the *Times*'s copydesk) to sound like the creakiest old man in the world, and a vaguely homophobic old man at that: "More convincing is his affection for Jerome Benton, a member of the Prince and the Revolution rock group, as his pal Tricky, who also likes to dress up when he isn't hanging around shirtless to show off his adorable chest." J. Hoberman, writing in the *Village Voice*, was one of the few who saw the fun in the film. He correctly located Benton's performance in 1930s musicals ("A gung ho second banana, Jerome Benton plays a street-smart Edward Everett Horton to Prince's dissolute Fred Astaire") and praised Prince's ability to simultaneously hog and share the spotlight ("Prince is the complete narcissist. What makes his egomania bearable is his sense of humor, as well as his generosity toward other performers"). He also took the time to process the ways in which the film advanced Prince's agenda, particularly when it came to dissolving conventional ideas of masculinity, race, and class: "I don't think I'd trust a revolution led by royalty (any more than a working-class hero they call 'the Boss') but, as current pop goes, Prince is radically subversive." No one wanted radical subversion, at least not in that form: the film sputtered to a ten-million-dollar domestic gross. After the superb *Sign O' the Times* concert movie, Prince went back to the fictional-film well a third time, for the largely worthless *Graffiti Bridge* (domestic gross: four million dollars; reviews: uniformly abysmal). The record company didn't even bother to send a promotions staffer to the premiere. George Clinton, one of the film's stars, called up the company's offices to ask why. "They got sarcastic with me," he wrote in his memoir. " 'We have more records to be worked,' they said."

The record company's indifference angered and confused Prince. In the early nineties, he decided that his Warner Bros. contract—not the original one that Husney had negotiated but an extension that he had signed after his first three records—wasn't serving him. New music was pouring out of him in torrents, and he wanted to release it as quickly as possible. Warner wanted to keep on as before: albums every year, traditional lead singles, a string of singles (at least two, up to four) played out over the course of months, tour at home or abroad, reset, repeat. This frustrated Prince further. He began to feel that the system was stacked against artists, and particularly against an artist like him. After reading paperwork, thinking, consulting with lawyers, and thinking again, Prince arrived at two realizations simultaneously: first, that Warner controlled all the music made under his name, and second, that he couldn't change the contract that had created that situation. He changed his name instead.

At the time that Prince vanished and Symbol Man appeared, Prince owed Warner five more albums. He had plenty of music already in the can, and he was willing to deal with a slower release schedule, assuming he could make new music under his new name for different labels. That didn't work for Warner. They wanted exclusivity. Negotiations continued. Prince knew he was at a disadvantage. George Michael, who had shot to fame as part of the pop duo Wham! and then become a megastar as a solo act, sued Sony in 1992 over his contract. The case didn't seem like it was going Michael's way. (In fact, it wasn't. His claims were rejected outright in 1994, and the Sony contract was judged to be reasonable and fair.)

The first compromise was a greatest-hits record that would be counted toward the remaining commitment. Prince made his unreleased material available, but only a few of those songs found their way onto the set. All started with "P," like the name he had left behind: the effulgent love song "Pink Cashmere," the funny rap "Pope," the doleful ballad "Power Fantastic," and the mediocre glam-blues "Peach." Still, the label refused to allow him to release music elsewhere.

Desperate for creative outlets, he poured himself into whatever projects the contract permitted. He created a stage musical called *Glam Slam Ulysses*, which wrapped new songs around a plot loosely based on Homer's *Odyssey*. He contributed music to movies like *Girl 6* and *I'll Do Anything*. He also forged a new relationship with the press. Once, Prince had been a difficult interview but spirited when he opened up. Now, he spoke extensively, with a grim mix of bitter philosophy and misplaced hope. He would sometimes assure interviewers—or, rather, assure himself by speaking out loud to interviewers—that the problem with the label was about to be resolved. During this time, he started spending lavishly again, the same way he had in the late eighties, when he was determined to outdo the *Purple Rain* tour no matter what the cost. Back then, he spared no expense on the *Lovesexy* tour and also indulged less sensible whims, including his insistence that while he was on the road, a baby grand piano had to be lifted by crane into every hotel room. In the eighties, urged to rethink his spending habits, he instead went, scythe in hand, through Paisley Park, cutting down managers, business managers, and lawyers. In the mid-nineties, he was told again to curb his spending, and he responded similarly.

He set about satisfying the terms of his contract, not with love anymore but with passion, the passion to be free of it all. He turned in two new records, the muted, chilly *Come* and the angry, jagged *The Gold Experience*. He asked Warner to release them on the same day—both because that was the fashion at the time (Guns N' Roses had done it with *Use Your Illusion I* and *II* in September 1991, and Bruce Springsteen with *Lucky Town* and *Human Touch* in 1992), and because they were, to him, two sides of the same coin, yet another illustration of duality. Warner wouldn't play along.

Already consumed by his own powerlessness, Prince suffered another devastating blow when he discovered that he didn't own his own masters. Recording contracts worked like particularly punitive long-term loans: Labels, when they first signed artists, forwarded them a large sum of money in return for ownership of their master recordings. Even when an artist repaid that initial loan, the masters stayed with the label. Prince coined a phrase, "If you don't own your masters, then your masters own you" and began to appear in public with the word "Slave" inked on the side of his face. This, of course, was a pointed provocation. During the Civil Rights era, the power to name was equated with the power to define and to control, and many African-Americans rejected the process by which they had acquired their birth names. Most famously, Malcolm Little had become Malcolm X in 1950, casting off what he called the "white slavemaster name" that had been "imposed upon . . . paternal forebears." The Black Muslims who followed suit in the sixties and seventies were similarly motivated; Cassius Clay became, briefly, Cassius X. Clay and then Muhammad Ali; Lew Alcindor became Kareem Abdul-Jabbar. By invoking Black Power and slavery, Prince connected with a long tradition of self-determination as a remedy for victimization.

The message made its way into every gesture. When Prince

played Radio City Music Hall in 1993, he wore a police hat from which a curtain of chains hung down, covering his face, and sang into a handheld microphone shaped like a gun. The symbol that was now his name hung from his neck, silver on a silver chain. In a long string of startling looks, this one stood out. It was truth to power but also an uncomfortable form of hiding in plain sight, a conspicuous concealment.

In a dark period, there was (dark) comedy. Prince was briefly considered for the starring role in Luc Besson's sci-fi fantasy *The Fifth Element*. He took a meeting with Jean-Paul Gaultier, who was designing the costumes for the film. "I showed him my drawings, but he didn't say a word," Gaultier later revealed, during a talk at the Brooklyn Museum. "I had had an idea for a really funny costume with netting which quite long body hair would pass through, and I had done front and back versions of it. So then I explained to Prince: 'Eet eel fake 'air, you know, and eet eel beaucoup, beaucoup, airy, vraiment fun, and ze back is made of sat, and on ze back were eez ze faux cul, you know, a very big faux cul,' and I slapped my buttocks to show him how the back of the costume would be designed." Prince gazed flatly at his bodyguard—Gaultier remembered it as a "Charlie Chaplin kind of look"—to signal that it was time to go. Later, he called Besson to decline. The costume, he said had been too effeminate. But he had another complaint as well. He had misheard Gaultier, and when the designer was saying "faux cul," Prince heard only "fuck you." He must have felt like he was hearing it from all angles.*

---

* *The Fifth Element* may not have been a good fit, but one of the best roles got away from Prince. The movie side of Warner Bros. had just acquired the rights to remake *Willy Wonka and the Chocolate Factory*. At the time, it wasn't yet Tim Burton's movie— rumors mentioned a variety of directors, including Martin Scorsese—and it wasn't Johnny Depp's role. Prince, I thought, would be perfect for the part. To start with, there was all the purple, and for a time, he even played "Pure Imagination," the Wonka theme song sung in the original film by Gene Wilder, over the PA system to

WHAT'S MY NAME **177**

+ + +

In early 1994, Prince recorded a new song, "The Most Beautiful Girl in the World." It was an inoffensive ballad with a predictable romantic message—written for Mayte, most likely—and it didn't appeal to Warner, which heard it and rejected it. That created a rare opportunity to release music outside of the terms of the contract, and Prince immediately called the Memphis-based distributor Bellmark Records, which had worked with several Stax artists. Bellmark snapped up the song and, to their delight, found that Warner had made the wrong call. "The Most Beautiful Girl in the World" went top five in the United States—higher than "Pop Life" or "I Would Die 4 U" or even "Little Red Corvette"—and was his first number one in the United Kingdom.

Warner countered by putting out the pair of albums he had submitted, though they didn't comply with his wish that they be released simultaneously. First was *Come*, whose cover art showed a moody Prince standing in front of the gates of Antoni Gaudí's Sagrada Família in Barcelona, Spain, over a caption that included birth and death dates for his Prince identity. That came out in 1994, as did an official release of *The Black Album*, seven years late, still welcome. A year later, they were followed by *The Gold Experience*. *The Gold Experience*, not composed of vault material, remains the only album of new songs that Prince recorded while his contract dispute was ripping him apart and (he feared) tarnishing his legacy. As a result, it was a dyspeptic record preoccupied with the way that suffering produced a clearer idea of the self—or, at the very least, the space where the self used to be. Much of

---

crowds lining up outside Paisley Park. In 2006, after the Burton movie, Prince followed Wonka's lead by loading special tickets into a small number of copies of his new *3121* CD; listeners who found them were flown to Los Angeles to see a concert at his home. I wrote a long letter to Warner making the case but was too shy to send it.

it finds Prince bearing witness to his own restlessness and crudely staging the idea that he might put himself to rest. At the end of the galvanic "Endorphinmachine," one of the album's stronger songs, a voice, in Spanish, says "Prince está muerto," or "Prince is dead," echoing the cover photo of *Come*. "I Hate U" was another standout track in the persecution suite, a kiss-off to an ex-lover in which Price put her on trial and then sadomasochistically misused her. It was as if he had dragged Lady Cab Driver into court: "I'd like to have the defendant place her hands behind her back / so I can tie her up tight and get into the act . . . I want it to be so good she falls back in love with me."

She didn't. Instead, Prince, gritting his teeth, submitted two more albums to Warner.

These were contractual-obligation records in the purest sense, material collected from the vault with perfunctory scorn.* The first, *Chaos and Disorder*, hit stores the next July. It was clear about the fact that it had been created under duress, with an album booklet filled with photocollages that read as heavy-handed political cartoons. One image showed a dollar bill stuffed inside a syringe. One showed a heart floating in a toilet. One showed the Paisley Park vault (in case anyone had forgotten where the songs came from), the walls covered with gold records (in case anyone had forgotten what Prince had accomplished). The songs were a mixed bag, some good ("Dinner with Delores"), some bad ("Right

---

* Even Prince's version of perfunctory scorn included a significant amount of craft. In the history of contractual-obligation albums, it doesn't come close to the spit-in-your-face disdain of the tracks Van Morrison recorded in 1967 to fulfill his contract with Bang Records. Morrison went into the recording booth with an acoustic guitar and one chord and vomited out thirty-one songs with nearly identical melodies and lyrics that consisted of nothing more than the title phrases, which included "Twist and Shake," "Shake and Roll," "Stomp and Scream," "Scream and Holler," "Jump and Thump," "Blow in Your Nose," "Nose in Your Blow," and the immortal "Ring Worm."

the Wrong"), some energetic but witless ("I Rock, Therefore I Am"). The whole thing felt haphazardly thrown together, like clothes in a hastily packed suitcase. Again, there was a querulous highlight: this time, it was "Dig U Better Dead," where he expressed frustration at the way Warner Bros. had forced him to kill himself off. The final Warner album, *The Vault: Old Friends 4 Sale*, without much to recommend it at all (mediocre jazzy ballad: "Extraordinary"; mediocre swinging funk: "It's About That Walk") wasn't released until 1999, in what seemed like an especially manipulative move (or a misguided attempt to maximize value). By that time, fans had chosen sides, and most had chosen Prince's side. It was the first Prince album in years I didn't buy on its release date, and the last one.

✦ ✦ ✦

The moment Prince turned in his final albums to Warner Bros., he celebrated his freedom with a record release. The label this time was his own new NPG Records, working in conjunction with EMI. When he had sung "Free" almost fifteen years before, on *1999*, freedom was a natural state ("Be glad that you are free"). Now, the natural state was bondage, and freedom had to be achieved, which is why Prince named the album—a three-disc, thirty-six-song chronicle of that achievement—*Emancipation*. *Emancipation* was too much music to take in all at once, or maybe ever. On first listen, it sounded underwhelming, low-energy given the high stakes. Over time, songs began to assert themselves: the sparkling "Damned If I Do," which opened with a little "Girls and Boys" drum tattoo; the irrepressible "Get Yo Groove On"; the simple and direct love song "Dreamin' About U"; and the labyrinthine "Joint 2 Joint."

Emancipation delivered new material, but it also told an old story. It reached back years, to the beginning of the conflict with

Warner Bros., and decades, to the beginning of the relationship with Warner Bros. It also looked back centuries, into the history of slavery in America, and millennia, into Biblical history. The album had its roots (all puns intended) in *Exodus*, a New Power Generation album he had released the year before. The album was essentially a P-Funk workout, refracted through the prism of Prince's backing band, that culminated in a ten-minute Afro-Futuristic concept piece, "The Exodus Has Begun." The song recounted a world in which people could be forced into bondage, compelled to work without being properly compensated: "Though their lives were made bitter with hard labor and no pay / these are the children that will come to save the day." This subjugation, of course, echoed the first Exodus—the one three thousand years earlier in which the Jews, led by Moses, fled the pharaoh and the chains of Egyptian slavery. This story had been appropriated before by other musicians, especially reggae artists—Bob Marley and the Wailers built an entire album around the theme in 1977. "Send us another Moses," Marley sang, "from across the Red Sea."

Just as in the Bible, *Emancipation* followed *Exodus* and elaborated upon its themes. Even its party songs and its love songs were loaded with lines about freedom or bondage. Some, like the midtempo "White Mansion," addressed the problem elegantly: not too direct, not too oblique, with a sense of humor to offset the serious matters at hand ("Sell my publishing? / What a laugh! / I don't know Bo, but I do know math"). Others jumped in with both feet. During the *Emancipation* sessions, Prince recorded a track called "Slave 2 the System" that addressed issues of identity, power, and property (both intellectual and otherwise). He must have judged it too on-the-nose. "Slave 2 the System" evolved into another song, "Slave." Sadder and darker, resting on a bed of moody electronica, it focused on the pain of that situation, and

Prince's martyrdom within that pain. "I tell you," he sang, anguished, "they just keep tryin' to break my heart."

In the homestretch of *Emancipation*, Prince focused on a specific aspect of bondage—imprisonment in the corporeal world, and the belief that faith and art could connect him to a more spiritual dimension. In "The Human Body," he thanks God for creating physical pleasure, though the term of that pleasure is short-lived: he ends the song with a chant of "Slave, slave, slave," and two songs later, in "Face Down," that human body is buried in the grave. What will liberate it from death? Prince offers a partial answer by covering "One of Us," an Eric Bazilian–penned song about God returning to earth that had been a big hit for Joan Osborne. "One of Us" adds a Christian dimension, and a messianic one, but it doesn't shift the terms of the discussion too drastically. Prince understood the record not only as evidence of liberation, but as evidence of rebirth. Freedom as an artist had recharged his powers. The title song, placed last on the record, draws together all these strands. It takes a final swipe at Warner Bros., whose money has turned "from green to brown." It takes pride in the tenacity that has allowed him to "break the chain." Now "free to do what [he] wanna," Prince pledges to his fans that he will see them "in the purple rain." *Emancipation* recalled *Purple Rain* in another regard: since the independent-distribution model allowed Prince to keep a much greater share of the profits of the album's sales than the corporate model, he claimed to have made more money from it than any record since his 1984 megahit.

+ + +

Prince didn't wait long before turning the tap back on and flooding the market again. In early 1998, a little more than a year after *Emancipation*, he released *Crystal Ball*. The late-nineties *Crystal Ball* shared only its name with the shelved mid-eighties mega-album that became *Sign O' the Times*; this was a four-CD compilation that included thirty songs, some new, some culled from the vault. In what was quickly becoming par for Prince's divot-filled course, *Crystal Ball* frustrated fans long before they even heard a note. Throughout 1997, he took preorders through his toll-free number (800-NEW-FUNK) and his website. The price was fifty dollars, which wasn't so steep considering that Prince assured fans that it was the only way the album would be sold. At the last minute, Prince cut a deal with companies like Blockbuster and Musicland. They would sell the record in their stores, which included Sam Goody and Media Play, for $29.95. Fans who had paid the fifty dollars to 800-NEW-FUNK rebelled and were given not a refund but a free additional disc that included the score of the Kamasutra ballet, a work he had created for Mayte and the NPG dance company.*

Crystal Ball's rocky release would be no more than a comedy of errors about an independent artist with entrepreneurial aspirations if it weren't for the fact that it contained more than three hours of music. The opening song was the title song, a Holy Grail among Prince collectors that had been heard across the years on bootlegs, sometimes under the title "Expert Lover." Prince, over a slow groove festooned with whistles and a Clare Fischer orchestration, sang hypnotically about lust and loss. Lyrically, it was a close cousin to "Sign O' the Times": "As bombs explode

---

* The same bungled launch would repeat in the digital age, almost twenty years later, with Kanye West's *The Life Of Pablo*, which was promised as a Tidal exclusive and attracted millions of users to the service, only to then turn up on other streaming services a few months later. West was sued by a fan named Justin Baker-Rhett, who claimed that the false promise of exclusivity caused millions of people to subscribe to Tidal and surrender valuable information to the service. As his lawyer said, "Mr. Baker-Rhett believes that superstars are required to follow the same rules as everyone else. Even if their streaming service is struggling, they can't trick millions of people into paying money (and giving up personal information) just to boost valuation numbers."

around us and hate advances on the right," Prince sang, "the only thing that matters, baby, is the love we make tonight."

The rest was a grab bag, though much of what it grabbed was welcome. "Good Love" was the most optimistic song that Prince ever recorded in his Camille persona, a slice of multitracked bliss that had only previously appeared on the *Bright Lights, Big City* soundtrack. Two songs were straight Time: the befuddled-ladies-man comedy "Movie Star" and the wicked improvised workout "Cloreen Bacon Skin." "Calhoun Square" was a nice little rock number, and "She Gave Her Angels" a comfortably pillowy ballad. But "Ripopgodazippa" left no impression other than time passing, and "Love Sign," a duet with Nona Gaye (daughter of Marvin, onetime girlfriend of Prince), languished. The other lost eighties epic on the set, "Dream Factory," proved a disappointment, with preachy antidrug lyrics and inelegant psychedelia. When it came to Prince's ongoing battle with Warner Bros., only the angry, anguished "What's My Name" was dispositive. "Take my name, I don't need it," he opened, and then offered up his fame as well. "You never would have drank my coffee," he sang, "if I had never served you cream."

"What's My Name" was recorded in 1993, and the cream that he had served, presumably, was "Cream," which had hit number one in 1991. But even as he asserted his independence from Warner, he seemed to be taunting his fans for their loyalty; there was, as in many of his songs of the period, a strong streak of self-annihilation working in tandem with an equally strong streak of self-celebration.

Crystal Ball had a companion album called *The Truth*: all-new material, but mostly acoustic and destined to be mostly forgotten. That was a shame since it contained some of Prince's best singing of the decade and some of his most bitter lyrics. "Don't Play Me" earned every bit of its double meaning—it picked up where

"What's My Name" left off, warning Warner Bros. not to toy with him and warning listeners not to underestimate him: "My only competition," he sang, "is, well, me in the past." On the love songs ("Circle of Amour" and "Dionne"), Prince was more generic, and songs like "Animal Kingdom" were little more than special pleading for vegetarianism. But the album remains a straightforward declaration of artistic intent, consistent in tone at a time when Prince was all over the map.

+ + +

In the fall of 1998, it seemed likely that 1999 (the year) would infuse new energy into "1999" (the song). How could radio programmers resist? The *Los Angeles Times* reported that it was the top request from ad agencies nationwide, with bids to use it in commercial campaigns starting at one million dollars, four times what was usually paid. The song's owner was certain to make a mint. There was only one problem with this scenario: Prince didn't own "1999." Warner still held the masters, and they were moving to capitalize on that fact. They sent promotional copies of a reissued single to radio stations in November and planned to ship new copies of the album with stickers highlighting the song.

What would Prince do? Would he sit back and grumble? Would he try to push copies of his newer, Warner-evading albums like *Emancipation* or *Crystal Ball*? Or would he do what he had, for the latter half of 1998, been insisting he could do: vanish into his studio for a day or so, whip up a note-for-note replica of the original song, and release the new version, the master copy of which he would wholly own, as competition for the original "1999"?

In early February, *1999: The New Master*, which featured the song buttressed by six remixes, was released on NPG Records. The idea of an artist remaking his own songs wasn't without precedent. Early rock stars such as Chuck Berry, Carl Perkins, and

Jerry Lee Lewis all rerecorded their greatest hits after leaving their original labels, often for the same reason as Prince: to confuse the listening public, or at least to give them a choice between versions. One of the most famous cases was Roy Orbison's 1987 *In Dreams*, which Virgin released to capitalize on the appearance of the title song in the David Lynch film *Blue Velvet*. Orbison's ersatz approach was apparent. By 1987, his voice, while still pure, had lost much of its power, and the glossy production hamstrung the new versions. Prince, on the other hand, had access to the same instruments and production techniques, and his vocal abilities were intact. Listening to the two versions side-by-side was a fascinating experiment. Prince had not only added a feature by Tony M. but also tacked on keyboard and guitar flourishes. Still, the likeness was strong; when I played a part of the new master for Shazam, the music-identifying app, it named it as the original "1999."

Whether or not Shazam could tell, the record-buying public could. The new master peaked at number 150, while Warner's rereleased version of the original single went into the top 40. But the new master of "1999" produced one of the best stories in all of Prince apocrypha. Love4OneAnother.com, one of the primary Prince fan sites, claimed that Prince had rerecorded every Warner Bros. track and would be systematically releasing his own new versions. The process of releasing a new master of "1999" had seemed strategic; the prospect of rereleasing a new master of every other song seemed like something out of Borges. No others have ever materialized.

✦ ✦ ✦

At the Equitable Center in midtown Manhattan in September 1999, Arista records staff showed us to our seats. There was a sense of ceremony in the room; Prince was back with a major label. Since his break with Warner Bros., he had operated independently, releasing a triple album (*Emancipation*) and a quadruple one (*Crystal Ball/The Truth*) while Warner continued to scrape the sides of the vault for old tracks that would fulfill the terms of his contract. After Warner dumped *The Vault: Old Friends 4 Sale* into stores in August of 1999, Prince could finally find another corporate partner. He picked Arista, run by the legendary Clive Davis, who had been instrumental in the rise of Sly and the Family Stone, Santana, and Earth, Wind & Fire (all three high in Prince's pantheon); had steered Arista through the eighties with stars like Aretha Franklin and Barry Manilow; and had cofounded soul and hip-hop labels like LaFace and Bad Boy.

Prince wore a kind of red sleeping cap. Clive Davis wore a gray suit. They looked about as poorly matched as two people could be. It didn't help matters that the album they premiered, *Rave Un2 the Joy Fantastic*, contained Prince's weakest set of songs since *Diamonds and Pearls*, propped up by pointless celebrity cameos. Prince (still the glyph) traded vocals with Gwen Stefani on "So Far, So Pleased" and innuendos with Eve on "Hot Wit U." Sheryl Crow added glamour to "Baby Knows," and Chuck D added grit to "Undisputed." The most substantial additions to his catalog were the loose-limbed title track and "The Greatest Romance Ever Sold," a grand ballad that became a minor international hit. Buried in the middle of the running order was the compelling "I Love U, But I Don't Trust U Anymore," which painted a detailed portrait of an emotionally destructive affair. It seemed to be about a specific, if unidentified female protégée ("You tricked me—but you will not anymore"), but it could have been about a specific, if unidentified, corporate ex.

Later that year, speaking to Larry King, Prince was more circumspect about Warner's role in the ordeal: "They're businessmen," he said. "They're doing what it is that makes their business successful, and I also am allowed to do things that make my business successful. And for me, that would be to own my work. So I just chose to step away from that. And knowing that, I sent a nice letter to the president—then-president because they changed a lot, weekly, during that time—and I told him that I loved him, and that, you know, I was glad that I had this experience, you know."

He didn't seem glad. The Spike Lee movie *Bamboozled*, released in 2000, was a scattershot satire of media and race. The accompanying soundtrack included contributions from Stevie Wonder ("Misrepresented People" and "Some Years Ago"), Erykah Badu ("Hollywood"), and Chuck D with the Roots and Zack de la Rocha (an amped-up cover of Public Enemy's "Burn Hollywood Burn"). Prince pitched in with "2045 Radical Man," a hell-for-leather attack on the record industry that had stretches of the lyrics that were almost prose ("How can a non-musician discuss the future of music / from anything other than a consumer point of view?").

The following year, Warner counterpunched with yet another greatest-hits album, *The Very Best of Prince*. Four months after that, Prince released *The Rainbow Children* on NPG Records, with distribution by Redline, a label owned exclusively by Best Buy. *Musicology*, in 2004, was distributed by Columbia; *3121*, in 2006, by Universal; *Planet Earth*, in 2007, by Columbia again. The three-album *Lotusflow3r* set, in 2009, was released by NPG and sold exclusively at Target stores. It didn't feel like a plan. It felt more like a series of experiments. But it felt most like wandering.

Closure came, finally. In April 2014, Prince re-signed with Warner Bros., which agreed to distribute his forthcoming album, *Art Official Age*. That was the minor deal point. The major one was that Warner also agreed to return ownership of Prince's master recordings to him. There were immediate financial benefits for Prince: *Billboard* estimated that catalog royalties in 2013 earned Prince more than six hundred thousand dollars; had he owned the masters, he would have made three times that. (The estimate is eye-opening in two respects: First, Warner was keeping two-thirds of Prince's money. Second, the royalty figures cited are modest at best for a star of his stature.)

The decision may have seemed magnanimous. In fact, it was purely strategic. According to the Copyright Act of 1976—which actually took effect in 1978—an artist could file a termination of copyright notice that would return master recordings to them at the conclusion of a thirty-five-year term. *For You*, Prince's 1978 debut for Warner, had been eligible for copyright termination and rights reclamation the year before. *Prince*, his 1979 follow-up, was just moving into place. The big ones—*Dirty Mind*, *1999*, *Purple Rain*—were on the horizon. The label was working against the clock, negotiating while it still had leverage, securing promises regarding Prince's willingness to participate in deluxe-reissue packages, boxed sets, and more.

A deluxe reissue of *Purple Rain* was announced immediately, with assurances that it would be released in time for the movie's thirtieth anniversary in the summer of 2014. It wasn't. In October of 2016, it was announced again, this time as part of the first wave of reissues following Prince's death. It would be a joint release of Warner Bros. and NPG Records—together at last, under the saddest of circumstances.

MPLS

How His Hometown Made Him
and How He, in Turn, Made It

ANKLE-DEEP IN THE MINNEAPOLIS WINTER, WATCHING THE WIND TURN the snow into sheets, I came up Minnehaha Avenue, turned left onto East Thirty-Fourth Street, made another left, and found myself in front of a small two-story structure: four windows on the first floor, two on the second, a path leading from sidewalk to front door—it was under the snow now, but I had seen it in photographs. This was 3420 Snelling Avenue: the Prince house. The Snelling address wasn't the apartment where Prince's mother had lived before he was born, or the Cymone home on Russell Avenue where Prince had slept when his stepfather had thrown him out during his teens. But it was the Prince house that everyone knew, the one from *Purple Rain*.

Even thirty years later, substantially worse for wear, it was still a movie star. Standing out front, it was impossible not to replay the film in my mind: the scene in which Prince charged through the front door to stop his movie father from hitting his movie mother; the scene in which Prince and Apollonia got together in the basement; the scene in which he busted up the place and found his father's sheet music. The Beatles had the crossing at the intersection of Abbey Road and Grove End Road, Bob Dylan had the alley behind the Savoy Hotel, where he filmed the "Subterranean Homesick Blues" video, and Prince had the *Purple Rain* house.

Minneapolis was an unlikely home for a funk superstar. Even on days without snow, it was far whiter than other cities in the upper Midwest; its African-American population was roughly 20 percent, about half that of other northern cities. That relative homogeneity resulted in relative intolerance—incidences of racial discrimination were common in the early twentieth century, and in 1946, the journalist Carey McWilliams, writing in *Common Ground* magazine, called Minneapolis "the capital of anti-Semitism" in the United States. Its African-American music scene suffered under that sameness. Minneapolis didn't have the blues tradition of Chicago (Buddy Guy and Chess Records in the fifties), the soul tradition of Detroit (Motown and George Clinton in the sixties and seventies), or even the surprisingly vibrant funk tradition of a smaller city like Dayton, Ohio (Ohio Players, Slave, and Zapp in the seventies). Before Prince, the city was mostly known for garage rock, and at the height of his fame, the only nationally notable local acts who weren't connected to him in some fashion were college-rock groups like the Replacements and Hüsker Dü. But in other respects, Minneapolis mirrored Prince's personality perfectly. It had a doubleness built into its foundation: the name was half Dakota Sioux (*minne* means water) and half Greek (*polis*, of course, means city), and it was also half of the Twin Cities, paired and partnered with St. Paul since the mid-nineteenth century.

Over the years, I had come to the city a handful of times, mostly for book tours, sometimes to visit friends. Whenever I was in town, I made a point of driving by First Avenue, the nightclub that featured prominently in *Purple Rain*. In real life, Prince had only played there about a dozen times (his first show there, in March 1982, consisted of a sharp seven-song set that opened with "Bambi" and ended with "Sexuality"; tickets cost four dollars), but the relationship between artist and club acquired the weight of legend. I had even driven to Henderson Station Road, where Prince rode his motorcycle through the country. But I had never before visited the *Purple Rain* house. It had recently changed hands. In the summer of 2015, 3420 Snelling hit the market for $110,000, with a listing that sounded some optimistic notes ("Newer boiler in 2010," "Close to Light Rail on a quiet street in the Longfellow neighborhood") and some cautious ones ("This home needs to be rehabbed," "Buyer to assume any R and R's on the TISH"). It eventually sold for $117,000, to an anonymous buyer. In 2016, after Prince's death, I was looking around for information and discovered that the buyer was no longer anonymous: Hennepin County records revealed that the property had been acquired by NPG Music Publishing, one of Prince's companies.

✦ ✦ ✦

For the final decades of Prince's life, the key local site wasn't even in the city proper. In the mid-eighties, Prince built the so-called Purple House on Lake Riley, in Chanhassen, a suburb to the west of the city; after a few years, he passed it along to his father, who lived there until his death in 2001. Prince gifted the Purple House to his father for a simple reason: he built himself a bigger place. Prince had a vision for an integrated residential-recording complex, and he and a young architect named Bret Thoeny, who had designed a recording studio in the Purple House, set about realizing that vision.

Paisley Park, a 65,000-square foot complex located on nine acres in Chanhassen, opened for business in the fall of 1987. It shared its name with Prince's imprint label, which in turn shared its name with a song on *Around the World in a Day*. The facilities included four different studios. There was Studio A, the largest at 1500 square feet; it included two isolation rooms dubbed the Granite and Wood Rooms after the composition of their walls. Studio B measured a thousand square feet, and there were two smaller studios, Studio C and Studio D. Paisley Park also had a large soundstage for live performances, video shoots, and tour rehearsals. There were offices, variously designated depending on what needed to be done: costume design, travel plans. And then there was Prince's private sanctum, which served as both office and living quarters and included a queen-size bed and oversize bathtub. Few people got to see it in person, but they could get a sense of it both from photographs and from Prince's mid-nineties CD-ROM *Prince Interactive*, which included a virtual tour through the facility.

Prince not only produced his own records at Paisley Park but brought in the other artists on his label, including George Clinton and Chaka Khan. Prominent bands of the late eighties and early nineties made the pilgrimage to Minneapolis to use the state-of-the-art facilities: The Fine Young Cannibals recorded some of *The Raw and the Cooked* there. R.E.M. recorded some of *Out of Time* "Cruella DeVille" there. The Replacements recorded their cover of "Cruella DeVille" there, and Paul Westerberg, in a piece he wrote for *Rolling Stone* after Prince's death, recalled the sessions fondly:

> He became comfortable enough to grace us with his presence, not bejeweled and not dressed up. He'd be wearing

maybe his jammies and sweat pants or maybe . . . jeans and sneakers. He could sort of just hang out. He may have been a little more normal than he would've liked people to know. That's the treasure that we got, to be able to sit in the big atrium where you're taking a break and Prince shuffles by in his slippers and makes some popcorn in the microwave.

In 1996, nearing the end of his protracted battle with Warner, under financial duress, Prince fired most of his staff and closed Paisley Park to outside recording, though it continued to function as his headquarters for studio work, late-night jam sessions, and impromptu concerts. Through the late nineties and on into the next century, he played dozens of home-field dates. In the summer of 2000, the complex hosted a weeklong festival called "Prince: A Celebration." Tickets entitled fans to tour the grounds, view memorabilia that included the *Purple Rain* motorcycle (by that point, it had been painted black and gold for *Graffiti Bridge*), and even vote on track lists for future works via an interactive exhibit.

Prince went away more than once. In 1998, after the death of Boy Gregory, Prince and Mayte bought a villa in Spain—located west of Marbella, in the El Paraíso hills—and decorated it lavishly, in the style of Paisley Park. When the couple divorced, the property was sold. In 2000, when he married Manuela Testolini, he took up residence in Toronto, in the upscale Bridle Path neighborhood. The city's skyline was featured on the back cover of *Musicology*. And in 2004, as he was beginning work on *3121*, he rented a West Hollywood mansion that belonged to NBA power forward Carlos Boozer; it had ten bedrooms and eleven bathrooms that cost Prince seventy thousand dollars per month. Prince's stay in the house was not without incident; Boozer told his teammate Jason Williams that he drove past the property and didn't recognize it as his own. He delivered a cure-or-quit letter and then filed a lawsuit in which he held that Prince had violated the lease by painting the house purple, adorning it with his pictonym, and adding the number "3121" (though the address was in fact 1235 Sierra Alta Way). That was just the outside. Inside, Prince tampered with the bedrooms, adding new carpeting in the master and, in a guest bedroom downstairs, installing "beauty salon chairs" that required additional plumbing. The suit was settled quickly; Prince wrote Boozer a check. Boozer later said there were no hard feelings.

He went away, but he always came back. He made his records at Paisley Park as late as the second half of *HITnRUN*. He played live shows there, including a warm-up gala for his Piano & a Microphone Tour. He hung out there, driving to the Dairy Queen in his BMW when the mood struck or to Caribou Coffee, where he paid in cash, often with a hundred-dollar bill, and never asked for change. And he was there in April 2016, strung out on fatigue (and, as it turned out, Fentanyl), shaping new music, and finally shuffling off this mortal coil. Staff reportedly found him unconscious in an elevator. On the 911 call released later by the Carver County Sheriff's Office, the male voice asking for an ambulance didn't know the street address. "We're at Prince's house," he said. He came back and then he went away.

After his death, his estate opened Paisley Park to the public, as a museum. The most I could bring myself to do was stand across the street and look at it. It was ungainly—three long, square warehouse buildings overlapping one another, and a circular silo nearby—and also too clean and minimalist for the roiling emotions it inspired. A friend of mine, an Elvis fanatic, had surprised me once by telling me that he was never going to go to

Graceland. "For starters," he said, "my connection to him comes through his work. Also, it's a private relationship. I don't want to see other people poking around in the space where he used to be, talking about him, saying things I either know are true or know aren't true at all." At the time, I had thought him hypersensitive, and said so, but everything I heard about the Paisley Park tours made me feel exactly the same way, most notably the fact that Prince's cremation urn was on display inside the building. It wasn't your run-of-the-mill bronze urn; rather, it was a scale model of the entire Paisley Park complex, complete with a bedazzled Love Symbol and a removable front wall that pulled away to show miniature doves and a replica of his purple Yamaha grand piano. Prince's ashes were in one of the front columns. In a sense, the urn was redundant. Prince designed Paisley Park as a combination of workspace and residence, but it served another function as well. The miniature, just like the actual building, featured pyramids prominently. "He loved pyramids," Bret Thoeny remembered in *Billboard*. "The glass pyramid marked the entrance to the building, and there were skylight pyramids on top of his office." He also loved Egyptian mythology and invoked it in his work, from the "hundred-percent Egyptian lace" he gave as a romantic gift in "Adore" to the extended narratives of the straight-to-video movie *3 Chains o' Gold* and the epic narration "Muse 2 the Pharaoh" on *The Rainbow Children*. Pyramids, of course, were used in ancient Egypt as elaborate aboveground tombs. The fact could not have escaped him.

✦ ✦ ✦

Prince mentioned other cities in his songs, of course. He could get away with talking about Detroit (specifically, "talkin' 'bout the Detroit crawl" in "It's Gonna Be a Beautiful Night"), because the city's music, particularly through the P-Funk of George Clinton, had furnished him with a foundation for his funk.* He could get away with Paris or London (or, on *20Ten*, with naming a song "Lavaux," after Swiss vineyard terraces) because they burnished his cosmopolitan credentials. But the most frequently and most credibly mentioned location was home. "MPLS," an unreleased song from 1992, tours his own past, name-checking local venues like Archie's Bunker. In 1995, after Lenny Kravitz had a minor hit with "Rock and Roll Is Dead," Prince answered back with "Rock and Roll Is Alive and It Lives in Minneapolis," a hometown ode with crunchy guitars and local color. That never appeared on an album, but the album that he did release that year included a song called "Billy Jack Bitch," a tight bit of invective supposedly directed at a Minneapolis *Star Tribune* gossip columnist. "White Mansion," a vaguely autobiographical song from *Emancipation*, took a swipe at Warner Bros. but also offered an affectionate, rueful look at his hometown: "Back to Minneapolis, there you go / You can't find your house underneath the snow." And back he went, again and again: for "Calhoun Square," a tribute to a local indoor mall, for "Northside," a tribute to the African-American neighborhoods where he spent his youth. When he was young,

---

* There was even more specific overlap between the two cities. The Electrifying Mojo, a Detroit DJ, was one of Prince's first important boosters, and various hangers-on from the P-Funk scene made their way to Minneapolis. Billy Sparks, who played the club owner in *Purple Rain*, had gotten his start selling bootleg P-Funk merchandise, and other members of the camp, including Greg Brooks (best known as the Davy Crockett cap–wearing supporting player in the *Sign O' the Times* concert film) and Wally Safford (who worked as a backup singer and dancer for Prince), were also Motor City migrants. Prince even wrote a song called "Wally," in which he imagined speaking to Safford about his sadness over his breakup with Susannah Melvoin. It was mostly an unaccompanied piano piece in which Prince asked Safford (unheard) if he could borrow some money and sunglasses to impress his girl; later, he explains that he doesn't need them anymore because she's broken things off. Prince, uncomfortable with the starkness of the song, kept adding tracks despite the objections of Susan Rogers, his recording engineer. The track remains unreleased.

he had complained to his high school newspaper that being marooned in Minneapolis limited his chances at stardom. Once he was a star, he went back there again and again, both in his life and in his music.

In January 2010, when the Vikings, led by the aging Brett Favre, upset the Dallas Cowboys in the first round of the NFL play-offs, Prince was among the 63,000 fans in attendance. The victory inspired him to whip up a theme song for the team. "Purple and Gold" wasn't his finest moment, and it may have been one of his worst—it was too simplistic musically and over-compensated lyrically by a wide margin. There was a "veil of the sky," the "roar of the chariots," and "walk[ing] upon water like solid ground," and that's just in one verse.

On the scattershot album *20Ten*, the following year, one of the standouts was "Laydown," a nervy, insistent public service announcement trumpeting the benefits of Minneapolis ("Let me show you how / we do this thing / up in funky town"). The song, which wasn't even officially listed on the record—it surfaced as a hidden track after six minutes of silence—nodded to *Star Wars* with one of Prince's funniest couplets: "From the heart of Minnesota / Here comes the Purple Yoda."

It was an instructive nickname: Yoda was two foot two. Prince was slightly taller. Yoda wore robes with nothing underneath. Prince wore trench coats with nearly nothing underneath. Most important, they were both masters of the Force who shared the same philosophy: Do or do not—there is no try.

12

CALL THE LAW

How He Grew Frustrated with
Fans and the Internet

On October 1, 1991, the same day that Prince released *Diamonds and Pearls*, a group of journalists who were also diehard fans (or was it the other way around?) began publishing a new magazine devoted to his music. Originating out of a southern Swedish town called Linghem, the magazine was called *Uptown*, after the *Dirty Mind* song, and the first issue gave a good indication of what was to come. The music writer Per Nilsen, the author of a book titled *Dance Music Sex Romance: Prince: The First Decade*, took a closer look at the Nude Tour, detailing the set list for every show. A second feature listed all of Prince's cowrites and ghostwrites, from the obvious (the Time) to the odd (Kenny Rogers) to the unthinkably obscure (the Japanese pop star Kahoru Kohiruimaki, who recorded two virtually unknown Prince compositions, "Mind Bells" and "Bliss"). The magazine was simple and straightforward, obsessed and unashamed of it. Where else could you find a structural and thematic analysis of the 1993 album *Come*?

> The first two songs . . . serve as a general invitation to "come" to a world of sexual salvation, the middle five songs . . . seem to reflect various conflicts and issues that need to be dealt with to free one's mind, and the final three selections . . . are the culmination of the journey.

Uptown preceded the Internet, but in a sense it was the Internet. It united members of a community despite geographical distance, and permitted—even encouraged—the obsessive parsing of details and an unabashed boosterism. In the mid-nineties, as Web technology advanced, *Uptown* migrated online, though it still published in print. There were other projects like it in which fans reviewed music, new and old, commented on shows they had attended, posted set lists, and speculated on unreleased material.

In 1999, editors at *Uptown*, along with ten other Prince sites and publications, were served with a trademark and copyright infringement lawsuit. The suit, filed in New York federal court, claimed that the sites had maliciously infringed copyright through "unauthorized use of the symbol," not to mention Prince's "name, image, and likeness." *Uptown* was singled out in the suit, supposedly for claiming a quasi-official relationship with Prince's NPG Records. Prince and his lawyers sought to halt all publication, whether print or online, and collect compensatory and punitive damages. A fan site was just a party, and parties weren't meant to last.

Copyright lawyers across the country leaned back in expensive chairs and considered the suit with interest. Most judged it without merit; fan sites and zines had historically been allowed to proceed unmolested, in large measure because they gave artists publicity and expected nothing in return. At the same time, though, editors at the zines, both online and off, leaned forward slightly in their less expensive chairs and felt their blood run cold. Nine of the eleven sites decided to shut down immediately rather than face any further legal action. Only *Uptown* and one site that reprinted Prince lyrics, dttlyrics.com, kept going.

After a little while, *Uptown* found a lawyer who was willing to take its case. Alex Hahn, based in Boston, had been a Prince devotee since college. At times, it had been a risky proposition: in 1988, he and hundreds of other fans were camped out overnight outside Tower Records to buy Prince concert tickets when a car lost control, hopped the curb, and plowed into the line, killing one person. Hahn, just beginning work at a small intellectual-property firm, felt that the suit against *Uptown* had no merit. "It was frivolous to the point of being ridiculous," he told me. Working pro bono, he designed an argument that proceeded along two fronts: first, that the sites had First Amendment protections; and second, that Prince had forfeited his ability to control Love Symbol #2 when he had sent out floppy discs to news media. In addition, there was the matter of profit, or rather the absence of it. Prince's arguments that the sites were making money from his name were flawed on their face; the sites broke even at best or operated at a slight loss. Many of the lawyers and editors targeted by Prince felt that the suit was simply a business strategy. In 1997, Prince had launched Love4OneAnother.com, which invited writers and editors from various fan sites to relinquish their individual projects and join a fan community. Prince, in an on-site interview, explained that he was ceding control of it to people in his camp: "My own personal objectives [for the site] change daily . . . that is y eye defer 2 the people at Paisley Park that eye love and respect the most. 4 me the initial objective was 2 have a visible place 4 my thoughts." The legal threats, seen through the prism of his own site's launch, seemed like an attempt to create an effective monopoly for Love4One Another.com.

The narrow contentions of the lawsuit opened outward into larger questions of fandom and fame. The line between commercial ventures and protected speech was a blurry one, especially when the object of that speech was a celebrity. What Prince was trying to do, some commentators felt, was not any different from trying to stop a newspaper from commenting on a new album, or an editorial cartoonist from drawing a Prince-like figure. *Uptown* hit back. With Hahn's help, the zine countersued Prince, prominently mentioning the Love4OneAnother .com theory. They also demanded that Prince himself be deposed. Prince, notoriously private, refused, and Prince's lawyers began to back down, claiming that he had only ever wanted to eliminate the bootleg listings in the back of the magazine for collectors and traders. *Uptown* readily agreed to that, in exchange for the freedom to write about Prince in any other fashion they wished—they could even write about unreleased songs, so long as they identified them as such. Hahn wrote a postmortem that was posted online, at multiple sites:

> I suspect for many others who support and read the magazine, it is a fairly joyless victory. The editors of *Uptown* never viewed this lawsuit as some public relations boon. They found it exhausting and at times frightening. They were worried about having to travel to New York to be questioned by Prince's lawyers, and about having to tear apart their offices and apartments to find documents.

It was a short lawsuit that came and went, with no real effect other than to alienate fans. It was also the beginning of a pattern.

✦ ✦ ✦

In "My Name Is Prince," Prince sang, "If you want to play with me, you better learn the rules." But learning them was nearly impossible—there were so many, and they kept changing. In 2007, Stephanie Lenz, a young mother living in the Bay Area, posted a twenty-nine-second clip to YouTube of her two-year-old son dancing as "Let's Go Crazy" played in the background. "Dancing" is perhaps an exaggeration: he bounced up and down, wearing a red shirt, pushing a blue cart along the floor.

A few months later, the song's copyright holder, Universal, contacted Lenz and asked her to take down the video under the Digital Millennium Copyright Act (DMCA). Though Prince and Universal had been at odds over the years, this time it seemed like the company was acting on his wishes. Within a few months, Lenz was not Prince's only target. He hired Web Sheriff, a "creative protection" firm, to comb YouTube and locate any additional clips that contained his songs, even as background music. He announced that he planned to file a series of lawsuits against any site that enabled the distribution of copyrighted materials, not only YouTube (for their videos) but also eBay (for any memorabilia) and the Pirate Bay (for torrents of both official albums and bootlegs). And two months later he sent cease-and-desist letters to fan sites like Prince.org and Housequake.com that demanded the removal of not only song lyrics and concert set lists but also Prince-adjacent content like photos of Love Symbol #2 tattoos and idiosyncratically spelled license plates (IDRV4U).

Lenz, represented by the Electronic Frontier Foundation (EFF) and the San Francisco law firm of Keker & Van Nest, sued Universal over the takedown letter, claiming that she was entitled to fair use of the material. Other fans banded together into an organization called Prince Fans United that reaffirmed that online fandom was simply a matter of providing commentary on Prince's activities (and largely positive commentary at that). Prince's response? A new song, called "PFunk" and then later changed to "F.U.N.K." (the "F.U." was the operative part of the title), that weighed in on the YouTube brouhaha with high-pitched vocals and a screeching guitar solo. But Prince was punching down, gratuitously belittling his fans ("The only reason to say my name is to get your fifteen secs of fame / Nobody's even sure what you do"), and his insistence on the redemptive powers of music ("the best remedy for a basket full of lies is funk") felt hollow.

Donated with ironic generosity, at best, the song was e-mailed from fan to fan as proof both of Prince's talent and of his petulance. Neither seemed to be in danger of disappearing. In 2008, he appeared at Coachella, where he played a long, lavish set that included a cover of Radiohead's "Creep." When a fan posted a video of the "Creep" performance, Prince's lawyers fired off yet another DMCA takedown notice. Sites complied, for the most part, but it wasn't clear that they had any reason to do so—the song's copyright was owned by Radiohead, and Thom Yorke was clear in his stance on the matter: "Tell him to unblock it. It's our song."

Many of the lawsuits were settled quickly, as the copyright-infringement suit against *Uptown* had been a decade earlier. But *Lenz v. Universal* dragged on, and the "dancing baby" suit, as it became known, helped to define larger issues around digital copyright. In September 2015, the Ninth Circuit ruled against Universal, stipulating that copyright holders had to consider whether or not fair use was applicable before even sending a takedown notice; previously, they had sent letters demanding that those posting content prove fair use. Fair use was not, as Universal's previous practice suggested, a secondary argument to be made by the accused site or citizen but rather a primary right.

Lenz agreed with the ruling, but felt that it still disadvantaged those victimized by frivolous takedown letters by leaving them without a practical path to redress. She asked the Ninth Circuit to rehear the case en banc (in other words, with all its judges). In March 2016, the court declined to rehear the case. The EFF, still representing Lenz, summarized the ruling in a post on its website: "After more than eight years, this litigation continues. EFF will continue to fight for fair use in this case and others." In August 2016, the organization asked the Supreme Court to review the lawsuit. The case has now outlived Prince himself.

+ + +

Prince's mistreatment of his fans stemmed at least in part from a powerful sense of privacy: once he gave people his songs—in recorded form, in live shows—he felt he wasn't obligated to accommodate them any further. His fan base, hungry for product, could also amplify the misdeeds of his record label and make a bad situation worse. But Prince's quarrel was also with the Internet itself. He didn't dislike the Internet only for copyright reasons; he disliked it for all reasons. He thought that it dulled human experience, that it corrupted private space, that it purported to encourage self-expression when in fact all it did was create new storefronts where companies could co-opt and monetize people's thoughts. He railed against the Internet whenever he could, both in interviews and in song. Though he was skilled with recording technology, he never quite got the hang of computers in general; more than one person described his approach to the computer mouse or track pad as "interesting." Yet he was also a relatively early adopter when it came to the Internet. In 1994, he released *Prince Interactive*, which was billed as a CD-ROM video game, though it was more like a scavenger hunt through a digitally recreated version of Paisley Park. On Valentine's Day 1996, he launched TheDawn.com, a website that promised exclusive music, videos, and games. A few months later, Warner Bros. threw up a rudimentary site for *Chaos and Disorder* and uploaded his new single, "Dinner with Delores." These tentative first steps evolved into a full-blown Web-based subscription service. In 1998, Todd Rundgren, long an inspiration of Prince's, had launched a site called PatroNet. Rundgren's goal was to create direct communication between artists and fans. For a single yearly fee, people had access to an artist's full released output; the artist could collect the money up front and use it to fund recording. Prince rolled out his own version in 2001, again on Valentine's Day. His model was pricier, and also Princier: for a monthly charge of $7.77, fans would get at least three new Prince songs each month, along with videos and an hour-long radio show. The annual premium membership, just a touch more expensive at $100 (or $8.33 a month), brought preferred seating at concerts, along with a free copy of Prince's most recent album, *Rave Un2 the Joy Fantastic*. As with other Prince initiatives, early customers got a raw deal. The price was soon slashed, to $2.50 for the monthly and $25 for the annual.

Content was released through the site, true enough. The first *NPG Ahdio Show*, in February 2001, knit together more than a dozen songs from Prince-affiliated artists like Rhonda Smith, Ani DiFranco, Cindy Blackman, and Carmen Electra, along with new Prince compositions such as "When I Lay My Hands on U," "Mad," and "Funky Design." The second installment skimped on the studio recordings but delivered live versions of "Letitgo," "Vicki Waiting," and "We March." The third debuted "The Work Pt. 1," which would later appear on *The Rainbow Children*, and the Jimi Hendrix–derived "Habibi." It wasn't a bad way to consume the music, though the monthly releases hamstrung Prince when it came to developing consistent themes. Still, he stuck with the NPG Music Club almost a year, an eternity by his standards. The eleventh and final audio show, in January 2002, included a cover of Joni Mitchell's "A Case of You," and two new songs, "Breathe" and "Madrid 2 Chicago." The latter was surprisingly carnal given his recent Jehovah's Witness conversion. Prince wondered "How am I gonna make this connection when I got nothing but you" while backup vocals, almost inaudibly, piped up with "Nothing but eatin' that pussy."

When the radio show stopped, the site stayed on, though it was kind of like an abandoned house, and by 2006 it was leveled. It lasted from Valentine's Day to Independence Day, symbolically paralleling Prince's usual course, from love to liberation. The farewell statement was gnomic at best.

> The achievements of the past cannot be questioned and we r truly grateful 4 everything that has been accomplished. But in its current 4m there is a feeling that the NPGMC has gone as far as it can go. In a world without limitations and infinite possibilities, has the time come 2 once again make a leap of faith and begin anew? These r ?s we in the NPG need 2 answer. In doing so, we have decided 2 put the club on hiatus until further notice.

Prince was back online again in 2009, with LotusFlow3r.com, which was launched to accompany the trio of new albums he was releasing. Again, he leaned on sevens: the initial subscription cost was seventy-seven dollars. There were three floating planets, each representing one of the albums that Prince also released that day. The most compelling thing about it was the standby music, an instrumental piece called "Disco Jellyfish." There was more language about serving fans and seizing on possibilities, but the site went down in a matter of months.

+ + +

His talent outlasted his capacity for profound mismanagement. Back in 1985, in the wake of *Purple Rain*, Prince had released *Around the World in a Day*, an album that sold four million copies and was considered—depending on whether you were a fan or a record company executive—either a modest success or a moderate failure. In 2015, those numbers would have put the album in a solid second place in yearly sales, behind only Adele's *25*. But in its day, *Around the World in A Day* didn't even scratch the top ten, which included Whitney Houston's debut (14.2 million copies sold), Phil Collins's *No Jacket Required* (13.9 million), Dire Straits' *Brothers in Arms* (12.9 million), Tears for Fears's *Songs from the Big Chair* (5.9 million), and ZZ Top's *Afterburner* (5.3 million).

The gradual and inexorable downturn in record sales, aided and abetted by digital downloads, music piracy, and the rise of streaming services, affected Prince along with everyone else. One of the results was that albums that sold poorly could still achieve a high chart position, sometimes higher than earlier albums that had sold much better. *Musicology* moved two million units and got to number three on the charts, but it was his last album to go platinum. *3121* went to number one in 2006, partly on the strength of "Black Sweat," a funk single as tough as ripstop nylon. But it leveled off at gold, and *Planet Earth* didn't even do that well, despite the fact that a copy of the album was given away with every copy of the UK newspaper *The Mail*.

With sales flagging, not just for his own albums but for nearly every album in the pop world, Prince began to reexamine his strict anti-Internet policy, instead opting for a haphazard mix of enthusiastic participation and sudden disappearance. He was on Twitter, under the 3RDEYEGIRL name, and then he was off it. He was on Instagram, joking that it should be called Princetagram, and then he was off it. Month by month, his Internet presence was like a mood ring, changing unpredictably, never an actual indication of any real state.

His final partnership was with Tidal. The streaming service, which had launched in 2014 before selling to a group headed by Jay Z the following year, billed itself as an artist-friendly environment, and they went after big names to prove their point. Prince was announced as a participating artist during Jay Z's first press conference, and he pledged that he would do right by subscribers: he would pull his music off all other streaming services and also release exclusive content through Tidal, including videos, stand-alone singles, concerts, and something he called the Purple Pick of the Week, a curated weekly song. It was, like nearly every other online initiative Prince designed, maintained erratically at best—it degenerated into a mix of Prince outtakes, material by other artists, and even, occasionally, songs simply pulled from official Prince albums.

Prince stayed on Tidal, and in the last years of his life, used it the way he promised he would, give or take. He streamed his Rally 4 Peace concert from Baltimore on the service. He gave Tidal exclusive rights to *HITnRUN Phase One* in 2014 and *HITnRUN Phase Two* in 2015. Prince's final release was a Tidal-only live single of "Black Sweat," illustrated, puckishly, with a picture of the actor Edward G. Robinson (Prince had referred to Robinson and his "funk face" in the performance). When Prince died, Tidal was the only place fans could stream his music, and they did, in large numbers. He died two days before Beyoncé released *Lemonade*, her eagerly awaited sixth album, also a Tidal exclusive; the two factors, one tragic, one triumphant, gave Tidal its best month ever.*

✦ ✦ ✦

When I finished writing this section, I suddenly felt tired. Prince's time on the Internet was a story of small-mindedness and high-handedness, and it was wearing me out. I got in the car and drove for an hour until I found myself by a river in a town where I knew no one. A cloud of starlings was in the sky, in the middle distance, moving together: flight time. I sat down on a bench and put on headphones. At first I listened to nothing, I just felt the snug of the ear buds. Then I let my iPhone pick a random song for me. It was "When 2 R in Love," which Prince originally recorded for *The Black Album* and then, after shelving the album, kept for *Lovesexy*. In the context of either album, the dense funk of *The Black Album* or the polyrhythmic spirituality of *Lovesexy*, it was an anomaly, a mellow make-out song with some of his loveliest natural imagery: "When two are in love," he sang, "the falling leaves appear to them like slow-motion rain." There was no rain, and no falling leaves either, but the starlings were in full murmuration, moving fluidly, all of them, however many that was, making shapes: now a sheet that folded over on itself, now a spiral, now a ribbon running rapidly toward the corner of the sky. My phone vibrated: a message coming in. I ignored it. I tried to pick out individual birds in the cloud—impossible—and then individual notes in the song, harder than I thought it would be. My phone vibrated again. I turned it facedown, and then my

---

* Because it was Prince, and because it was the Internet, things got knotty. In November 2016, his estate sued Jay Z's Roc Nation over the terms of Tidal's streaming, claiming that the service improperly streamed too much of Prince's content. Roc Nation disputed the claim.

impatience got to me and I turned it faceup. It was, of course, a reminder of what I had driven an hour to escape: an e-mail from a friend of mine, a lawyer, who wanted to tell me that he had just discovered that his wife, also a lawyer, had a secret past with Prince. That piqued my interest. I read on. In the late nineties, she had worked for a firm that represented Prince (she hadn't told him exactly what business they had conducted, and he hadn't asked—lawyers), and the firm had had to invest in new typesetting software to write their briefs, because they were absolutely required to refer to him as the symbol in court documents. I closed my e-mail. The song, still going, was doing what soul music was supposed to do: transporting, uplifting, giving shape to hope. "Nothing's forbidden and nothing's taboo," he sang, "when the two are in love." The starlings were showing off now with their shapes: an upright crescent, a manta ray, a long, tapered cylinder that looked like a zeppelin taking off. They never got around to making the shape of the symbol, and eventually I had to go.

13

IT'S GONNA BE A
BEAUTIFUL NIGHT

When He Was Onstage

PRINCE AND HIS BAND WERE PLAYING THE BIGGEST GIG OF THEIR YOUNG lives, opening for the Rolling Stones at the Los Angeles Memorial Coliseum. It was 1981, October. The previous year, *Dirty Mind* had attracted the attention of the rock cognoscenti, including Mick Jagger, who went to see Prince perform in March at the Ritz in New York. Jagger liked what he saw—he may even have recognized some of his old dance moves—and he offered Prince a supporting slot for two shows in LA and two more in Detroit in December.

Opening for the Stones meant playing for a big crowd, maybe as many as a hundred thousand, and Prince had never been in front of that many people. He wasn't the only opener—J. Geils and George Thorogood were there, too—but he was the only black opener, and he was a black artist of a different generation (the Stones had toured with African-American acts as tour support before—with Ike and Tina Turner, and with Stevie Wonder—but those acts were their contemporaries). Whatever reservations Prince had, the size of the opportunity overpowered them.

Prince and his band had wound down the *Dirty Mind* tour in April, and after a handful of summer shows, including a gig at Dez Dickerson's wedding in June, they took the stage at the Coliseum. Prince dressed as he often did in 1981: trench coat over black briefs, thigh-high socks and boots, and a bandanna. His leopard-skin guitar strap cut him crossways. The second he appeared, people in the crowd started to point. He was, if not a laughingstock, at least a gazingstock.

The set opened with "Bambi," which showcased Prince's sizzling guitar heroics, and "When You Were Mine," which was, despite its ménage à trois subject matter, a classicist and even conservative composition. So far, so good. Then things went a little haywire. The third song on the set list was "Jack U Off," and it's possible to see why Prince thought it was a good idea. The Stones were no strangers to innuendo and had been sexually explicit in songs like "Some Girls" and "Star Star." But something about "Jack U Off" landed wrong. Maybe it was the New Wave keyboards, or the fact that the title might have made it seem like the song was about pleasuring another man (it wasn't—Prince considered the act of masturbating a woman a form of jacking off). Something set the crowd off, and that's when the booing started. On bootlegs of the performance, you can hear it. One male voice said, "One more like that and they'll be throwing stuff." As rock-and-roll insults go, it isn't exactly "Judas!" But it was accurate—a beer can or two sailed toward the stage, and then a soda can hit Dickerson, and then a bottle of Jack Daniels narrowly missed Prince. He was rattled. "Uptown" was next up, a good match for the crowd, but Prince walked offstage without even telling the band to stop. He was done. He took a car to the airport and flew back to Minneapolis. Both Jagger and the promoter Bill Graham, who had berated the rowdy crowd following the incident, called Prince to coax him back West for the second show two nights later. "If you get to be a really big headliner," Jagger said, "you have to be prepared for people to throw bottles at you."

Prince relented. He went back west. By then, LA morning radio had ginned up the conflict, bringing more anti-Prince forces out of the woodwork. Dez Dickerson said he saw someone in the parking lot unloading a plastic bag filled with "old gray chicken parts." During "Bambi," a whiskey bottle came flying in. Plastic bottles of juice followed, as well as tomatoes, but the band got all the way to the fifth and final song of its set, the newly relevant "Why You Wanna Treat Me So Bad?" Twenty years later, Prince was still fuming when he recounted the incident for Robert Hillburn of the *Los Angeles Times*:

> Don't say that was because of me—that was the audience doing that. I'm sure wearing underwear and a trench coat didn't help matters, but if you throw trash at anybody, it's because you weren't trained right at home. The reason I left is that I didn't want to play anymore. I just wanted to fight.

✦ ✦ ✦

Most of the time, he wanted to play. In his *American Bandstand* interview in 1980, Dick Clark asked Prince about his plans to take his album out on the road. "We have a tour," he said coyly. It was a brutal understatement. He would finish up a run of shows in support of his *Prince* album on February 17 in Boston, and then, five days later, take the stage in Fort Worth opening for Rick James, which would keep him on the road for three more months, and not a leisurely three months either—they barnstormed across the eastern half of the country, playing forty dates in seventy days: Shreveport, Greenville, Saginaw, Jackson, Landover. In March, after playing a show at the Dorton Arena in Raleigh, North Carolina, Prince and his band returned to the downtown Holiday Inn where they were sleeping. That same night, North Carolina State University's Sigma Pi fraternity was holding their spring formal in the hotel's ballroom. Prince approached the stage and asked if he could play when the party band took a break. He and his band performed a short set, shook some hands and left. Colby Warren, now a designer, remembers being impressed. "We were an all-white frat at the time," Warren told me, "but I was a hardcore funkateer." It is not known exactly what attracted Prince to Sigma Pi, though their crest was lavender and white.

Prince came off the road after the Rick James tour, recorded *Dirty Mind* in his home studio in Minneapolis, and was back onstage before the end of the year, playing thirty dates between Buffalo in December and New Orleans the following April. In February, he was in New York to perform on *Saturday Night Live*. The musical guest that night was Todd Rundgren, one of Prince's musical idols. The Philadelphia-born Rundgren, who had started off in blues bands and cofounded the psychedelic-rock group Nazz (at their early best, an American version of the Who), had, as a solo artist, become the original one-man band, recording several of his albums completely on his own. He had also (as Prince would) passed restlessly through a series of creative incarnations: twee singer-songwriter, snot-nosed prankster, self-indulgent artiste, back-to-basics pub rocker. That night, Rundgren was promoting his album *Healing*, a suite of subdued, spiritual pop songs. Prince and his band, added at the last minute as a second musical guest, played one song only, "Partyup." Prince wore a gray-purple overcoat accented by a red bandanna, and the second the song ended, he rushed his band offstage—it was a common practice at the time, designed to project punk impatience. By the end of 1981, he had recorded *Controversy*, suffered his sticks-and-Stones debacle, and embarked on a mammoth national tour of more than sixty dates. The *1999* tour was even more break-neck, with forty-one dates in sixty-eight nights. And while the *Purple Rain* tour is remembered most for the closing show in Miami, much of that tour operated as a series of residencies: the band did six shows at the Forum in Los Angeles, seven at Joe Louis Arena in Detroit, five at the Rosemont Horizon in Chicago, five at the Omni Coliseum in Atlanta, six at the Summit in Hous-ton. That's only a thumbnail of Prince's first half decade as a stage performer; three more decades followed suit. Across the years, from the early tours (the fast food on the interstate, the motels with popcorn ceilings) to the late ones (room service in five-star establishments, baby grand pianos craned up to the suite), the job was the same: go out, move the crowd. All told, he played more than two thousand concerts over the course of his life. If you missed out, it was on you.

✦ ✦ ✦

In Miami in 1985, I missed the Purple Bowl—not because my parents thought that I was too young, not because the tickets were too pricey. I just didn't do it. It was on me.

A few years later, I made up for lost time by watching the *Sign O' the Times* movie three times in three nights at York Square Cinema in New Haven, Connecticut. Prince had originally intended to build it around performances filmed that summer in Rotter-dam and Antwerp, but the footage was too uneven, especially in sound quality, and he had to recreate nearly the entire show on Paisley Park's large soundstage. The movie transformed his best album into something even better. "Play in the Sunshine" was joyfully acrobatic; "Forever in My Life" was improved by a bluesy acoustic guitar intro and a powerhouse backing vocal from Boni Boyer; and "I Could Never Take the Place of Your Man" extended the instrumental breakdown before Prince drove back in to take his solo so fiercely and confidently it was as if he was riding his *Purple Rain* motorcycle again.

The movie propelled me directly into the *Lovesexy* tour, and specifically into Prince's September 1988 show at the Hartford Civic Center. The show was a birthday present from me to myself: I dipped into my meager savings for the funds, and a college roommate and I took the bus up from New Haven, eating four-dollar convenience-store sandwiches as we walked from station to stadium. My devotion to *Lovesexy* carried me through the show, which was not a perfect concert and maybe not even a good one. Prince had produced so much good music so quickly that he had to incorporate six classic albums worth of material, and as a result songs came fast and furious, crammed into medleys, sometimes cutting off before the chorus. Momentum was elusive. The music was also overwhelmed a bit by the staging, the multitiered set with its playroom feel and basketball hoop. He stopped the concert twice to dribble and try to pop a fifteen-foot jumper. As I remember, he made both shots.* The highlight was the solo piano set in the second half of the show, during which Prince sat quietly and played "When 2 R in Love," "Starfish and Coffee,"

---

* Magic Johnson, appearing on *Jimmy Kimmel Live!* after Prince's death, discussed Prince's on-court demeanor. It was, in the words of one of his songs, "a double, a double arrogance": "He talked so much trash—he thought he had a real jump shot," Magic said. "I had to remember it was Prince that I was playing against, so I had to back off. But he really thought he could play basketball." What he could really play, evidently, was Ping-Pong. There are dozens of stories of Prince taking a break from recording to go play Ping-Pong; the table was right outside the studio. Few people could keep up with him, either in terms of his table skills or his trash-talking skills.

"Venus de Milo," "Condition of the Heart," and more. He had lots of hair that year, curly, less an afro than a sort of mane, and he kept sweeping it back as he played. His fingers moved more than his arms did, and his shoulders hardly moved at all inside his suit coat, which was purple and covered with white squiggles. "He should do an entire show like this," my roommate said.

"I don't see it," I said.

"Why not?" he said. He was right. I was wrong. On the way out, I bought a tour shirt: black, with his name written in rainbow that looked like it had been scratched out in the manner of one of those children's drawing boards that covered back over the scratched-out lines with black oil the second that pressure was no longer applied. What were they called? The Internet must know. Marvin's Magic Drawing Boards.

After the *Lovesexy* tour, Prince came off the road. Or rather, he came off the road for me and millions of other American fans. He toured in Europe and Asia with the Nude Tour in 1990; the Diamonds and Pearls Tour in 1992; the Ultimate Live Experience in 1995. He stopped off for Rock in Rio in 1991. Shows in the States were generally benefits, hometown gigs, or televised performances like the infamous assless-pants "Gett Off" performance from the MTV Video Music Awards. In 1994, he opened a trio of Glam Slam nightclubs—one in Miami, one in Los Angeles, and one in Minneapolis—and booked himself as his own headliner whenever possible. As 1999 approached, and with it promises of renewed Stateside relevance, he suited back up for America with the Jam of the Year World Tour (which, despite its name, was only an American tour), which rolled into the New Power Soul Tour and then the New Power Soul Festival Tour and then the One Nite Alone . . . Tour (again a misnomer: Prince recorded the album alone but took a band out on the road with him).

✦ ✦ ✦

Did the road wear on him? It must have, but he betrayed none of the exhaustion of albums like the Kinks' *Everybody's in Showbiz*, on which the process of touring becomes intolerable tedium: "There goes another night, here comes another flight / Can't stop gotta go, here comes yet another show." Instead, he celebrated the concert experience, as on the slight if energetic "We Gets Up," from *Emancipation*: "We gets up, everybody gets down." He did, nearly every night. This was no small feat.

And yet, he changed over time, and there are a number of diagnostics available to detect that change. How taut was the riff of "When You Were Mine"? Did the preprogrammed drums drag while he played "Mountains"? Did he run the band through the one-minute prog-rock outro to "1999"? Some years he seemed as though he was in the grips of bad sound design or an indifferent band. Other years, he sounded crisp and power-ful. His set lists were always a kind of psychological profile. They could suggest the presence of an artist anxiously proud of his achievement and eager to show it off through overstuffed medleys that reduced many of his hit compositions to minute-long snippets (see: *Lovesexy* tour). But he could also play his best songs at full length and added in carefully selected cover ver-sions (see: "Chain of Fools"/"My Name Is Prince" medley from Diamonds and Pearls Tour). He could mine for ore in his deep back catalog, too (see: "I Wonder U," played only occasionally during *Parade* shows; "The Ballad of Dorothy Parker," played a handful of times over the years, almost always with Madhouse's "4" wrapped around it; "Anna Stesia," played during the *Lovesexy* tour and unwrapped later only during One Nite Alone . . . ; "Vicki Waiting," played only in Japan in the mid-nineties). As with Minnesota's other great rock star, Bob Dylan, Prince's onstage evolution not only echoed his studio work but provided a parallel narrative.

Live shows were also where audiences got to see Prince dance. He worked his body as hard as any rock star of his era: he would be on a platform and then sailing through the air toward the stage; or on the microphone until he stepped away for a series of moves. Starting with Janet Jackson, dancing in pop music became increasingly choreographed and martial. Prince flew solo, even when he had backup dancers. He danced like a rock star, never letting his great ability eclipse his individuality. In that he was like Mick Jagger before him, or James Brown before that, but unlike the other great star of his era, Michael Jackson. Jackson planned every last flick of the finger, and his extreme premeditation allowed him to become something monumental. Prince moved his body where his music took him. Zadie Smith, writing in the *Guardian*, discussed the ways in which Prince's dancing, more elusive than Jackson's, was nonetheless more meaningful: "Prince represents the inspiration of the moment, like an ode composed to capture a passing sensation. And when the mood changes, he changes with it: another good lesson."*

Live shows introduced another dimension of Prince's duality. He was torn between the complete control he wielded when he created songs in the studio and the cooperation and coordination needed to reproduce those songs onstage. Bandleaders might imagine that their bands are simply projections of the music they

---

* There was an early-career moment that distilled this difference. In August 1983, James Brown was performing at the Beverly Theatre in Los Angeles, and he heard that both Prince and Michael Jackson were in the audience. Brown summoned them both to the stage. Jackson got there first and out–James Browned James Brown; it was clear that he had studied the man, and the man's film, for years. Prince was carried to the stage by bodyguards. He didn't dance as much. Instead, he played the guitar and then leaned against a lamppost he thought was real. It wasn't. He fell, Buster Keaton–like, right through it.

hear in their heads, but that's a fragile idea, immediately rattled. You can hear the tug-of-war in 1985, as the Revolution sound-checks for the final stop on the *Purple Rain* tour at the Orange Bowl in Miami. The concert itself would be largely a greatest-hits affair. But in rehearsal, the band is out in the sticks. They roar through a set of rarities, mostly: "17 Days," "Erotic City," which had been released as the B side to "Let's Go Crazy," and the mid-seventies James Brown cut "Body Heat" (a staple for Prince and his bands). At the end of the rehearsal, Prince leads the Revolution into an extended jam. On bootlegs, it's broken up into two sections, a long one called "Groove in A" and a shorter one called "Groove in F," but really it's one long workout. Prince calls for Eric Leeds on saxophone and lets that run for a little while. He calls for Dr. Fink on piano. He calls for only the bass and drums. There's no call for a guitar solo—or rather, one appears without him calling for it. That's because he's the one playing it. And the second he does, it's apparent that (and why) he's in charge: the sound on the thing is huge. It just soars over the rest of the band, like the air force is flying jets over the stadium. And then he returns to his taskmaster duties. Here, the word is precise. He's trying to get the band to master tasks: "Play straight drums, A, good God!" More than ten minutes in, he barks "B!" Then Wendy flubs something, or Prince thinks she does, and his tone hardens: "Guitars and drums . . . you weren't listening . . . B. Say it, say it into the mic, weak. Say it so all of Miami can hear it. You didn't know what key we was in. Cool." Wendy says "No! Big no!" He badgers her further: "Say it into the mic: I'm weak." It's jokingly insulting and yet clearly insulting. It was a common occurrence. During a later rehearsal at Crosstown Circle warehouse in Eden Prairie—a recording space Prince had set up after the *Purple Rain* tour—the band is rolling through a take of "Data Bank" when Brown Mark stumbles. "Hold up, hold up," Prince says.

"Mark, come on. You're in the wrong key, cousin. No, no, wait! Augh!" The band doesn't wait. Prince is displeased. "What happened to that melody we had? What is . . . We're just gonna groove? We're just gonna groove or what? Well, somebody's got to solo or something. Well, I don't know." When the horns horn in, that exhausts what little patience he has left: "I didn't call the horns. Why y'all gotta play? I don't wanna hear no horns, I just want to hear Lisa. Oh that's dog, that's dog. I didn't call that either. I quit. I'm quitting. Lisa: stop." They don't listen. "Susan," he says, appealing to Susan Rogers, his recording engineer, "fade this shit out. Yeah, I know. Fade it out." She does. "Data Bank" will later resurface on the Time's *Pandemonium*, in a version that has none of the chaos of the Crosstown Circle take and also none of the appeal. The band, missing its marks in rehearsal, challenges authority while also acknowledging it, both defying Prince and also defining him.

✦ ✦ ✦

Prince's September 1998 show at Madison Square Garden had a stronger Vegas vibe than I would have preferred. He started promisingly, opening with "Push It Up" and "Jam of the Year" and covering James Brown ("Talkin' Loud and Saying Nothin'"), but then it was mostly hits, and mostly underwhelming.

But the night wasn't over. At one in the morning, I was standing outside of Tramps—a thousand-capacity nightclub on Twenty-First Street. The doors opened around two thirty, I think, and just after three, Prince and his band strode back onto the stage. The Tramps show kicked off with a loose, long take on "Days of Wild" that folded in various Sly and the Family Stone songs, especially "Thank You (Falettinme Be Mice Elf Agin)," in part because the bassist Larry Graham, who had been a founding member of the Family Stone, was in attendance. Prince continued along those lines with Graham Central Station's "The Jam," followed by the Ohio Players' "Heaven Must Be Like This," Chuck Brown's "That'll Work," and Madhouse's "Asswoop." Every song smoked because every song was on fire. The rapper Doug E. Fresh performed the hip-hop novelty "La Di Da Di" (though no one did the Dougie), and Chaka Khan showed up to sing Steve Winwood's "Higher Love" (she had contributed backup vocals to the original), Aretha Franklin's "Baby I Love You," and two of her own hits with Rufus, "Sweet Thing" and "You Got the Love." Prince was especially compelling on the two Rufus songs: on the former, he spun out jazzy guitar chords with a contemplative calm that was just above resting pulse; on the latter, he built fat stacks of riffs. Though there wasn't a Prince song proper in the whole set, the night was revelatory, as successful as the show I had seen at Tramps a year before, after a show at Jones Beach that I had missed. That time, D'Angelo had shown up and accompanied Prince on "The Ballad of Dorothy Parker," and the touchstone had been the sixties rather than the seventies: the final run of songs included James Brown's "I Got the Feelin'," the Temptations' "The Way You Do the Things You Do," and the Isley Brothers' "Shout."

The Tramps shows were part of the shadow canon of Prince's concerts: the aftershows. When Prince played in your city, you waited around for news. People would start to whisper. Maybe a club in town would unexpectedly cancel their regularly scheduled dance party for a "special event" or book another one with a suspiciously generic name ("Celebration of Music"). While the regular tour stops had to go off as planned, which meant a relatively firm set list to match lighting cues and complex choreography, the aftershows could range across his catalog, and—as Tramps demonstrated—extend into the catalogs of others. Prince fans love to talk about "Sunday songs," contemplative works that were a personal church service. Aftershows, by comparison, were Saturday-night affairs, places for him to air out everything else. (The blues scholar Albert Murray has written about this "Saturday Night Function," where the blues is exorcised and sexuality exercised before spirituality reasserts itself the next morning.)

Every Prince fan has a favorite aftershow. There was the November 1994 date at the Tränenpalast in Berlin, where he delivered stripped-down versions of most of the songs on the overproduced *The Gold Experience*, including "Days of Wild," "Now," and "Shhh." There was the marathon three-hour show at Le New Morning in Paris in 2010, where Prince covered Sly and the Family Stone again, added in the Rolling Stones ("Miss You"), and uncorked rarities like "2045 Radical Man." I nominate the oft-bootlegged July 1988 Camden Palace show, during which the band celebrated Cat Glover's birthday and sculpted an extended groove that threaded through "Forever in My Life," "Strange Relationship," and a cover of "Just My Imagination." And I wish I remembered more of the June 1994 show he played at the opening of Glam Slam East, his nightclub in Miami Beach. My brother and I went, and after only one drink, I was crouched on the ground, head on knees, seeing blue spots in the air. My brother insists to this day that I must have been drugged. I recall only a rubbery cover of Stevie Wonder's "Maybe Your Baby."

Of all the aftershows Prince ever played, only one was ever officially released: *One Nite Alone . . . the Aftershow: It Ain't Over!* Compiled from a set of aftershows over the course of 2002, it was released as part of the One Nite Alone boxed set. It's a strange artifact. Concert recordings make only occasional appearances in the official discography, from "It's Gonna Be a Beautiful Night" on *Sign O' the Times* to "The Ride" on *Crystal Ball*—not to mention, of course, the career-defining second side of *Purple Rain*, which was sweetened and sharpened in the studio. Here, that prowess is on full display. Prince's band delivered an angular take on "2 Nigs United 4 West Compton" that trumped the *Black Album* version; George Clinton showed up to chant along on "We Do This," a song from his second Paisley Park record, *Hey Man, Smell My Finger*; and there was a sustained jam based on "Peach" that incorporated several new ideas about what shape the song's central riff should take. But the real standout was "Joy in Repetition." It had its start, like so many Prince songs, in the summer of 1986, where it was sketched out the day after "I Could Never Take the Place of Your Man." As *Dream Factory* came together and came apart, "Joy in Repetition" bounced around, and the official recorded version didn't surface until *Graffiti Bridge*, three years later. On record, the song opened with a clamor of voices—buried in the mix, there was a reference to "Andre Crabtree III," a vaguely pimp-like character that also turned up in "Lovesexy"—and then Prince came on, speak-singing a portrait of a woman lured by music. Lyrics tumbled out as if they had been hoarded in a drawer that was suddenly pulled open. And then there was the guitar solo, which pooled and rippled and leaped and echoed. In live versions, it could stretch out forever but still keep him tethered, like an astronaut's umbilical line. When he finally stopped playing, the silence was everywhere.

✦ ✦ ✦

When American audiences embraced *Musicology* in 2004, giving Prince his first top-ten album since *The Gold Experience* in 1995, he embraced them back, mounting a grueling Stateside tour: ninety dates in six months, including three-night stands in New York, Chicago, Boston, and Philadelphia, and five nights in Los Angeles. Everyone got to see him again. After that, he shifted his strategy into residencies (one in Las Vegas, one in London) and high-profile one-offs.

Some were higher-profile than the rest. There was Coachella in 2008, where he brought along old friends like Morris Day, who opened the show by duetting on a pair of Time songs, and Sheila E., who helped out on an extended medley of Santana songs. That was the show where Prince famously covered Radiohead's "Creep."

But the pinnacle of late-career Prince performances had come a year earlier, in February 2007, on a rainy evening in Miami sandwiched between the two halves of Super Bowl XLI. The year before, the Rolling Stones had delivered a tight three-song set in Detroit; maybe that sparked his competitive instinct. Whatever the reason, Prince's performance was a consuming fire. It opened with the stomping and clapping of Queen's "We Will Rock You," and then there was a bolt of lightning that illuminated the Prince symbol on the center of the stage. Prince emerged, in a turquoise suit with an orange-sherbet shirt—a nod to the palette of the hometown Dolphins—and a black do-rag, and played "Let's Go Crazy" as dancers complied. "Are you all ready to get nuts tonight?" he asked. "Let me hear you scream!" But what he really meant was "let you hear me scream." Power flowed from his lips and fingertips. A snatch of "1999" shifted immediately into "Baby I'm A Star," accompanied by a marching band down on the field, and midway through Prince stalked to the front lip of the stage, leaned out like a perching bird, and called out an order: "Somebody take my picture of me with all this rain." The meat of the show was a series of thefts: he took other people's songs and took them over. He played "Proud Mary." He played a small portion of "All Along the Watchtower" (the crowd surged at the lyric "princes kept the view"). He played a larger portion of the Foo Fighters' "Best of You" (possibly as payback for their B side cover of "Darling Nikki"). He closed, of course, with "Purple Rain," ripping into the solo from behind a big scrim that made his guitar-wielding, do-rag-sporting silhouette look at once demonic and phallic. In the game, the Indianapolis Colts beat the Chicago Bears 29–17. Not quite a decade later, after Prince's death, the Colts' owner, Jim Irsay, bought Prince's Yellow Cloud guitar at auction.

✦ ✦ ✦

Rejuvenated by *Musicology*, sustained by the string of records that followed, Prince hit the road again between 2010 and 2013: he toured Australia, toured Europe, toured Canada. But the climate had changed again. Newer pop acts were putting on circus shows, heavy on special effects, light on songcraft. Pink's highly regarded 2013 tour incorporated aerial acrobatics and required a chartered 747 and nineteen semitrailers to transport more than four hundred tons of equipment, not to mention eighty crew members. Older acts became oldies acts, often performing single classic albums from beginning to end. Against this backdrop of large-scale artifice, Prince went small and natural. He announced a bare-bones tour, A Piano & a Microphone, which delivered exactly what it promised: Prince sitting down behind a custom purple Yamaha grand piano, playing songs and telling stories.

The tour, originally scheduled for Europe in the winter of 2015 and postponed after the terrorist attack on the Bataclan, instead started in Australia in February of 2016. He returned to North America in March. An April 7 doubleheader at the Fox Theatre in Atlanta was postponed when Prince fell ill—the reason given was the flu—and rescheduled for April 14. He made that date. During the Piano & a Microphone shows, he was alone onstage, but in some ways he was less alone than ever. He had his whole catalog to wander around inside, which meant that he could pull out deep cuts like "Rock and Roll Love Affair" and "Muse 2 the Pharaoh." More familiar songs were, as a matter of necessity, reinterpreted. "I Could Never Take the Place of Your Man" got remade as something both less steely and more ornate, notes flurrying on his fingers. He also had everyone else's catalog, and songs made surprising connections with one another—"Dirty Mind" opened up into Vince Guaraldi's "Linus and Lucy," and "Somewhere Here on Earth" grew out of "Somewhere Over the Rainbow." He had begun work on a memoir, which had put him in a reflective mood, and between songs he told stories: about Minneapolis in the early days, about school, about friends, about family. "My father taught me piano," he said, playing "Chopsticks," adding that his father also taught him that "funk was space." The shows had a memorial feel, which isn't to say funereal, though there were moments that addressed death directly. In Melbourne, before "Little Red Corvette," he paused to reminisce about Vanity, who had died the day before: "Her and I used to love each other deeply. She loved me for the artist I was, I loved her for the artist she was trying to be. She and I would fight. She was very headstrong 'cause she knew she was the finest woman in the world. She never missed an opportunity to tell you that." In Atlanta, he played a moving cover of David Bowie's "Heroes," just months after Bowie's death from cancer. That was in the earlier show of a doubleheader. The late show started at 10:00 p.m. and lasted just over an hour and a half, incorporating old hits like "Dirty Mind," new songs like "Black Muse," unreleased tracks like "Indifference," and covers like Bob Marley's "Waiting in Vain."

The live shows of a dead artist sometimes feel like a cruel trick, and the live shows from just before death are the most cruel. When Prince performed "Little Red Corvette" in Atlanta on the Piano & a Microphone Tour, he played one chord, and the crowd shrieked for thirty seconds, to the point where he had to lift his hands off the keys and wait. Listening to those final shows—

which are among the most straightforward documents of Prince tracing his path through human life—is tough because the life they illustrate is gone. They have to be used philosophically, to help us recognize that what befell him will one day befall us all. He ended the Atlanta show with a medley of "The Beautiful Ones," "Diamonds and Pearls," and "Purple Rain." The final note endured.

14

THE WORK

How He Produced So
Much for So Long

THE B SIDE OF THE "1999" SINGLE WAS "HOW COME U DON'T CALL Me Anymore," a bluesy ballad in which Prince searched for answers regarding a missing ex: "I always thought you'd be by my side / Now you're gone," he sang, and "You know I don't like being alone / Why must you torture me, why you gotta torment me so?" For a decade, it was one of the most coveted off-album Prince songs and a legitimate rarity, until it appeared, in quick succession, on the *The Hits/The B-Sides* package in 1993 and the *Girl 6* soundtrack in 1996. For me, it also became a kind of metaphor for the relationship between artists and fans. In *Being and Nothingness*, Jean-Paul Sartre proposed that absence was not simply the state of being missing but the state of being missing meaningfully. "I shall not say that Aga-Khan or the Sultan of Morocco is absent from this apartment," he wrote, "but I say that Pierre, who usually lives here, is absent for a quarter of an hour."

Pierre's absence is a nothingness, a not-being-there not just in fact (many things are not technically present in the place) but in consciousness. During the eighties and nineties, I often experienced this nothingness with regard to artists I depended upon. It might have been Lou Reed. It might have been Public Enemy. It might have been Aretha Franklin or Paul Simon or Living Colour or Liz Phair. When a certain amount of time had passed without a new album, I became irritable without knowing why. I couldn't read articles about them. Their old albums became irritants; I saw only the space where the new album was not. How come they didn't call me anymore?

With Prince, I never needed to wait long. He made records like clockwork, once a year, with rare exceptions. He missed 1983, but that was on the heels of a double album, and then he put out *Purple Rain*. He took 2005 off after releasing three records in 2004 (though two were collections of singles he had distributed through the NPG Music Club), and he was scarce for a stretch between 2010 and 2014, but he resurfaced with four records in two years: *PlectrumElectrum*, *Art Official Age*, and the two volumes of the *HITnRUN* series. The totals—more than forty officially released studio records, including two double albums, one triple album, and one quadruple album—outpaced other rock stars who came onto the scene twenty years before him. Bob Dylan, whose debut was released in 1961, had released thirty-five studio albums as of 2015. Stevie Wonder, who started as a twelve-year-old in 1962, had released thirty. Neil Young was the closest competition, with thirty-six.*

---

* Of course, there were Roger Maris–like exceptions. Frank Zappa, Prince's old PMRC comrade-in-arms, put out upwards of sixty records during his lifetime, and Jandek, the Houston-based avant–folk singer whose career has been shrouded in mystery, has put out more than seventy to date. Both of those tallies depended upon sustained periods of self-release and large numbers of live sets.

✦ ✦ ✦

How did Prince make so much music? For starters, hard labor. He may have written about sex, God, and race, but he also wrote about work ("Let's Work," "The Work, Pt. 1"), and when he did, he was writing what he knew. Owen Husney described the teenage Prince as "exhibiting the work ethic of a CEO of a Fortune 500 company." Professional athletes are an instructive comparison. In "Style," Prince sang the praises of "the face you make on a Michael Jordan dunk"; Jordan, of course, was legendary not only for his talent but for how hard he kept on himself. (His closest heir in this regard was Kobe Bryant; the NBA star Chris Bosh related a story about playing on the 2012 Olympic team and going to breakfast early the first morning. Bryant arrived late: "And Kobe comes in with ice on his knees and with his trainers and stuff," Bosh said. "He's got sweat drenched through his workout gear. And I'm like, 'It's eight o'clock in the morning, man. Where in the hell is he coming from?' ") But business and athletic analogues only explained part of the process. Producing creatively at a high rate and a high level, year after year, requires a special mental makeup.

Mihály Csíkszentmihályi was born in Hungary in 1934 and grew up in a world torn apart by the Second World War. After the cease-fire, he lived in the war's shadow; he and his family were held in an Italian prison camp until the Italian government could ascertain whether or not they were Fascists. In the camp, Csíkszentmihályi took solace in chess, which produced a mental state that was hard for him to describe: relaxation, in a sense, but more captivating. As he grew up, he noticed similarities between that sensation and the feeling produced by other activities. Rock climbing struck him as particularly comparable; on the mountain, he entered a state of heightened concentration and intense focus, a pleasurable absorption in the task.

Csíkszentmihályi became a psychologist, and in his professional life he began to study this state in a more organized fashion. He studied it in painters. He studied it in athletes. He studied it (or, just as often, its absence) in teens. And finally, he named it: flow. Flow was the umami of mental phenomena: many people had experienced it, but no one had taken the trouble to define and describe it. Csíkszentmihályi not only defined and described but also diagrammed it. In 1987, he and two colleagues published a flowchart (all puns intended) that mapped mental states on two axes, skill level and challenge. Flow occupied the prime spot, in the top right quadrant of the chart, high in both categories. Its opposite was apathy, which was at the bottom left, flanked by worry and boredom.

According to Csíkszentmihályi, flow required at least two ingredients: a challenge appropriate to the subject's skill level (a challenge that was too difficult would produce anxiety; one that was too easy would produce boredom), and a task of sufficient complexity (whether artistic, scientific, or physical). Simply walking a far distance would not engage the mind or extend its sense of itself. "The best moments in our lives are not the passive, receptive, relaxing times," he wrote, but rather those in which "a person's body or mind is stretched to its limits in a voluntary effort to accomplish something difficult and worthwhile."

Will Henshall was a founding songwriter and guitarist for Londonbeat, a British band that hit the charts in 1990 with the dance-pop love song "I've Been Thinking About You." In 2001 he founded Focus@Will, a company that built on the research of Csíkszentmihályi and others to explore the link between music and productivity. "It starts with the way your brain is built," Henshall told me. "And when we think of the way your brain is built, at least for our purposes, we think of the limbic system." The limbic system, a set of structures just beneath the cerebrum, controls some of our basic circuitry, including the fight-or-flight instinct. "Your brain is always looking out for your safety," Henshall explained, "and that process is driven by your ears. When you're doing a cave painting, you need to know what's there and what's not there. You need to know when the environment changes. Your limbic system, through your ears, is highly tuned for two or three things. One of the things is a change in the sound. If everything goes quiet, that means a large predator may be nearby. You notice the quiet."

Henshall devoted special attention to the limits of flow. Most research had found that the maximum length of a flow state was twenty to thirty minutes before the limbic system intervened. "It's great to be in a flow state, whether you're playing golf or riding a motorcycle or writing," he said. "You can do your best work there. But it's also dangerous because you are distracted from your surroundings. You're vulnerable to a predator. Your brain knows that, and the limbic system is always fighting to go back online. We wondered what would happen if we managed the limbic fight-or-flight response by controlling the sound field around people." Henshall set about designing music that would lengthen flow states. Some people, he said, had learned to extend flow on their own—they found their way to music that made them more productive, whether Mozart or Miles—but he believed that meticulously engineered sonic environments could extend flow states to as long as a hundred minutes.

Henshall had agreed to speak with me about the general dynamics of flow states, but as we talked, I started to wonder about Prince and his own capacity for concentration and creative production. I kept coming back to a trio of anecdotes. The first was something I had read about Prince as a child: When he took music lessons, he wouldn't concentrate on scales or chords. Rather, he would lose himself in playing original compositions—

not songs, exactly, but ideas. I was thinking also of the way he used to rehearse his bands, how he would start them on a groove and keep them there for five minutes, ten minutes, fifteen, while he moved from guitar to piano, adding in extra melodic and harmonic flourishes. What was that if not a flow state? The third story was something that Questlove had told me: When he would participate in jam sessions at Paisley Park, Prince would call out a song—say, the Ohio Players' "I Want to Be Free," play the perfect keyboard or guitar part for the intro, and then peter out as the first verse approached. "It was like he didn't know the lyrics," Questlove said. "I asked him how that was possible and he just shrugged. It was like those parts of the songs weren't on his radar at the moment." He was lost in his own thoughts of his own music.

Long before Csíkszentmihályi, long before Henshall, musicians already had phrases to describe getting enjoyably lost in the task at hand: they were "in the groove" or "in the pocket." But Prince possessed a special ability to stay there—not just during a lesson or a rehearsal but when he was eating lunch, or driving his car, or going to sleep, or (more likely) not going to sleep. What if he had developed, over the years, the ability to generate his own musically-aided flow state? What if, while ordinary people either made do with their natural twenty minutes or stretched it out with the aid of music, Prince could make music in his head that allowed him to make more music in his head? It would be a virtuous cycle, the closest thing imaginable to a perpetual-motion machine. But even this theory of an internally generated flow state offers only a partial account of Prince's prolific pop production. Csíkszentmihályi spent his early years interviewing and observing painters, whose relatively simple creative infrastructure—they needed only a canvas, brush, and paints—made them ideal subjects. But the process of creating a pop song

is significantly less autonomous. Pop musicians need collabora-
tors. If they are songwriters, they need singers. If they are singers,
they need musicians. If they are musicians, they need arrangers. If
they are arrangers, they need producers. Prince addressed that
problem by participating in all these processes at once. He could
pass from task to task, first programming a rhythm track, then
adding bass, then keyboards, all the while remaining in a flow
state. In fact, this was exactly what he did in his first audition at
Warner Bros. in 1977, and what he kept doing for years. He built a
rolling process for challenging his mind: challenge here, move
there, challenge there.

He also insisted on the importance of his own creative process,
sometimes ruthlessly. It wasn't just that it was his priority; it had to
be *everyone's* priority. In an interview with the Minneapolis *Star
Tribune* in 2004, the recording engineer Chuck Zwicky, who
worked with Prince in the late eighties and early nineties, remembered how single-minded he could be:

> You were given a pager, and he seemed to have an
> uncanny sense of when to call at the worst time. Right
> when the meal would arrive at a restaurant, the pager
> would go off. Crawl into bed with your girlfriend, the
> pager would go off. You'd get called in at very odd hours,
> set up and wait. Sometimes he'd show up, and sometimes
> he wouldn't.

This was at least partly the arrogance and narcissism of celebrity;
Elvis Presley, late in his life, believed that he could move clouds
and bushes with the power of his mind. But it was also partly
Prince's understanding that he had perfectly tuned his process
for high creative yield. He had a good thing going, and he didn't
want to do anything to disrupt it.

A continual flow state wasn't an unqualified good. Flow state brought with it certain risks, and not just the danger that your limbic system, lulled by creative satisfaction, might fail to notice an approaching bear. The more that Csíkszentmihályi studied flow state, the more he realized that it produced such a powerful sense of satisfaction that the pursuit of it could come to be an addiction. Those who refined their relationship to flow state— who learned how to enter it more efficiently, to prolong it more successfully, to repel distractions and disruptions—began to reject all activities that didn't bring them closer to it. Their lives became consumed with a small set of activities because those were the activities most likely to produce flow state. George Clinton, who recorded at Paisley Park in the early nineties, was one of many people who described Prince in terms of his single-minded dedication to working on music, to the point where he hardly seemed to do anything else.

Csíkszentmihályi did other work that's pertinent to Prince, including research that looked into how "creative individuals escape rigid gender stereotyping" by demonstrating aspects of both genders in their thinking. And while there's no evidence that he ever studied Prince, Prince may have studied Csíkszent- mihályi. In 1989, the *New York Times* published a lengthy profile of Csíkszentmihályi, summarizing his thought to date and not- ing that the following year, HarperCollins would publish a book on flow "for the lay person." The next September, a few weeks after the release of *Graffiti Bridge*, Prince laid down basic tracks for a new song. Heavily influenced by hip-hop, featuring a full verse performed by Tony M., it reasserted Prince's dedication to making music despite various distractions that included tabloid journalists ("Is it really important where I take my naps?") and ignorant fans ("Another fool don't know what she's talkin' about"). The name of the song? "The Flow."

+ + +

Another reason for Prince's prodigious output was that not every new song was entirely new. George Clinton, late in his career, made new music by revisiting old tracks, both released and unreleased, from the various bands in the P-Funk orbit. He pulled out a bass line from a hit or found a never-used keyboard figure and cultivated it until another song blossomed. To describe the process, Clinton used a drug metaphor, of course—he called these leavings "seeds and stems," no longer useful for smoking but useful for making new things to smoke.

Prince's obsessive dedication to the studio meant that he saved all his seeds and stems—and not only saved but cataloged them, kept them at hand, and planted them in fertile soil. Sometimes what he saved was rhythmic: the "Housequake" drums were recycled many times; the beat of "Erotic City" resurfaced in "1+1+1 Is 3" and elsewhere. Sometimes it was melodic: "Manic Monday" echoed "1999," and "Black Sweat" echoed "Kiss." Snippets might pop back up without warning: a little keyboard squiggle in "Glam Slam" could be traced back to "Automatic." And sometimes there was an elaborate family tree around a song. "Gett Off" was assembled from earlier songs like "Glam Slam '91" and "Get Off" (which itself was a spin-off of "New Power Generation" and a close cousin of "Loveleft, Loveright" and "The Lubricated Lady"); "Gett Off," in turn, spawned a set of songs like "Gangster Glam" and "Violet the Organ Grinder," which share so much with "Gett Off" that some people consider them remixes rather than independent compositions. That practice (reuse, recycle, renew) was most prominent during the period stretching from *Lovesexy* to *Diamonds and Pearls*, during which Prince's confidence in his own material was almost limitless: Why throw something away when it had emerged from a crucible of genius? This networked set of relationships sustained and enlarged itself. The more connections he made, the more connections he could make.

When I started working on this book, I promised myself that I would listen only to Prince's music. I had enough to last me months. But about six weeks in, the Prince-only diet started to feel claustrophobic and maybe even a little ghoulish. I had been reading about Paul Simon's new album, *Stranger to Stranger*, and I debated whether or not the Simon album would be my first non-Prince record. Would it be it a betrayal? Was it a necessary depressurization? While I was mulling it over, Simon taped an episode of *Austin City Limits*, and when I saw that he had come onstage in a satiny purple jacket, I felt authorized to make the leap. The lead-off track of *Stranger to Stranger*, "The Werewolf," was about death, which was figured as a movie monster that comes for us all, no matter our station in life, no matter our privilege or our talents. That had resonance. Its title was inspired by the fact that Simon was experimenting with a new instrument, a single-stringed drone lute called a gopichand or ektara, and, slowed down, it sounded like the English phrase "the werewolf." That sent me down a spiral of resignation about the hairy unpredictability of life—in Simon's song, the tenuousness of existence was revealed as simultaneously beautiful, horrible, and hilarious, and for a moment, that took some of the sting out of Prince's death. But it also sent me up a spiral of understanding regarding the ways in which artists were the ultimate conservationists. Hear an unfamiliar sound? Turn it into a title. Write a song around it. Fend off death, or even the idea of death, by bringing life out of chaos. Evade dissipation with rebirth. The idea was even stronger elsewhere on *Stranger to Stranger*. In the liner notes, Simon explained that specific sonic elements recurred from song to song: "I've re-used drum tracks several times from within the album to keep a sense of continuity of sound," he wrote, "and also because they still groove in different contexts." The final song on the record was the lovely "Insomniac's Lullaby," another echo. In the wake of Prince's death, his brother-in-law Maurice Phillips told the press that Prince had worked for a week straight, never sleeping. "Oh Lord," Simon sang, "don't keep me up all night / with questions I can't understand / While I wrestle my fears / the sound in my ears / is the music that's sweeping the land."

I went back to Prince, where I let my computer pick a random song. It picked "Future Baby Mama," a romantic ballad from the 2007 album *Planet Earth*. It sounded generically familiar: moody melody, feathery falsetto. But then, just like that, the familiarity was specific and conspicuous. In the bridge, Prince swiped the melody of "Thieves in the Temple" and, along with it, sang lyrics that seemed to acknowledge the debt ("Yeah, I know you might be fine but I've seen it all before"). If you steal from your own songs, are you actually stealing at all, or just grooving in a different context?

✦ ✦ ✦

People had been buzzing about the vault since the mid-eighties. Prince was putting out so many songs—on albums, on B sides, on maxi-singles. But there were other songs he wasn't putting out at all. Everyone had an estimate of how many songs there actually were. Brent Fischer—the son of the late Prince arranger Clare Fischer—estimated that for every released collaboration between his father and Prince, there were two dozen more songs that never came to light.

Of course, just because a song wasn't officially released didn't mean that it didn't find its way into the light. Much of the fun of being a Prince fan, especially in the eighties, was tracking down unreleased music. There was no Internet back then and consequently no digital downloading; locating those songs was a far more arduous process that involved traveling into cities, poring over racks of bootleg CDs and cassettes, sometimes writing letters to other fans in other cities and waiting to see if a cassette might show up in your mailbox. Once you had the songs in hand, once you had listened to "Sexual Suicide" or "Data Bank," it then became your responsibility to turn around and Johnny Appleseed them to someone else.

In the digital era, collecting and redistributing Prince rarities changed tremendously. The music was stripped of its physicality and idiosyncrasy: there were no more cassette boxes with amateurish drawings of Prince anymore; there were only folders filled with file names. They could be obtained from anywhere in the world, immediately, with the click of a mouse. Even worse, as the Internet gradually destroyed secrecy, the walls of the vault became transparent. Fan sites compiled lists of all the unreleased songs, sometimes with annotation—precise recording dates, personnel. These were unofficial inventories, of course, best guesses based on leaks and sleuthing. But whether they were accurate or not, whether they were comprehensive or not, they still disrupted the idea of the vault, which was to let fans think that Prince had stockpiled an unthinkable amount of content. Each individual song may or may not have been worthwhile on its own, but the overall concept of a vast storehouse of unheard (and maybe never-to-be-heard) music produced a magical aura. This aura, diminished by the Internet, dissipated entirely when Prince died. Newspapers ran lists of what the vault contained, and implicit in those lists was the knowledge that the contents were now definitively frozen.

Talk then turned to the disposition of the unreleased material. Would the contents of the vault be used as the basis for a Prince-only streaming service? Would the songs be signed over to a record label, maybe even Warner Bros., so that the milking could begin? One headline, trying for a note of admiration, instead struck one of alarm: "What's Left in the Vault Could Make for One Album a Year for a Century!" There was also a thuddingly literal dimension to the proceedings. For years, people assumed that the vault was only a figure of speech. But as it turned out, it was an actual secured location on the grounds of Paisley Park, built at the same time as the original compound and modeled after a bank vault, right down to the oversize round combination wheel—though traditional combination wheels aren't amoebic purple splotches. "He wanted a place to keep his master recordings," said Bret Thoeny of California's BOTO Design, the firm that designed the original complex in the mid-eighties. "But at the time it was very important to keep this a secret." After Prince's death, Bremer Bank, given control of the estate, drilled into the room. It seemed like a shockingly physical breach. And soon enough, product followed. Warner Bros. and NPG Records announced that they were partnering on two new records: a forty-track greatest-hits collection, *4Ever*, that would include the early-eighties rarity "Moonbeam Levels," and the long-awaited deluxe reissue of *Purple Rain*. But the math had reversed, and these were now subtractions.

✦ ✦ ✦

The vault was an account of both vast creativity and a powerful desire to conceal, and also an argument about the relationship between creativity and concealment. Many people believe that secrets are experienced as psychological (and even physical) pain. The young husband living a double life as a gay man, hiding that information from his wife and family, may experience anxiety. He may sleep fitfully; he may eat poorly. We tend to believe that coming out—bringing our secrets into a visible space—will increase our mental health. But exposing everything may be just as problematic, at least as far as creativity is concerned. Marcel Proust held that those hidden corners were the engine of art. "Real books," he wrote, "should be the offspring not of daylight and casual talk, but of darkness and silence." Under this theory, an artist needs a steady supply of secrets to replenish creative energies. It's worth thinking about, not only with regard to the vault but with regard to the rest of Prince's life. After his death, tabloids devoted themselves to unearthing and exposing what Prince had not, in life, been able to admit. The headlines were all about bringing these secrets into the light: "Prince: His Hidden Life," "How Prince Kept His Pain and Addiction Secret from Those Closest to Him." As that wave of coverage receded, what was left on the shore?

Section Four

MEMORY

15

SUCH A SHAME
OUR FRIENDSHIP
HAD TO END

SEPTEMBER 30, 2014 WAS A TUESDAY, AND FOR PRINCE, IT WAS A BUSY Tuesday. He released two new albums—*PlectrumElectrum*, recorded with his young all-female band 3RDEYEGIRL, and *Art Official Age*, a solo project—and celebrated with a concert at Paisley Park that included a rare performance of "What's My Name." Kendrick Lamar showed up to rap a verse. Prince also took to Facebook for an extended question-and-answer session with fans. The Q&A lasted three hours, in the sense that Prince started three hours late. Even then, he responded to only one question: "Greetings, my dear Brother . . . Please address the importance of ALL music being tuned to 432hz sound frequencies??? Thanks in advance!!! Warmest regards, Emanuel . . ."

Emanuel was referring to a New Age acoustical theory which held that the universal standard of tuning music to 440 hertz was inconsistent with human ears. A slightly shorter frequency, 432 hertz, was considered preferable. Prince subscribed to this theory, which he indicated by singling out Emanuel's question. He didn't really answer, except to name one of the songs from *Art Official Age*, "The Gold Standard," and link to an article that connected 432 hertz to the harmony of the universe itself:

> It is said that 432 Hz vibrates with the universe's golden mean PHI and unifies the properties of light, time, space, matter, gravity and magnetism with biology, the DNA code, and consciousness. When our atoms and DNA start to resonate in harmony with the spiralling pattern of nature, our sense of connection to nature is said to be magnified.

Harmony was the order of the day. One of Prince's two new records, *Plectrumelectrum*, was an energetic trifle, an exercise in playing off the three young women in his band. But *Art Official Age* was something else entirely. For the first time in his career, Prince had a coproducer: Joshua Welton, a young musician who was married to the 3RDEYEGIRL drummer Hannah Ford Welton. Welton had a definite aesthetic, and at first it seemed unfortunate. The opening track, "Art Official Cage," was a clamor of electronic dance music clichés and Europop propping up a grim assessment of modern society in which Prince declared his determination to "free [his] mind from this art official cage."

It was a mess, provocative but not remotely successful. The rest of the album, however, represented Prince's most coherent and satisfying work in more than a decade. *Art Official Age* didn't sound quite like anything Prince had made before—its gelatinous, futuristic R&B made extensive use of straightforwardly beautiful melodies, synthesized strings, and some of the most passionate singing Prince had ever done. More to the point, it pursued the argument of its opening track across its entire fifty-three minutes, turning what seemed like a vague philippic into a sustained discourse on sex, self, love, lust, loneliness, and life itself. It was, after decades of thesis and antithesis, a synthesis.

At first, the record mostly seemed like a pointed attack on the seductive malevolence of technology. "Clouds," the second track, set out the case. In the past, clouds had represented romantic dreaminess (in "Raspberry Beret," in which "something 'bout the clouds and her mixed") or whimsy (in "Starfish and Coffee," in which breakfast included "butterscotch clouds"). Here, though, when Prince sang "We don't need no clouds," he was both warning against fuzzy thinking and making a specific argument regarding the state of music distribution in the twenty-first century. All physical traces of music, as Prince knew, were disappearing as music was digitized and sucked up into distant servers. This troubled him greatly; he had spent years warning that streaming services would cripple music both financially and creatively. "Clouds" went after social media, too, lamenting the way it transformed ordinary citizens into social-media performers. (One lyric, "When life's a stage in this brand-new age / How do we engage?" could have been a précis of *Black Mirror*, the British television series that probed the dystopian aspects of technology.) As an antidote, the song proposed a return to the world of actual physical contact: "You should never underestimate the power of a kiss on the neck," Prince sang. The final stretch dissolved into a sci-fi monologue delivered by the British folk singer Lianne La Havas in which she notified Prince (she called him "Mr. Nelson," the most adult name available) that he had been in a state of suspended animation characterized by an inability to forge intimate bonds with others. The next track, the breathtakingly intense ballad "Breakdown," illustrated the consequence of this failure. Prince lamented that he had chosen money and fame over human connection. "Give me back the time," he sang in the song's most poignant, tortured lyric, "you can keep the memories."

The middle of the record contained a few moments that slipped back into pro forma dance-funk—"The Gold Standard" boasted about the benefits of real music in a clenched, Morris Day–style voice—but even those had an annealing power, heating things rapidly before they cooled back down into a stronger state. "U Know," built on a stuttering sample of the singer Mila J's "Blinded," alternated wordy half-rapped verses with an irresistibly seductive chorus. "Breakfast Can Wait" (whose single used a picture of Dave Chappelle dressed as Prince) was a sparkly little jewel about romance in the morning. And "This Could Be Us" had the wittiest and most barbed backstory of any song on the record. In the early months of 2014, one of the most popular online phenomena was the "This Could Be Us but You Playin'" meme, which reproduced pictures of couples in romantic situations. The idea was that one of the partner's transgressions (the playin') was preventing the couple from enjoying the romantic bliss represented in the photo. The meme spread and mutated. Sometimes the photos showed couples in more awkward moments. Sometimes they didn't even show people: popular #ThisCouldBeUs images included two puppies sleeping next to empty vodka bottles and a rabbit with a pancake on its head. Meme creators also plundered pop culture for pictures, and that's how someone came to tweet out a photo of Prince and Apollonia riding a motorcycle in full *Purple Rain* regalia. Much as he had with Jesse Jackson's *Shockadelica* album title, Prince took it up as a challenge and crafted a song by that title. The lyrics self-consciously invoked Prince's own past—he mentioned the color purple and doves—and didn't skimp on sex either. Since becoming a Jehovah's Witness, he had generally avoided explicit lyrics, but backup vocals, buried in the mix, showed off a still-dirty mind. "Let me lick your kitty clean," he sang, "and after that, you can put me on your back." The song also suggested Prince was once again addressing his relationship with his audience and lamenting the way that technology had come between them.

None of that, though, was sufficient preparation for the home-stretch of *Art Official Age*, which was where Prince stopped worrying about the future or the past and truly inhabited the present. "What It Feels Like," a duet with the Cameroonian-American singer Andy Allo, used the biblical figures of David and Saul to discuss the degeneration of a romantic relationship, and "Way Back Home" was a self-portrait painted in the strang-est and most accurate colors imaginable, a melancholy mix of confession and boast in which Prince copped to the fact that he felt out of place, out of sorts, pushed forward at times by desper-ation but "born alive" in a world where most people were "born dead." The capper was "Time," another duet with Allo that spent seven minutes exploring the fragility of love and the loneliness of the road. For "Time," Prince brought the tempo way down, focused on the nuances of his melodies, incorporated motifs from earlier songs on the album, and added a steady supply of surpris-ing touches. The superbly funky, if subdued, horn outro sounded as if Sly Stone came by Paisley Park, dozed off, and started talking to himself in his sleep—while Prince taped the whole thing.

Throughout *Art Official Age*, Prince was, finally, fully and only human. On "Breakfast Can Wait," he begged his lover not to "leave a black man in this state," explicitly identifying him-self with two categories he had not always straightforwardly embraced. And what was that state? The state of being in your fif-ties, grappling with loneliness, aging, self-doubt, a shifting cul-tural landscape, and a still-problematic understanding of the relationship between love and sex. The closing track, "Affirma-tion III," trotted out La Havas one last time. "How are you doing today, Mr. Nelson?" she said. "As you can see, we are now communicating telepathically, which makes things move so much faster here." The transformation was complete: technology was no longer an impediment; the limits of the body were no longer a source of anxiety. The music reprised "Way Back Home," emphasizing the clipped, angelic backing chorus. And then Le Havas delivered closing remarks:

> You've probably felt that in your former life, you were separate from not only others, but even yourself. Now you can see that was never the case. You are actually everything and anything that you can think of. All of it is you.

This was a revelation—not the capital-R Revelation in which the future is shown to a saint, but the lowercase-r revelation in which the present is shown to a Prince. For decades, Prince was driven by the paradox of internal contradiction. He trafficked in the faith that mysterious forces—creative, sexual, divine—could turn division into dualism and in the fear that they could not. The question both bedeviled him and spurred him to artistic heights. Even when he devised a series of personae to address those issues—New Wave–inflected provocateur, motorcycle-riding rock god, psychedelic introvert, pervert, seeker—those central problems, separation from others and separation from the self, remained. At some point, his creative strategies only intensified the disconnection. These guises were art, but they were also artifice, and over time they imprisoned him: as the pun of the album title suggested, it wasn't just the society that created the cage around the individual, but the official art, made for labels, sent to market. On *Art Official Age*, officially coproduced for the first time, often placed in duet settings, he seemed finally to have loosened his hold on ego and to have located himself. New directions in music, new directions in identity: Miles Davis would have been proud.

✦ ✦ ✦

And then, after waking, sleep. On April 15, 2016, Prince's private jet was forced to land in Chicago, supposedly to treat a lingering flu. Three days later, Prince was up and around again, reportedly on the mend. Three days after that, he was dead.

Within hours, rumors began to circulate that Prince was a drug user, and maybe a drug addict, that the emergency landing had in fact been the result of an overdose, and that paramedics had revived Prince by administering a "save shot" of the opiate antidote Narcan. A friend of mine who used to live in Minneapolis heard that a prominent local rehab counselor was contacted on April 20 regarding a high-profile client who wanted to enter treatment. "This will require absolute secrecy," the counselor was told. The next day, he was sent a follow-up message that his services were no longer needed. In the first week of June, the Midwest Medical Examiner's Office released an autopsy report that determined that Prince had died from an accidental overdose of Fentanyl, a synthetic opioid a hundred times more powerful than morphine.

Evidence mounted. Sheila E. revealed that Prince had been suffering from chronic pain, the result of years of splits and jumps. Records showed that he had visited a Walgreens near Paisley Park four times in the week before his death. And then, at the end of August, a further investigation revealed that pills found in Paisley Park labeled as prescription painkillers in fact contained Fentanyl. It didn't seem real, any of it. For years, Prince had preached clean living and even written songs that argued that the power of drugs could not approach that of music or faith.

There was "Purple Music," for starters ("Don't need no reefer, don't need cocaine / Purple music does the same to my brain"), and "Cindy C" ("Music is the key to set yourself free / from depression, drugs, and increasing poverty"), and "Musicology" ("Minor keys and drugs / don't make a roller-skate jam"), and "Sign O' the Times" ("In September my cousin tried reefer for the very first time / Now he's doing horse; it's June"). The songs had the ring of truth, which meant that anything that contradicted them was suspect. Facts are stubborn things, but fans are even more stubborn.

Reality settled. Or rather, I settled for reality. Gutted, dazed, I went to "My Little Pill," an unreleased song from the mid-nineties in which Prince, over a descending piano line, painted a portrait of a woman in search of pharmaceutical assistance:

> *Every time I pop my little pill*
> *A pixie does my laundry and the universe, my will*
> *All my cares and troubles dive right off my windowsill*
> *Every time I pop my little pill*

The song was written in the early nineties, for the James L. Brooks movie *I'll Do Anything*, during the period when Prince's deteriorating relationship with Warner Bros. forced him to seek out alternative markets for his music. Brooks developed the project as a musical comedy in which new songs by Carole King, Sinéad O'Connor, and Prince would be performed by the cast. Prince contributed four compositions, but when the movie tested poorly as a musical, Brooks cut out all the songs and retooled it as a conventional comedy. "My Little Pill" finally appeared on *The Vault: Old Friends 4 Sale*. The song's history is more than an extended liner note. It's a cautionary tale about control in the narrow artistic sense—a song cut from a movie in violation of the director's original vision that was then released on an album in violation of the artist's original vision—and also in the broad thematic sense. The song was written from a female perspective, but it describes Prince as well. He hired house staff and assistants to take care of mundane tasks so that he could focus on his creative work, which was so prodigious that it seemed like it might change the world. A pixie did his laundry and the universe, his will.

✦✦✦

Prince rarely made explicit mention of death in his song titles. When he did, he addressed the subject glibly ("Dead on It," in which he insisted that "the only good rapper is one who's dead . . . on it") or defiantly ("Dig U Better Dead," in which he pushed back against Warner Bros. for forcing him to temporarily abandon his birth name). Both of those felt considerably off the mark in the weeks after his own passing.

The main song that sprung to mind, for me and for everyone else, was "Sometimes It Snows in April." In a slightly different form, with orchestration added by Clare Fischer, the song served as the love theme to *Under the Cherry Moon*, or at least the costs-of-love theme. Prince's character, Christopher Tracy, attempts to elope with his girlfriend, but her powerful father instructs the police to shoot him dead. The first verse remembers Christopher in the moments just following the shooting, when he died "after a long-fought civil war" and went to an afterlife where he was "a whole lot better off than the fools he left here." As a metaphor for Prince's own death, this was a little bit on the nose (April, a long-fought civil war). There were other verses: in the second, the parallels between Christopher and Christ came to the fore ("Springtime only reminds me of Tracy's tears / Always cry for love, never cry for pain"); in the third, Prince imagined his alter ego in the afterlife ("I often dream of heaven and I know that

Tracy's there"). But the first verse loomed large. It was the only one Prince performed when he played the song live on the *One Nite Alone . . .* record. In the end, I couldn't get the song to solace me. It came off as a taunt, especially when I learned that it was recorded on April 21, 1985, exactly thirty-one years before Prince's death. Instead I listened to a strange, moody outtake called "2020," originally slated for *Emancipation*. In the song, Prince describes a futuristic Utopia—significantly less futuristic now than when he recorded the song in 1995—as a place of "peace and happy people" where the "walls between us soon all disappear." In a turbulent political year, that lyric hit hard. Peace and happy people seemed further away than ever. But what hit harder was the realization that Prince wouldn't even make it to 2020 to experience either his prophecy or, more likely, ordinary human disappointment.

✦ ✦ ✦

In the wake of Prince's death, other artists remembered him the best way they could, which meant playing his songs. Mostly, that meant "Purple Rain." Bruce Springsteen played it at Barclays Center in Brooklyn. Beyoncé let it run over the PA system at Marlins Park in Miami during a costume change. Stevie Wonder sang it through a megaphone at the New Orleans Jazz Fest. The cast of *The Color Purple* on Broadway performed it onstage. Dwight Yoakam, in the middle of recording a bluegrass album, added a cover version as a final track. Others opted for "Nothing Compares 2 U," especially country acts like Chris Stapleton and Lady Antebellum, though Madonna also performed it at the *Billboard* Music Awards. The cast of *Hamilton* went a third way, with "Let's Go Crazy," as did Paul McCartney, on tour in Minneapolis. (As always, McCartney's accompanying remarks sounded like pained small talk: "Prince, Minneapolis; Minneapolis, Prince. It goes together.")

Not every tribute was musical. Helen Mirren sported a Prince glyph tattoo during a White House visit. *Last Week Tonight with John Oliver* memorialized Prince in its witty opening-credit graphics, with the faux-Latin caption "Dovus Cryum." Albert Brooks, Prince's old *I'll Do Anything* colleague, tweeted a reminiscence: "Met Prince once. He was sitting elevated with literally 15 people at his feet. I said, 'Which one is Prince?' No laughs." And the hip-hop star Drake—Larry Graham's nephew—posted a photo that purported to show Prince in a live-action version of "When You Were Mine," naked beneath two naked young women. Some fans found it disrespectful, others triumphant.

Prince was the subject of loving tributes, and then he was a source of beloved objects. His Yellow Cloud guitar was sold to Indianapolis Colts owner Jim Irsay at auction for $168,000. The *Purple Rain* jacket and shirt went to an anonymous bidder for $192,000. Another bidder paid fourteen thousand dollars for a letter from Paul McCartney to Prince requesting money for a Liverpool performing arts school. The selling off of memorabilia was at once an act of devotion and a raiding of the tomb. But there were moments of quiet dignity, too. Three days before Prince's death, a woman named Heather Hofmeister saw Prince on a local bike path. Hofmeister had lived in Minneapolis for more than a decade but had never seen Prince in person; when she texted her husband to tell him, he encouraged her to take a photo. She did, and posted one of them to her Facebook page. A few days later, after his death, calls began to stream in from tabloids looking to buy the other images. She released the photos without taking payment. "I am not interested in profiting off someone's death, especially someone I have admired my entire life," she said.

"I just can't do it." Her photos served as a reminder of how difficult ordinary pleasures were for a celebrity like Prince, and how much he treasured them. "He looked so free and happy," she told *Entertainment Tonight*. "The wind was blowing through his hair. He just looked like he had no care in the world, and I just loved that."

Some fans took solace in conspiracy theories. There was no shortage of them; they mushroomed in the dank soil of the Internet. "Sometimes It Snows in April" wasn't the only prophetic song, apparently. Prince had died in an elevator, and he had written about elevators in "Let's Go Crazy." Prince had died at fifty-seven, and he had mentioned the number in "Positivity," in reference to the kind of gun that the devil would use to kill him. Prince had died on April 21, and he had released an album titled *3121*, and $3+1$ equaled 4, and April was the fourth month. A woman sitting near me in a Brooklyn coffee shop went on at length: "They cremated him. Cremated! They don't do that unless they're trying to hide something. I won't believe it until I see a body in the ground. There's a very real chance he's coming back." She was turned away from me, but I could see the face of her companion, and he was pained—maybe for Prince, maybe for her. I thought of an interview Prince did in the late nineties with Mel B. of the Spice Girls. The subject of birthdays came up, and Prince confessed that he didn't like to celebrate them, because they were the result of our fallen state. "We came here not knowing we were going to die," he said. "Somebody told us that. I'll celebrate the day I die." This stopped Mel B. for a second. "Because you're going to move on to the next path in life?" she said. Prince gave her a thumbs-up. "Yes," he said. Wouldn't that be cool?

✦ ✦ ✦

In 2009, after an uncharacteristically fallow period, Prince announced a triple album. The announcement included a little smoke and at least one mirror—the third record of the set was the debut by a protégée named Bria Valente, and while Prince wrote and played all of her songs, they never rose above undistinguished soul. That still left a solid double album. The first album of the package was *Lotusflower*, stylized, leetlike, as *Lotusflow3r*. It was composed primarily of ballads and midtempo musings, including the slinky "Wall of Berlin" and the preachy "$." There was no title track, exactly, but rather a two-part lotus-themed composition that served as the album's intro and outro. The lotus, of course, is a symbolically freighted plant. In Homer's *Odyssey*, Odysseus and his men are blown south from Cape Malea to an island whose inhabitants subsist on a "mellow fruit." The islanders give it to the crewmen, and those who indulge fall into a narcotic apathy. Robert Fagles translates:

> Any crewmen who ate the lotus, the honey-sweet fruit,
> lost all desire to send a message back, much less return,
> their only wish to linger there with the Lotus-eaters,
> grazing on lotus.

This is not the feeling of death so much as it is the death of feeling. Was *Lotusflow3r* a coded admission of drug use? Prince certainly knew the *Odyssey*; he had written *Glam Slam Ulysses* back in the early nineties. At the very least, he invoked the epic to suggest the notion of homecoming, which carried across to the second album of the package, the funk-inflected *MPLSound*. *MPLSound* was filled with inventive, energetic material. "Chocolate Box" had a guest spot by Q-Tip and a funny chorus—"I've got a box of chocolates that'll knock the socks off any girl that wanna come my way." "Dance 4 Me" was the last effective

Camille appearance. The album pulled out the full trick bag: distorted vocals, lavish synths (Moogs rather than Obenheims). But it felt aggressively retrospective. "Ol' Skool Company" was a late-career jeremiad, with lyrics that both called for a return to organic soul and criticized the handling of the 2008 financial crisis. And "Here," a slow-building, slow-burning plea to an absent lover, contains a nod to the soul singer Donny Hathaway that typographically suggests that Prince is speaking as much to himself:

> *"A Song 4 U" just ain't the same without you.*

The signal moment is the first track, "There'll Never B (Another Like Me)." It's refreshing to remember that even three decades into his career, Prince could still kick down the door with an album opener the way he did on *1999*, or *Purple Rain*, or *Sign O' the Times*. "There'll Never B (Another Like Me)" starts with a bouncing beat reminiscent of "The Question of U," tips into a roller-coaster scream that's a close cousin of "Anotherloverholenyohead," and then clears out for a soap-bubble synth-bass note that seems lifted from "Gett Off"—and that's just in the first fifteen seconds. The lyrics are equally self-directed:

> *I can get you what you want*
> *Anything at all girl*
> *All you gotta say is please*
> *Ask your mother your sister your brother*
> *There'll never be another*
> *Never be another like me.*

Presumably, they're the same mother, sister, and brother from Prince's first hit, "I Wanna Be Your Lover," still around, still happy to attest to his charms. And in a kind of tribute to (or reprise of) that earlier song, "There'll Never B (Another Like Me)" shifts at the two-thirds mark into a synth-and-guitar groove. It's the omega that returns to and recharges (while also mourning the loss of) the alpha.

+ + +

Prince was always out there, making music. That was a constant. And then, a desolation. The last batch of songs Prince officially released, collected on the *HITnRUN* albums in 2015, found him working amid expansive instrumentation and explicitly positive sentiment; tracks like "Groovy Potential," "Black Muse," and "Revelation" suggested a bright future, or at least an enlightened one. There were also songs left behind. While working on the social-protest anthem "Baltimore," the horn arranger Michael Nelson got a note from Prince that he wanted to "remake the Minneapolis sound." Nelson operated in the space around Prince's guitar solo, giving it an orchestral bed. Prince tinkered further, deleting the beginning of the solo, dropping the horn section further back into the mix, and moving a string melody. "It's like he shifted it by two-and-a-half beats, just something that made it completely different than what was intended," Nelson told *Rolling Stone*. "I tip my cap to the genius and I'm glad I was a part of it," he said. I wanted to hear that song, but it was nowhere to be found, only words on the page. I let my phone pick a random song from the catalog. It picked "Get Yo Groove On," a sunny party jam from *Emancipation*. "I got some money 'cause I just got paid," Prince sang. "It's time to get my groove on." He sounded so alive. I remembered all the stories I had heard over the years—the way he would call up friends and use funny accents on the phone, his habit of cooking breakfasts, his penchant for perfectly timed and shyly delivered barbs. I forgot, temporarily, the truth, which was that he had gone.

In the months that followed, as the specific tributes faded, it seemed as though Prince had been distributed across the universe. I started to see purple everywhere: in four separate coats in the subway one day, in the set of *Full Frontal with Samantha Bee*. I read a news story about gender-neutral bathrooms at a Vermont high school, and it was illustrated with a photo of two teens, one darker-skinned, one lighter-skinned, putting up a sticker whose purple icon combined the symbols for male and female. Then there were the other artists still making music in his absence, in his image, and in his shadow. Prince survives in the work of Miguel, Lady Gaga, Usher, Esperanza Spalding, Blood Orange, Of Montreal, Chance the Rapper, Solange, Beyoncé, and hundreds more. Not all the flowers that he planted in the backyard died when he went away.

As I thought about Prince—here, not here, vibrating eternally at 432 hertz—I was confused. I finally went where I always go when confronted with the impossible: I went to literature. I sought out passages that reminded me of what Prince was, and how the world was lacerated without him. I went to Mark Twain's "The fear of death follows from the fear of life; a man who lives fully is prepared to die at any time," and found it comforting but not true. I went to Samuel Beckett's "to open its mouth no more, confusion of memory and lament," and found it true but far too stark. I went to Henry James's "The Altar of the Dead," a story about how remembering those who have departed the earth is at once a form of solace and a form of bondage. "Mine are only the Dead who died possessed of me," says his protagonist, George Stransom. "They're mine in death because they were mine in life." That was less stark, but no more comforting. In the end, I came to Emily Dickinson. Dickinson started writing poems in the summer of 1858, a century before Prince was born. The first poem of her Time and Eternity set seems to reach across that hundred-year gap and anticipate Prince's life, especially in its first stanza, which is colored purple. For Dickinson, purple not only represented opulence and majesty but also death. After all, it was the color of dusk, and everyone's sun eventually set. The poem opens at life's close:

> *One dignity delays for all—*
> *One mitred afternoon—*
> *None can avoid this purple—*
> *None evade this crown!*

And none did.

LET'S WORK

Annotated Discography and Song Index

Prince left behind so much music that it's hard to keep track of it all. What follows is an inventory of all of his official albums, along with release dates and track lists. One song per album has been highlighted, usually for idiosyncratic reasons. This guide can be used as a playlist or a wish list. All songs have also been indexed to places where they are discussed in the text.

Prince, *For You*

Released April 7, 1978

1. For You, 184
2. In Love
3. Soft and Wet, 18, 28, 69
4. Crazy You
5. Just as Long as We're Together
6. Baby
7. My Love Is Forever
8. So Blue
9. I'm Yours

This song, Santana-flavored, was the definitive proof on the debut album that Prince was a force to be reckoned with on the guitar. The song was not performed live until 2009, when he played a special three-show engagement in Los Angeles to celebrate the release of *Lotusflow3r*. The middle of those shows was at the Conga Room, a thousand-seat club partly owned by Sheila E. Prince opened with "I'm Yours." Some people speculated that the song's romantic message was being turned to spiritual ends—it was March 28, the sixth anniversary of Prince's baptism as a Jehovah's Witness.

Prince, *Prince*

Released October 19, 1979

1. I Wanna Be Your Lover, 27, 28, 29, 30, 69, 71, 258
2. Why You Wanna Treat Me So Bad?
3. Sexy Dancer
4. When We're Dancing Close and Slow
5. With You, 111

Early on, Prince had a talent for innocence, especially in his love songs, and this is one of the best examples. It's also one of the rare cases where his original was bested by a cover—the version that Jill Jones sang on her eponymous solo debut.

6. Bambi, 48, 191, 212, 213
7. Still Waiting
8. I Feel for You, 50, 62, 94
9. It's Gonna Be Lonely

Prince, *Dirty Mind*

Released October 8, 1980

1. Dirty Mind, 227
2. When You Were Mine
3. Do It All Night, 70
4. Gotta Broken Heart Again
5. Uptown, 148
6. Head, 70, 71, 93
7. Sister, 70
8. Partyup, 87, 214

For a song with a straightforward message, "Partyup" is shrouded in mystery. Morris Day wrote it for his band, Enterprise. Prince liked it and offered Morris a flat payment, which Morris took. Prince may or may not have intimated that he'd throw an entire band in for good measure. But the deal was struck, and "Partyup" became, for legal purposes, a Prince composition.

Prince, *Controversy*

Released October 14, 1981

1. Controversy, 81, 93, 121, 151
2. Sexuality, 53, 71, 75, 81, 150, 191
3. Do Me, Baby, 71, 87
4. Private Joy, 71, 80, 151
5. Ronnie, Talk to Russia
6. Let's Work

For me, this is Prince's definitive early song—not because it's his best, not because it's his most interesting, but because it's his most undeniable, especially in its first seconds: chanted title, synth swoop. It just takes off, the drums (played by Prince) pulled along by the taut bass line (played by Prince) and surrounded by three different keyboard parts (Prince, Prince, Prince). Prince opened for the Rolling Stones about a month after this, and about five years after that, Mick Jagger nicked the title for the lead single of his second solo album, *Primitive Cool*—a song that suggests that the way to "kill poverty" is for the poor to stop being lazy ("No sitting down on your butt / The world don't owe you").

7. Annie Christian, 146
8. Jack U Off, 52, 71, 74, 133, 168, 212

Prince, *1999*

Released October 27, 1982

1. 1999, 25, 34, 61, 93, 110, 123–24,
   125, 147, 148, 184, 185, 218, 225,
   229, 237
2. Little Red Corvette, 30, 32, 72–74, 87,
   89, 93, 109, 133, 227
3. Delirious, 30, 47, 54, 74, 93, 125
4. Let's Pretend We're Married
5. D.M.S.R., 55, 75

1999 was an album about technology, in more ways than one. It was the first record on which Prince started to explore more complex drum-machine patterns and keyboard textures, and also the first record to be released on CD (pop-music CDs debuted in October 1982 in Japan and reached the States by March 1983). Because of the limitations of early CDs, tracks sometimes had to be removed to fit double albums; in the case of the first *1999* CDs, "D.M.S.R." was removed.

6. Automatic, 2, 47, 54, 55, 237
7. Something in the Water (Does Not
   Compute)
8. Free, 179
9. Lady Cab Driver, 46, 59, 75, 110, 150
10. All the Critics Love U in New York,
    46, 155, 168
11. International Lover, 51, 54, 75

Prince and the Revolution, *Purple Rain*

Released June 25, 1984

1. Let's Go Crazy
2. Take Me with U, 78, 168

3. The Beautiful Ones , 2, 35, 51, 52, 78,
   90, 228
4. Computer Blue, 34, 55, 89

Though it was edited down to pop-single length on the album, "Computer Blue" was originally a fourteen-minute piece that included a long speech in which Prince constructed an epic metaphor comparing his complex emotional state to a house with many hallways: lust, fear, insecurity, hate, and pain. The full-length version is easy enough to seek out, and well worth it.

5. Darling Nikki, 34, 76, 77, 90, 93, 122,
   130, 225
6. When Doves Cry, xii, 2, 3, 22, 31, 32,
   33, 34, 46, 58, 94, 109, 123, 125
7. I Would Die 4 U, 23, 35, 125, 168,
   177
8. Baby I'm a Star
9. Purple Rain, xii, 3, 40, 48, 61, 84, 90,
   92, 126, 225, 228, 254

Prince and the Revolution, *Around the World in a Day*

Released April 22, 1985

1. Around the World in a Day, 61
2. Paisley Park

The song gave a name to his home and his recording studio. That's unfortunate, in a sense, because the monumental associations of the name overshadow the song itself. It's a trifle, but a beautiful one. The girl on the seesaw laughs, the place imparts love—it's a remarkably lyrical lyric for such a young man, and one whose counterparts on the pop charts were not interested in (or capable of) such nuanced imagery. In the end, he insists, "Paisley Park is in your heart."

Prince and the Revolution, *Parade*

Released March 31, 1986

The second side of *Parade* came bounding out of the gate with "Mountains," a Wendy and Lisa composition with Prince lyrics (though Prince, of course, took credit). Before the three massive classics that closed the record, there was "Do U Lie?" which is a modest song with an entirely immodest Prince vocal, in the sense that it's at least three vocals, style after style. The most thrilling section is Prince's Sarah Vaughan impression, which is more than mimicry. (Vaughan, who started her career as a vocalist with the Earl Hines band in 1943, was still active in 1986 and had released a video of a concert from Monterey, California, just a few years earlier.)

Prince, *Sign O' the Times*

Released March 31, 1987

This mellow love song seemed like a hangover from *Under the Cherry Moon*, vaguely European in its sensibility, especially the part where Prince took a bubble bath with his pants on. What stuck, mainly, was the keening falsetto, the Joni Mitchell reference, and the notion of Prince just hanging out with a beautiful waitress, trying to forestall the moment when he'd have to go back to that violent room.

15. It's Gonna Be a Beautiful Night
16. Adore, 52, 80, 135, 195

Prince, Lovesexy

Released May 10, 1988

1. Eye No, 53, 130
2. Alphabet St., 130, 133, 158
3. Glam Slam, 2, 3, 83, 84, 123, 131, 132, 237

Like "Paisley Park," this song became central to the Prince lexicon—it gave its name to the ill-fated theatrical production *Glam Slam Ulysses* in 1993 and a trio of nightclubs the following year. The song isn't worthy of that attention; it was neither the catchiest song on *Lovesexy* nor the most powerful nor the most romantic. But it also contained some of Prince's most gnomic lyrics, including a few lines in a row that guaranteed he'd never get a soda endorsement deal, a lawn-care endorsement deal, a skin-care endorsement deal, or a butterfly endorsement deal ("Sun is risen, moon is gone / Soda fizzin' on the lawn / Come a butterfly straight on your skin").

4. Anna Stesia, 116, 117, 131–32, 218
5. Dance On, 3, 54, 149
6. Lovesexy, 99, 123, 224
7. When 2 R in Love, 209, 216
8. I Wish U Heaven, 3, 132
9. Positivity, 133, 134, 256

Prince, Batman

Released June 20, 1989

1. The Future
2. Electric Chair, 4, 135

3. The Arms of Orion
4. Partyman, 160
5. Vicki Waiting, 205, 218

This slender pop song has glimmerings of maturity; Prince wonders, from behind Batman's perspective, about starting a family: "Talk of children still frightens me / Is my character enough to be / one that deserves a copy made?" But he also turns nightclub comic for one glorious moment, retelling the old joke about the woman who asks her lover, "Why is your organ so small?" His answer: "I didn't know I was playing in a cathedral." It's a rare moment of overt humor, along with a canny commentary on the relative power of human sexuality and divine grace.

6. Trust
7. Lemon Crush
8. Scandalous, 54, 135
9. Batdance, 3, 4, 5, 48, 134

Prince, Graffiti Bridge

Released August 20, 1990

1. Can't Stop This Feeling I Got
2. New Power Generation, 52, 62, 237

"Let down your funky weapon," he says, and instead the vocals go up in a jubilant "woo!" The song, which would furnish a name for his backing band, is filled with sound effects, from whooshes to ninja sounds, that mark it as a cousin to Michael Jackson's "Bad." The maxi-single includes "Loveleft, Loveright," a loose, propulsive sequel to "When You Were Mine" that forgoes emotional depth for intricate vocal effects (layered, slowed, sped), layered polyrhythms, and filigreed funk guitar; it's one of the strongest songs that never appeared on a proper album, sort of a nineties "Shockadelica."

3. Release It
4. The Question of U, 258
5. Elephants and Flowers
6. Round and Round
7. We Can Funk
8. Joy in Repetition, 48, 224
9. Love Machine, 84
10. Tick, Tick, Bang, 83
11. Shake!
12. Thieves in the Temple
13. The Latest Fashion
14. Melody Cool
15. Still Would Stand All Time, 135
16. Graffiti Bridge
17. New Power Generation, Pt. II

Prince and the New Power Generation, *Diamonds and Pearls*

Released October 1, 1991

1. Thunder
2. Daddy Pop
3. Diamonds and Pearls, 228
4. Cream, 3, 84, 183
5. Strollin'
6. Willing and Able, 62–63
7. Gett Off, 24, 52, 84, 85, 217, 237, 258
8. Walk Don't Walk
9. Jughead, 61
10. Money Don't Matter 2 Night
11. Push
12. Insatiable, 54
13. Live 4 Love

Prince rarely did character work. "Live 4 Love" offers a portrait of a fighter pilot who takes enemy fire and, in that moment, appeals to his maker. On an album filled with lackluster songs, this is at least distinctive and legitimately spiritual.

Prince and the New Power Generation, ⚥

Released October 13, 1992

1. My Name Is Prince, 136, 163, 202, 218
2. Sexy M.F.
3. Love 2 the 9's
4. The Morning Papers
5. The Max
6. Segue
7. Blue Light
8. I Wanna Melt with U
9. Sweet Baby
10. The Continental
11. Damn U

This song is a reminder of Prince's range as a singer: it moves from the highest falsetto down into deep bass. It's strangely phrased: he doesn't carry his vowels here like anywhere else. And then there are the lyrics: "Damn this kooky love affair," he sings, like he's Sammy Davis Jr., or Paul Shaffer. Retro, silly, unaware of its neighbors in the way of much of this record (the faux reggae of "Blue Light" is miles away from the techno of "I Wanna Melt with U," even though they're right next to each other), it's a winning one-off.

12. Arrogance, 99
13. The Flow, 236
14. 7, 52

15. And God Created Woman
16. 3 Chains o' Gold
17. Segue (Pt. 2)
18. The Sacrifice of Victor

The New Power Generation, *Goldnigga*

Released July 26, 1993

1. Goldnigga, Pt. 1
2. Guess Who's Knockin'?
Paul McCartney played "Let's Go Crazy" as a tribute when Prince died, but had McCartney dug a little deeper, he could have also played his own "Let 'Em In," which was the basis for this song—so much so, in fact, that Prince removed it from all subsequent pressings of the album.
3. Oilcan
4. Segue
5. Deuce and a Quarter
6. Segue
7. Black M.F. in the House
8. Goldnigga, Pt. 2
9. Goldie's Parade
10. Segue
11. 2gether
12. Segue
13. Call the Law
14. Johnny
15. Segue
16. Goldnigga, Pt. 3

Prince, *Come*

Released August 16, 1994

1. Come, 53, 55
2. Space

3. Pheromone
4. Loose!
5. Papa
6. Race
7. Dark, 52
Though this album was one of the nails in the coffin of Prince's Warner years, there's plenty to love here. "Dark" is the album's most beautiful moment, a moving, angry song about romantic betrayal and pain that showcases a fantastically slow-building horn section. There's a version later that he did with Andy Allo that includes samples from the *Chappelle's Show* Rick James sketch.
8. Solo
9. Letitgo, 205
10. Orgasm

Prince, *The Black Album*

Released November 22, 1994

1. Le Grind, 129
2. Cindy C, 129, 252
3. Dead on It, 62, 133, 253
4. When 2 R in Love, 209, 216
5. Bob George, 129
6. Superfunkycalifragisexy, 129
7. 2 Nigs United 4 West Compton, 224
8. Rock Hard in a Funky Place
In this set of sly, slinky funk anthems, this isn't the best, the nastiest, or the most visionary—but it is the only one that's explicitly about an erection and how he hates to see it go to waste. He's pounding on the skins, if you know what he means.

The New Power Generation,
Exodus

Released January 1, 1995

1. NPG Operator Intro
2. Get Wild
3. Segue
4. DJ Gets Jumped
5. New Power Soul
6. DJ Seduces Sonny
7. Segue
8. Count the Days, 48

Prince has many underrated songs, for the simple reason that he has so many songs, but this is one of his least known and most rewarding, a gentle and restorative melody yoked to a rough tale of urban threat and romantic betrayal. It's also Prince's opportunity to namecheck an underrated artist, the great eighties soul singer Frankie Beverly.

9. The Good Life
10. Cherry, Cherry
11. Segue
12. Return of the Bump Squad
13. Mashed Potato Girl (Intro)
14. Segue
15. Big Fun
16. New Power Day
17. Segue
18. Hallucination Rain
19. NPG Bum Rush the Ship
20. The Exodus Has Begun, 180
21. Outro

⚥, *The Gold Experience*

Released September 26, 1995

1. P Control, 160

2. NPG Operator
3. Endorphinmachine, 52, 178
4. Shhh, 223
5. We March, 205
6. NPG Operator
7. The Most Beautiful Girl in the
   World, 161, 177
8. Dolphin

There's a strange history of dolphins in pop music. There's Fred Neil's folk standard, covered most famously by Tim Buckley; the Byrds hymn "Dolphin's Smile"; and the jazz ballad "On Green Dolphin Street." This airy pop confection has a literary pedigree all its own. It was originally a part of *Glam Slam Ulysses*, Prince's retelling of the *Odyssey*, and in Homer it's an important plot point: Odysseus is rescued by a dolphin and then conveyed to Miletus accompanied by a school of them.

9. NPG Operator
10. Now
11. NPG Operator
12. 319
13. NPG Operator
14. Shy
15. Billy Jack Bitch, 196
16. I Hate U, 178
17. NPR Operator
18. Gold, 61

Prince, *Girl 6*

Released March 19, 1996

1. She Spoke 2 Me
2. Pink Cashmere, 174
3. Count the Days, 48
4. Girls and Boys, 179

5. The Screams of Passion
6. Nasty Girl, 108
7. Erotic City, 77, 137, 220, 237
8. Hot Thing
9. Adore, 52, 80, 135, 195
10. The Cross, 128, 138
11. How Come U Don't Call Me
    Anymore
12. Don't Talk 2 Strangers
13. Girl 6

Spike Lee's phone-sex-worker comedy used only Prince and Prince-related material on its soundtrack. The title song was a collage piece, sort of like "Purple Music," but more properly a forecast of the autosampling he would do on songs like "Musicology."

𝄞, *Chaos and Disorder*

Released July 9, 1996

1. Chaos and Disorder, 133
2. I Like It There
3. Dinner with Delores, 178, 205

A comic song about a woman with an appetite ("like a brontosaurus, she was packing it in"), this quick little pop piece is supposedly about Prince's mother-in-law, Mayte's mother. Questlove thinks it has the best ending in pop music: after a short and sweet return to the chorus, Prince sings, "No more—that's the end," and it is.

4. The Same December
5. Right the Wrong
6. Zannalee
7. I Rock, Therefore I Am
8. Into the Light
9. I Will

10. Dig U Better Dead, 179, 253
11. Had U

𝄞, *Emancipation*

Released November 19, 1996

1. Jam of the Year, 221
2. Right Back Here in My Arms
3. Somebody's Somebody
4. Get Yo Groove On, 179, 259
5. Courtin' Time
6. Betcha by Golly Wow!
7. We Gets Up, 49, 218
8. White Mansion, 180, 196
9. Damned If I Do, 179
10. I Can't Make U Love Me
11. Mr. Happy
12. In This Bed I Scream
13. Sex in the Summer, 133
14. One Kiss at a Time
15. Soul Sanctuary
16. Emale
17. Curious Child
18. Dreamin' About U
19. Joint 2 Joint, 55, 56, 179
20. The Holy River, 56
21. Let's Have a Baby
22. Saviour, 116
23. The Plan
24. Friend, Lover, Sister, Mother/
    Wife
25. Slave, 175, 180, 181
26. New World
27. The Human Body
28. Face Down, 181

The spikiest song of Prince's mid-nineties wilderness years, "Face Down" calls out all the unbelievers who counted him out. There's an unforgettable vocal sample ("Dead like Elvis"), an insistent keyboard wave, enough funk bass to flood the place, and many great lyrics, including the conceit of the title: get buried facedown so they can kiss your ass.

29. La, La, La Means I Love U
30. Style, 161, 231
31. Sleep Around
32. Da, Da, Da
33. My Computer
34. One of Us, 181
35. The Love We Make
36. Emancipation

☥, Crystal Ball

Released March 3, 1998

1. Crystal Ball, 55
2. Dream Factory, 183
3. Acknowledge Me, 63
4. Ripopgodazippa, 183
5. Love Sign (Shock G's Silky Remix)
6. Hide the Bone
7. 2morrow
8. So Dark
9. Movie Star, 105, 183
10. Tell Me How U Wanna B Done
11. Interactive

Originally the title song of a CD-ROM, the song employed many of Prince's mid-nineties conceits: a fake-out introduction that mimicked the process of booting up a computer program, a bloodcurdling scream, and an insistent guitar riff. Luckily, the riff was wickedly catchy enough and the song that he built around it sturdy enough to outlast its novelty origins.

12. Da Bang
13. Calhoun Square, 183, 196
14. What's My Name
15. Crucial
16. An Honest Man
17. Sexual Suicide, 240
18. Cloreen Bacon Skin, 183
19. Good Love, 96, 130, 183
20. Strays of the World
21. Days of Wild, 63, 221, 223
22. Last Heart
23. Poom Poom
24. She Gave Her Angels, 183
25. 18 and Over
26. The Ride, 223
27. Get Loose
28. P Control (remix)
29. Make Your Mama Happy
30. Goodbye

☥, The Truth

Released March 3, 1998

1. The Truth

Prince often flirted with larger questions, and this is one of his most expansively philosophical lyrics. While he expresses his desire to hear "the Truth" (the capitalization is spiritual, and telling), he also asserts that "everybody's got a right to lie." He wonders if time's only purpose is to give us all something to fear. He directly probes the heart of human life and its significance ("Questionnaire, what did you stand for? Questionnaire, who did you save?"). And he ties it all together with an odd dessert metaphor ("the choice you make ain't no piece of cake / it ain't no motherfucking piece of pie").

2. Don't Play Me
3. Circle of Amour, 184
4. 3rd Eye
5. Dionne, 184
6. Man in a Uniform
7. Animal Kingdom, 184
8. The Other Side of the Pillow
9. Fascination
10. One of Your Tears
11. Comeback
12. Welcome 2 the Dawn, 137

The New Power Generation,
New Power Soul

Released June 30, 1998

1. New Power Soul
2. Mad Sex
3. Until U're in My Arms Again
4. When U Love Somebody
5. Shoo-bed-ooh
6. Push It Up, 221
7. Freaks on This Side
When George Clinton led his P-Funk army in concert, he often split the crowd into halves. One side would say, "We all funking over here / Over there ain't shit," and then the other side would do the same. This song originated with Prince's version of this practice; he would instruct his audience to chant the title.
8. Come On
9. The One
10. (I Like) Funky Music
11. Wasted Kisses

Prince, *The Vault: Old Friends 4 Sale*

Released August 24, 1999

1. The Rest of My Life
2. It's About That Walk
3. She Spoke 2 Me
4. 5 Women
Prince's songs ended up in many surprising places, but few were as surprising as Joe Cocker's throat. Cocker's version of this urban blues ballad predated Prince's, appearing on his 1992 album *Night Calls*. While Prince was invited to play guitar on Cocker's version, he couldn't make the time. Prince reclaimed the song, or Warner Bros. reclaimed it on his behalf, for this contractual-obligation record.
5. When the Lights Go Down
6. My Little Pill
7. There Is Lonely
8. Old Friends 4 Sale
9. Sarah
10. Extraordinary, 179

⚥, *Rave Un2 the Joy Fantastic*

Released November 2, 1999

1. Rave Un2 the Joy Fantastic
2. Undisputed, 64, 186
3. The Greatest Romance Ever Sold, 186
4. Segue (silent)
5. Hot Wit U, 186
6. Tangerine
7. So Far, So Pleased, 186
8. The Sun, the Moon and Stars
9. Everyday Is a Winding Road
10. Segue (instrumental)

11. Man 'O' War

12. Baby Knows, 186

13. I Love U, But I Don't Trust U Anymore, 186

14. Silly Game

15. Strange But True

Prince's songwriting inspiration flagged significantly around this time, which made it doubly unfortunate that he was counting on *Rave Un2 the Joy Fantastic* to return him to commercial prominence. Most of the songs here are synthetic or derivative. "Prettyman" is James Brown via the Time. "Silly Game" is silky seventies soul, in the style of the Delfonics or Stylistics (both of whom he had covered on *Emancipation* back in 1996). "Strange But True" is the one time he cuts to somewhere new, a half-spoken abstract piece that's within spitting distance of "Irresistible Bitch" but so self-referential (and self-reverential) that it's hermetically sealed. "Where I was and who I am / The only Prince that will ever rule this holy land / All understand and all stand under this affirmation now / By the power invested in me by God, all negativity bows." When he reconceived the album as *Rave In2 the Joy Fantastic*, this was the only original song he removed.

16. Wherever U Go, Whatever U Do

17. 1-800-NEW-FUNK Advertisement

18. Prettyman

Prince, *The Rainbow Children*

Released November 20, 2001

1. Rainbow Children

2. Muse 2 the Pharaoh, 195, 226

3. Digital Garden

4. The Work, Pt. 1, 231

5. Everywhere

6. The Sensual Everafter

7. Mellow

8. 1+1+1 Is 3, 139, 237

9. Deconstruction

10. Wedding Feast

11. She Loves Me 4 Me

Prince was courting Manuela Testolini during this record, and this song is a sweet testament to their blossoming love. "This one I can take over to my momma's house / and I don't have to worry what goes in and out her mouth." Prince's mother was still alive, though she would die the following February. Her obituary in the *Pioneer Press* inexplicably misspelled his name as "Prince Roger."

12. Family Name, 140, 141

13. The Everlasting Now, 140, 141

14. Last December

Prince and the New Power Generation, *One Nite Alone . . .*

Released May 14, 2002

1. One Nite Alone

On an album that's mostly Prince at the piano by himself, the falsetto-drenched opener finds him arranging a brief affair. He asks a woman her name; she tells him; he says that his tongue wants to never speak it again, because it's their little secret. Let the speculation begin.

2. U're Gonna C Me

3. Here on Earth
4. A Case of U
5. Have a Heart
6. Objects in the Mirror
7. Avalanche
8. Pearls B4 the Swine
9. Young and Beautiful
10. Arboretum

Prince, *Xpectation*

Released January 1, 2003

1. Xhalation
2. Xcogitate
3. Xemplify
4. Xpectation

Prince's first all-instrumental album was supposed to be called *Xenophobia*, but at the last minute he scrapped the title track and promoted this one, which is a nasty little squiggle of horns and guitar, with some wobbly keyboards and proggy drums thrown in for good measure.

5. Xotica
6. Xogenous
7. Xpand
8. Xosphere
9. Xpedition

Prince and the New Power Generation, *C-Note*

Released January 3, 2003

1. Copenhagen
2. Nagoya
3. Osaka
4. Tokyo
5. Empty Room

Most of C-Note is sound-check jazz—the cities in which Prince recorded furnish the acronym of the title. "Empty Room" is the exception, a bit of melancholy bombast left over from the mid-eighties in which Prince laments his failing relationship with Susannah Melvoin.

Prince, *N.E.W.S.*

Released July 29, 2003

1. North
2. East
3. West

The album makes me think of Hans Christian Andersen's "The Garden of Paradise," where a prince (not Prince, I don't think) visits the Cavern of the Winds and meets the four winds: North, South, East, West. All the tracks on this record are exactly the same length, though different in feel. "West" has the most guitar, gentle at the start, driven at the end. It remains Prince's poorest-selling record, though it earned him a Grammy nomination for Best Pop Instrumental Album.

4. South

Prince, *Musicology*

Released April 20, 2004

1. Musicology, 252
2. Illusion, Coma, Pimp and Circumstance, 79
3. A Million Days
4. Life o' the Party
5. Call My Name, 51

6. Cinnamon Girl
7. What Do U Want Me 2 Do?
Price's late songs could sometimes be ornate to the point of embarrassment. This one stays simple, and benefits from it; even when the lyrics make no sense ("Quit trying to get me under / that icy plunder"), it makes sense.
8. The Marrying Kind
9. If Eye Was the Man in Ur Life
10. On the Couch
11. Dear Mr. Man
12. Reflection

Prince, *The Chocolate Invasion*

Released March 29, 2004

1. When Eye Lay My Hands on U
2. Judas Smile
3. Supercute
4. Underneath the Cream
5. Sexme, Sexmenot
6. My Medallion, 8
7. Vavoom
8. High
9. The Dance
10. Gamillah
11. U Make My Sun Shine
The Chocolate Invasion, composed of singles released through the NPG Music Club, is a mixed bag at best. But it ends well, on this warm, organic duet with Angie Stone. After the irresistible chorus, when Stone picks up the second verse to run with it, it's like Allyson Felix at the Olympics. She brings it home fast.

Prince, *The Slaughterhouse*

Released March 29, 2004

1. Silicon
2. S&M Groove, 63
3. Y Should Eye Do That When Eye Can Do This?
The guitar sample is from Sly and the Family Stone, which Prince tips off with his "boom-shaka-laka-boom" chant. But rather than wanting to take you higher, Prince wants to remind you that you're lower than him: "If I didn't try to school you I would be remiss."
4. Golden Parachute
5. Hypnoparadise
6. Props'N'Pounds
7. Northside, 196
8. Peace
9. 2045 Radical Man, 187, 223
10. The Daisy Chain

Prince, *3121*

Released March 21, 2006

1. 3121, 194
2. Lolita
Most of the reviews focused on "Black Sweat," among his last great singles, but "Lolita" is noteworthy for different reasons: Prince demonstrates his appreciation for an attractive young girl by sending her home. It's a song of personal evolution that ends with a call-and-response chant that revises and extends the Time's "Cool": "Fellas, how bad is this girl? / (Bad) / Then what

you wanna do? / (Whatever you want)
/ Then come on, let's dance."
3. Te Amo Corazón
4. Black Sweat, 54, 207, 208, 237
5. Incense and Candles
6. Love
7. Satisfied
8. Fury
9. The Word, 142
10. Beautiful, Loved and Blessed
11. The Dance
12. Get on the Boat

Prince, *Planet Earth*

Released July 15, 2007

1. Planet Earth, 61, 150
2. Guitar
3. Somewhere Here on Earth
"Guitar" was the single, and not an
especially good one, and "The One U
Wanna C" was the best pop song, but
the otherwise lackluster *Planet Earth*
only really soars here, with this
creamy late-period falsetto workout.
Here, as elsewhere, technology is figured as the enemy of intimacy ("In this
digital age, you could just page me / I
know it's the rage but it just don't
engage me"), though mentioning pag-
ing technology seems almost defiantly
old-fashioned.
4. The One U Wanna C, 92
5. Future Baby Mama
6. Mr. Goodnight
7. All the Midnights in the World
8. Chelsea Rodgers
9. Lion of Judah, 92

10. Resolution, 92

Prince, *Lotusflow3r*

Released March 29, 2009

1. From the Lotus . . .
2. Boom
3. Crimson and Clover
There are many original touches on
Lotusflow3r—the satisfying crunch of
the guitar on "Boom," the strange
lyrical conceit of "Wall of Berlin," the
blaxploitation-meets-swing feel of
"$"—but one of the album's strongest
moments is its least original, this
clunky but enjoyable mashup of the
Tommy James bubblegum classic and
the Troggs' "Wild Thing."
4. 4ever
5. Colonized Mind
6. Feel Good, Feel Better, Feel
   Wonderful
7. Love Like Jazz
8. 77 Beverly Park
9. Wall of Berlin, 257
10. $, 257
11. Dreamer
12. . . . Back to the Lotus

Prince, *MPLSound*

Released March 29, 2009

1. (There'll Never B) Another
   Like Me, 258, 259
2. Chocolate Box, 257
3. Dance 4 Me, 257–58
4. U're Gonna C Me
5. Here

6. Valentina

"Valentina" is a friendly uncle's note to Salma Hayek's daughter that nicks the melody of Lionel Hampton's "Hey Ba-Ba-Re-Bop." It starts off as if it's a come-on ("Hey Valentina, tell your mama she should give me a call"), but quickly shifts into babysitting mode ("when she gets tired of running after you down the hall"). Hayek's praised fulsomely, as a "Mexican bombshell" who's "curvier than a Fender Stratocaster guitar," equally attractive to men and women, and while Prince seems at times to be carrying a torch, he keeps returning to celebrate her maternal virtues. Whether booty call or Mother's Day card, it's a pleasant oddity.

7. Better with Time
8. Ol' Skool Company, 258
9. No More Candy 4 U

Prince, 20Ten

Released July 10, 2010

1. Compassion
2. Beginning Endlessly
3. Future Soul Song
4. Sticky Like Glue
5. Lavaux, 152, 196
6. Act of God

Despite its title, this is not a religious song, unless by "religious" you mean the intersection of spirituality and social revolution. "Act of God" is a surprise, frankly, a righteous, fractious broadside that hydroplanes along on a tide of synth-bass and whose arrangement is filled with sub-

tly placed grace notes: here an atonal keyboard wobble, there a filigreed funk guitar. In a sense, it's a companion piece to "Money Don't Matter 2 Night," a frank look at the way that power not only corrupts but deflects, especially when it comes to finance (the first verse is about a bank foreclosing on a family's home) and war (second verse: "Tax dollars build a plane drop a bomb / Supposedly to keep us all safe from Saddam / Bringing bad news to another woman / Call it an Act of God"). It's also proof that even at this late date in his career, Prince, like Paul McCartney, could still deliver inspiring songs on otherwise lackluster albums.

7. Walk in Sand
8. Sea of Everything
9. Everybody Loves Me
10. Laydown, 197

Prince and 3RDEYEGIRL, *Plectrum-Electrum*

Released September 30, 2014

1. Wow
2. Pretzelbodylogic

Alongside the fully realized *Art Official Age*, *PlectrumElectrum* can feel perfunctory, and the best songs are the least ambitious ones, like this lickerish little ode ("Dreaming of each other on each other's tongue").

3. Aintturninround
4. Plectrumelectrum
5. Whitecaps
6. Fixurlifeup

7. Boytrouble
8. Stopthistrain
9. Anotherlove
10. Tictactoe
11. Marz
12. Funknroll

Prince, *Art Official Age*

Released September 30, 2014

1. Art Official Cage
2. Clouds, 247
3. Breakdown, 247
4. The Gold Standard, 246, 248
5. U Know, 248
6. Breakfast Can Wait, 59, 248, 249
7. This Could Be Us, 248
8. What It Feels Like, 249
Duets were always an odd process for Prince. "U Got the Look" was sung with Sheena Easton, and "Why Should I Love You," on Kate Bush's *The Red Shoes,* was sung with Bush, but neither song was sung together. The most high-profile duet he ever did was "Love Song," a track on Madonna's *Like a Prayer.* It was hyped as a big deal, and why not? It was a summit meeting between two of the most important pop stars of the day. But the song fell flat. In part, that may have been a result of the circumstances of its composition. Madonna visited Minneapolis to write with Prince, but most of their collaborations didn't pan out. Only "Love Song" seemed promising, and they couldn't finish it before Madonna had to leave: "Quite frankly, I couldn't stand Minneapolis," she told Yahoo.

"When I went there, it was like 20 degrees below zero, and it was really desolate. I was miserable and I couldn't write or work under those circumstances." This duet, late in the game, showed that Prince had learned to increase the size of the collaboration by shrinking his own role slightly.
9. Affirmation I & II
10. Way Back Home, 249, 250
11. Funknroll
12. Time, 249
13. Affirmation III, 249

Prince, *HITnRUN Phase One*

Released September 7, 2015

1. Million $ Show
2. Shut This Down
3. Ain't About to Stop
4. Like a Mack
5. This Could B Us
6. Fallinlove2nite
7. X's Face
Spooky, spiky, and slick, this kiss-off is probably Prince's last great song. It originally surfaced in the time after *Art Official Age,* and sonically it belongs to that record, though the sentiment is probably too corrosive. The song got some flack for what some listeners perceived as racially insensitive lyrics ("Black don't crack, beige don't age / Come on, take that banana, get back in your cage"), but the confident falsetto and skeletal arrangement are what distinguish it.
8. Hardrocklover
9. Mr. Nelson

10. 1000 X's & O's
11. June

Prince, *HITnRUN Phase Two*

Released December 12, 2015

1. Baltimore, 154, 259
2. Rock and Roll Love Affair, 226
3. 2 Y. 2 D.
4. Look at Me, Look at U
5. Stare
6. Xtraloveable, 259
7. Groovy Potential, 259
8. When She Comes

9. Screwdriver
10. Black Muse, 154, 227, 259
11. Revelation, 259
12. Big City

The last song on Prince's last officially released record is buoyant and hopeful, with a Sly Stone quote in its lyrics ("Everybody is a star") and an implicit callback to the equally optimistic "Good Love." The second half explodes into a kaleidoscope of live instruments and affirmative sentiment. "Where's my guitar?" Prince asks after the breakdown, and then finds it.

SOURCES

There are many Prince books out there in the world, and many good ones. I read several of them as they came into the world, but reread none of them as I worked on this book; I didn't want to inadvertently borrow or have the field of argument narrowed or distorted. I did, however, make extensive use of the Internet, particularly the wave of coverage that followed his death.

As for other books and other authors in other fields, I want to thank Joshua Wolf Shenk, whose book *Powers of Two* is an excellent study of creative pairs, a topic that was uniquely irrelevant for Prince but helpful in my thinking about Wendy and Lisa. I want to thank Mark Lamster, who has written about Rubens and baseball and is also a gimlet-eyed architectural critic, for talking through various issues surrounding Paisley Park. Greg Tate has always been a North Star for me, and his *Flyboy in the*

Buttermilk has few equals. Everyone knows Paul Beatty now, because of the immense success of *The Sellout*, but the poetry books he wrote when he was young, especially *Joker, Joker, Deuce*, remain high in my mind. Ishmael Reed has always been a forward thinker, and going back through his work proves it; few people have thought as vibrantly about how cultures can share space without sharing aims, and how they both make and unmake one another. I also want to thank Emily Dickinson, and Hafiz, and William Blake, and Kurt Vonnegut Jr., and Stanley Elkin, and Elmore Leonard, and John Berger, and Pierre Guyotat, and Mary Robison, and Joy Williams, for doing amazing things with the language.

Here is a list of some of the works I have cited.

Adler, Bill. "Will the Little Girls Understand?" *Rolling Stone*, February 19, 1981.

Barbin, Herculine, and Michel Foucault. *Herculine Barbin: Being the Recently Discovered Memoirs of a Nineteenth-Century French Hermaphrodite*. Translated by Richard McDougall. New York: Pantheon, 1980.

Barnes, Julian. *Keeping an Eye Open: Essays on Art*. New York: Knopf, 2015.

Beauvoir, Simon de. *The Second Sex*. 1949. Reprint, New York: Knopf, 2010.

Bennett, Kim Taylor. "The Man Who Discovered Prince." *Noisey*, May 24, 2016. https://noisey.vice.com/en_us/article/the-man-who-discovered-prince-owen-husney.

Carter, Judy. "Sad Day When Your Prince Dies." *Psychology Today*, April 21, 2016. https://www.psychologytoday.com/blog/stress-is-laughing-matter/201604/sad-day-when-your-prince-dies.

Christgau, Robert. "Dirty Mind: A." Christgau's Consumer Guide. http://www.robertchristgau.com/get_artist.php?name=Prince.

C.J. "PR Exec Refused to Profit off Prince's Death by Selling Photo of Him on Bike." *Minneapolis Star Tribune*, April 26, 2016.

Clinton, George, with Ben Greenman. *Brothas Be, Yo Like George, Ain't That Funkin' Kinda Hard on You?* New York: Atria, 2014.

Cohen, Finn. "The Day Prince's Guitar Wept the Loudest." *New York Times*, April 28, 2016.

Cornish, Audie. "'His Music Does the Talking': Manager Owen Husney on Prince's Legacy." NPR, April 21, 2016. http://www.npr.org/2016/04/21/475161524/his-music-does-the

-talking-manager-owen-husney-on
-princes-legacy.

Csikszentmihalyi, Mihaly. *Flow: The Psychology of Optimal Experience.* New York: HarperCollins, 1990.

Danois, Ericka Blount. "Prince and André Cymone Formed the Band Grand Central While Still in High School." *Wax Poetics.* http://www.waxpoetics.com/blog/features/articles/prince-and-andre-cymone-formed-the-band-grand-central/.

Davis, Miles, with Quincy Troupe. *Miles: The Autobiography.* New York: Simon & Schuster, 1989.

Du Bois, W. E. B. *Black Reconstruction.* New York: Harcourt Brace, 1935.

Goodman, Jessica. "Destiny's Child Remembers Prince's Visit to Concert." *Entertainment Weekly,* April 21, 2016. http://ew.com/article/2016/04/21/prince-dead-destinys-child/.

Hoffman, Claire. "Soup with Prince." *New Yorker,* November 24, 2008. http://www.newyorker.com/magazine/2008/11/24/soup-with-prince.

Holland, Nancy J. "Purple Passion: Images of Female Desire in 'When Doves Cry.'" *Cultural Critique,* no. 10 (Autumn 1988): 89–98. http://www.jstor.org/stable/1354108.

Homer. *The Odyssey.* Translated by Robert Fagles. New York: Penguin, 1997.

Hunt, Dennis. "Revolution Frees Lisa and Wendy." *Los Angeles Times,* September 13, 1987. http://articles.latimes.com/1987-09-13/entertainment/ca-7727_1_lisa-coleman.

Plato, *Selected Dialogues of Plato.* Translated by Benjamin Jowett. Edited by Hayden Pelliccia. New York: Modern Library, 2000.

Pleij, Herman. *Colors Demonic and Divine: Shades of Meaning in the Middle Ages and After.* Translated by Diane Webb. New York: Columbia University Press, 2004.

Rabin, Nathan. "T.C. Ellis vs. T.S. Eliot: Men of Words." The Onion A.V. Club, August 25, 1999. http://www.avclub.com/article/tc-ellis-vs-ts-eliot-1371.

Raftery, Brian. "The Oral History of 'Purple Rain.'" *SPIN,* July 2009. http://www.spin.com/2016/04/prince-the-oral-history-of-purple-rain-brian-raftery/.

Smiley, Tavis. "The Prince I Knew." *USA Today,* April 22, 2016. http://www.usatoday.com/story/life/people/2016/04/22/tavis-smiley-prince-dies/83381318/.

Smith, Zadie, "Dance Lessons for Writers." *Guardian,* October 29, 2016. https://www.theguardian.com/books/2016/oct/29/zadie-smith-what-beyonce-taught-me.

St. Onge, Elina. "Here's Why You Should Consider Converting Your Music to A=432 Hz." *Collective Evolution,* December 21, 2013. http://www.collective-evolution.com/2013/12/21/heres-why-you-should-convert-your-music-to-432hz/.

Tate, Greg. *Flyboy in the Buttermilk: Essays on Contemporary America.* New York: Simon & Schuster, 1992.

———. "Black Jazz in the Digital Age." *Critical Studies in Improvisation* 3, no. 1 (2007). http://www.criticalimprov.com/article/view/287/431.

Teachout, Terry. *Duke: A Life of Duke Ellington.* New York: Avery, 2013.

Updike, John. *Roger's Version.* New York: Knopf, 1986.

Watercutter, Angela. "Alpocalypse Now: Weird Al Says 'Twitter Saved My Album.'" *Wired*, June 20, 2011. https://www.wired.com/2011/06/weird-al-yankovic-alpocalypse/.

Westerberg, Paul. "I Can't Think of Anyone Better." *Rolling Stone*, April 22, 2016.

ACKNOWLEDGMENTS

I'd like to thank my brothers: Aaron, who is as obsessive a Prince fan as I am, and Josh, who is as obsessive a writer as I am. Aaron is the one who, as an undergraduate at Amherst a million years ago, mined the origins of Camille for the connection-to-Herculine-Barbin theory. Josh, from suburban Miami in the eighties through to present-day Brooklyn, has put up with me and Aaron talking about Prince and then e-mailing Prince-related links back and forth, clotting his in-box. My parents deserve credit for not locking us all in a van in the middle of the forest and driving a second car home.

My children, Daniel and Jake, got exposed to Prince early, but for the purposes of infecting rather than inoculating. It took. Daniel, fifteen during the creation of this book, helped to compile the discography.

My wife, Gail, was not natively a Prince person; she went more for the Beatles and Johnny Cash. Over the course of this project, she came to admire or at least to pretend to admire him.

Friends are always central in any book-writing process, if only for the purposes of keeping an author sane. I'd like to thank Nicki Pombier and Lauren Mechling, Harold Oster and Rhett Miller, Steve Weinstein and Cal Morgan and Nicole Spector and Dave Jaffe. They all contributed in different ways, sometimes by talking to me directly about the material, sometimes by distracting me from it, sometimes by providing inspiration on the writing front, sometimes just by existing. I'd also like to thank Richard Nichols, who is no longer here on this planet, but is certainly on some planet somewhere (and maybe more than one), for his tireless commitment to endless conversations about nearly everything.

This book itself could not have come into the world without my agent, Nicole Tourtelot, and my editor, Gillian Blake. Thanks to both of them for focused intelligence and intelligent focus.

Special thanks to Prince and U.

ABOUT THE AUTHOR

BEN GREENMAN is a *New York Times* bestselling author and *New Yorker* contributor who has written both fiction and nonfiction. His novels and short-story collections include *The Slippage* and *Superbad*, he was Questlove's collaborator on *Mo' Meta Blues* and *Something to Food About*, and he has also written memoirs with George Clinton of Parliament-Funkadelic and Brian Wilson of the Beach Boys. Greenman's journalism, criticism, and fiction have appeared in *The New Yorker*, *The New York Times*, *The Washington Post*, *The Paris Review*, *Zoetrope*, *McSweeney's*, *Miami New Times*, and elsewhere, and his work has been widely anthologized.

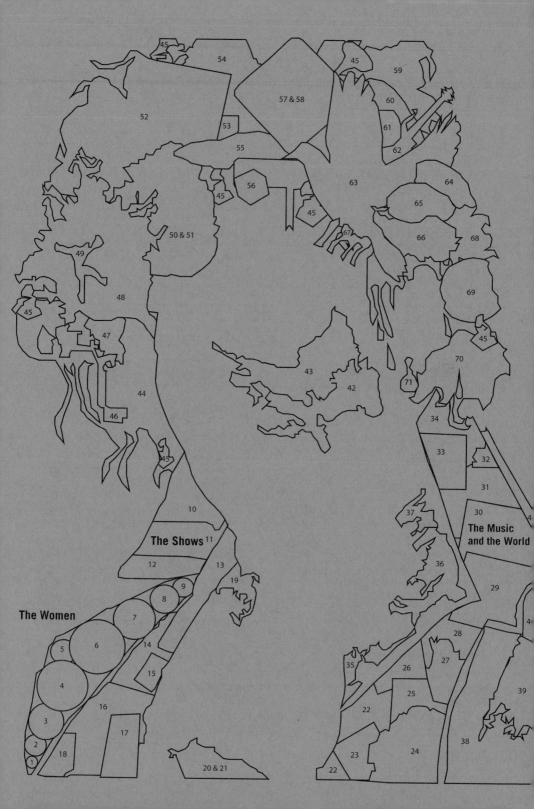